Bryan Islip

Me, my life

SO WHAT?

A genuine autobiography

SO WHAT?

ISBN 978-0-9555193-7-6

Copyright © Text Bryan H Islip 2016
Copyright © Cover artwork Bryan H Islip 2016

The author asserts the moral right under the Copyright, Designs and Patents Act 1988 to be identified as the author of this work.

All Rights reserved. No part of this publication may be reproduced, stored in a retrieval system, or transmitted, in any form or by any means without the prior written consent of the author, nor be otherwise circulated in any form of binding or cover other than that in which it is published and without a similar condition being imposed on the subsequent purchaser

Published by Bryan Islip:
Aultbea, Ross-shire, Scotland, IV22 2JN
March 2016

****

Why the use of the word 'genuine' on the front cover? Simply because a genuine auto-biography is a life written entirely by its subject - as opposed to being dictated or suggested by its subject to the actual writer of the words you read.

The front cover photograph of me was taken by Joan, my wife to be, during our Scottish holiday together in 1953. We were both eighteen. Actually it is two photographs - an accidental double exposure on our borrowed Box Brownie camera. We were on Ayr's seaside pitch and putting green.

The author's preamble

About a year after being diagnosed with advanced prostate cancer my youngest son remarked quite casually that he enjoyed reading my occasional blogs. But because I, his father, obviously enjoyed writing them, 'why not blog about your life?' he suggested, adding that people seldom know very much about their parents' early lives and are always curious. So I started blogging in November 2014 It took me about a year to cover, through eighty four irregular essays my life between 1939 and 2015. This autobiography is a self-published compendium.

I blogged about the things I have done and those I have left undone. Trouble is, I guess like most of us I tend to forget, accidentally or on purpose, the actions or experiences of which I am not proud or which made me and sometimes mine unhappy. The reverse is also true. I have to remember that the words of an old man with little to lose can still hurt. Notwithstanding all that, what you read here is the truth and nothing but the truth as I recall it. Naturally, I cannot claim it to be the whole truth. Nothing written down by mankind ever is.

Why should I put myself through the toil and sometime pain of remembering and producing with as much care as I can a one hundred thousand word autobiography? It has nothing to do with ego. There are warts in abundance within the life described here and I can hardly be proud of them! On the contrary, whenever I might bother with any useless introspection I would consider myself a humble kind of a man … Shakespeare's Julius Caesar comes to mind … *I cannot tell what you and other men / Think of this life; / but, for my single self, / I had as lief not be as live to be / In awe of such a thing as I myself.*

Soon enough I shall embark on my final adventure. I shiver with excitement at the prospect of meeting each of my wives soul to soul, perhaps even the author of the quotation in my last paragraph alongside the other poets, writers and artists who have paved with their star spangled lustre this man's often pain-filled pathway through his life on earth.

Bryan Islip - December 2015

Previous publications by the author ... (I have included their ISBNs in case you should seek to buy!

More Deaths Than One - a novel - ISBN 978-0-9555193-2-1

Going with Gabriel - a novel - ISBN 978-0-9555193-1-4

Twenty Bites - a compendium of short stories - ISBN 978-0-9555-3-8

Twelve of Diamonds - shorter short stories - ISBN 978-0-9555193-4-5

On Wester-Ross - 24 paintings, verse and narrative - 978-0-9555193-0-7

Life in the Highlands - 24 more paintings etc - 978-0-9555193-5-2

SO WHAT?

1. Early days

My birth certificate tells us I was born to Marie and Edwin Islip in Chigwell, North London, on the 23rd of October 1934. My father tells me I was born dead and was granted an existence only by the good doctor who persisted in swinging me about by my baby ankles. Welcome, Bryan Henry Islip, to this Vale of Tears.

My only pre-world war two memory is of a family picnic / fishing day out in Epping Forest, just to the northeast of London. Quite recently I wrote a long narrative poem about my early love of the piscatorial arts. It included these lines ...I would have been aged about four ...

> *But I remember the finger-feel*
> *of warm black earth, uprooted turf*
> *that we hand-dug in search of bait*
> *from the soft bank, wriggly worms,*
> *for whom I felt that sadness:*
> *and still I feel the sleepy weight*
> *of summer through sun-shaft foliage*
> *overhead; green, golden, shifting,*
> *and still the moving water glistens;*
> *I hear the ruckle of its slow running,*
> *swirling, cold to my bare feet,*
> *and the insect drone of tiny wings*
> *amidst the waxy drowse of that forest.*

I have to assume that mother, father, two years old sister Shirley and now baby Bryan were living in some kind of modest suburban affluence, for shortly after the outbreak of the second world war I have a fractured memory of getting used to our 'just-for-practice' nights in the Anderson bomb shelter at the bottom of our garden. At any rate, unless memory plays me false I am sure my five years old self was, with the rest of the nation, crowded around our radio as Mr Nevelle Chamberlain spoke so very sonorously that we were *now in a state of war with Germany*. As the echoes of world war one must still have been sounding and most of my little boy toys were military I do remember that this didn't seem to me to be at all bad news.

Father's position as a quantity surveyor with The Ministry ensured that he was needed more for the construction of war-time airfields than the wearing of any uniform other than that, eventually, of the Home Guard. His work on the giant USAF airbase at Burtonwood in Lancashire led to the whole family, now increased to myself and Shirley plus Tina and Maureen, migrating north, away from London's bombing.

I understand that soon after we left Chigwell an enemy bomb landed foursquare on our Anderson shelter, leading to the local newspaper's obituary account of the complete demise of the entire Islips!

One of my earliest clear memories is of the long car ride from Essex to Lancashire in father's Morgan sports car. Traversing a bridge over the river Ribble my daddy stopped the car. I watched him as he scrambled down to the waterside and came back up after a while carrying a mighty salmon that by his account had stranded itself in a bankside pool. Fish and fishing would become a fixation, one that would last all of my life. This is another little extract from my poem 'Fisherboy' …

> *…but this is fishing, nineteen forty two.*
> *Lancashire pond, shiveringly deep*
> *rush fringed, overhanging willows,*
> *dark skies, menace, mirror calm,*
> *whatever monster lurks down there?*
> *My father is handing me his rod,*
> *shiny soft feel of its cork handle*
> *tiny bobble float red and white,*
> *with quill upright out in the middle.*
> *'Watch it, now, pay attention',*
> *he instructed, (as if I needed it),*
> *and yet I miss the strike when, dis-*
> *believing, I no more see a float,*

> *just plop within those circle ripples,*
> *gone. 'Too late, Bryan', father says,*
> *and I feel his disappointment*
> *in me in spite of all my good intent,*
> *and in myself, all passion spent.*

I think I must have been something of a risk taker even then, for to this day I bear a scar central on my forehead from an injury sustained in falling off some wall on to an iron railing. Much blood, much panicked mummy! I detested infant school in my new home village of Walton-le-Dale. In fact I'm not sure if I was or wasn't in the act of absenting myself when falling off that wall. But I so well remember sitting with mummy and daddy in the headmaster's office; the latter, stern of face, asking me whether I *really* wished to let down my family so much? I understood that by my family he meant my maternal grandfather Albert Osborne, then the world-wide General of the Salvation Army. I remember him well, grandfather Osborne; a very big man in all senses.

When the U.S.A. entered the war on our side huge convoys of American vehicles would crawl up Chorley Road past our house. This is an extract from another of my long, autobiographical poems, the one I call Early Stirrings ...

> *There's this eight year old in war-*
> *time Lancashire when the door*
> *to England opens wide as his eyes,*
> *and they're singing or humming*
> *all about The Yanks Are Coming,*
> *mother says they'll help us win*
> *whilst father mutters better late ...*
> *And me? I'm bedazzled, silent,*
> *standing outside our garden gate*
> *at the village roadside, puzzled,*
> *when that great convoy passes.*
> *Puzzled by Yankee imprecations*
> *in language strangely accented*
> *whilst they throw out small tins*
> *of proper coffee and Wrigley's*
> *much sought after chewing gum*
> *for us to scramble over: but why*

*would they want to meet the girls
of Walton-le-Dale? I wonder,
for girls are so boring, at least,
as are my sisters three to me
and girls can't even fight the
German Hun or Eyeties, anyone.
But still there are more interesting
things than where the fighting's been
or what goes on unseen behind
the sightscreen on the green:
like exploring the summer fields,
and fishing (if father was home)
or watching him shoot bottles
off our fence, or birds alive
with his Home Guard forty five
(he let me hold it, unloaded),
and learning from a local boy
to tell an ordinary rabbit hole
from a breeding burrow, pull
out a baby with a bramble, so
at school I tried to please but
it was not there I felt at ease,
and my classes dragged along,
and learning right from wrong,
and how the price of wrong is pain
and 'Bryan, don't do that again',
yes, my world is full of fears
as dreams turn often into tears,
'til came the time in that farmer's
barn with its piled high bales
of straw, where up on top I hide,
watch that Yankee soldier ride
a breathless, laughing village girl
with all that grunting, groaning
ending in strange female crying,
and I feel unreasoned anger
although lustful wings are whirring
and thus there is that early stirring.*

No doubt totally the wrong kind of sex education, but I had begun to notice the biological differences between myself and my sisters three.

I learned to fear my father - or rather his inexplicably foul moods when the rest of us so wanted him - and us and everything - to be happy. One Christmas we had all been sitting with mother ahead of father's return from his work in London for what seemed like ages making paper chains with which to decorate the house When daddy arrived he took no notice of our decorations. Soon enough the shouting began; that is, father shouting, mother saying nothing, which simply resulted in the upping of his volume. He raged around, tearing down our careful work, yelling inexplicably about how there could be no Christmas in this house!

It's the little things that years later are still there in the forefront of one's mind. It must have been for my seventh birthday that my parents presented me with what automatically became my prized possession: a pearl handled penknife. A few days later I was by myself in the nearby woods, cutting my initials on to a tree when along came three much bigger boys. One of them said he'd teach me to throw my knife from a distance so that it would stick in the tree trunk. Needless to say that was the last I would see of my precious possession. I ran home in tears. Daddy asked me what was wrong. When I told him he ordered me to go back to the wood, find those boys and retrieve the knife. I roved around in the trees until dark, of course without finding them - in fact dreading to find them for what was I to do if I did? As punishment for that I was made to bend over for a good hiding with a carpet slipper, my mummy crying in the background. I was lucky. The more extreme punishment came via daddy's leather leather belt.

I think I must have been quite a shy little boy. The time came when, instead of being escorted to the barber shop by mother, father gave me the money and told me to go by myself. I was racked with embarassment. On returning home father flew into a rage, declaring that the barber had 'hardly touched' a part of my hair. I was to go back by myself and demand a 'proper haircut', he said. For ages I walked up and down outside the shop. I think the barber must have seen me and understood this strange little eight year old's problem, for when I did finally pluck up courage to go back in he made no fuss about it; made no extra charge, either.

In spite of all I really loved my father; idolised him in fact especially when he donned his officer's Home Guard uniform and practiced firing his sten gun, shooting, or trying to shoot tin cans off our back garden fence. But it was mother who I loved the most. I recollect the sheer beauty of the woman and I truly relished the comforting warmth of her love for me. But strangely disturbing things were to happen. Mother put Shirley, aged twelve and myself aged ten on a London bound train at Preston. I could not understand it when I realised that she was not coming with us. I see her still; she is waving as our train pulls away, tears sparkling on her face. I would neither see nor hear from my mother again for the following forty two years.

2. In the aftermath

I can say that I was, and still am most unhappy about my parents' divorce and the permanent splitting up of the family into which I was born. To this day I think divorce is far too easy and much too damaging a choice. I think any sworn agreement between responsible adults should be a permanent deal for better or for worse - whatever one's or one's partner's frailties. Oh yes, I know these frailties well enough. But surely, if one cannot make matrimony work happily one should still grit one's teeth and get on with it, taking care above all not to damage one's progeny. It is they who are the primary reason for one's life on earth. Should the couple be childless of course all bets could be off. To those who claim that divorce does no damage to children I say that is just rubbish. Forget the palliatives and self-justifications. Staying with the deal may be tough but, in my own view at least, it is always one's best and noblest choice.

Naturally I have to exclude from these comments the situation where physical or mental trauma is involved. But that should, in this man's obviously controversial view be justification for criminal prosecution, not simply for running away - aka 'divorce'. Evidence these days is ultra easy to come by.

I was very unhappy about the loss of my mother when my father took me away from her and committed me to boarding school at age eleven. It took me a number of years to find an acceptable balance.

Shirley and I were met off that train from Preston by father, who took us to his/our new home in London's Pimlico, close by that massive block of upmarket apartments, Dolphin Square on the Embankment. But very soon both Shirley and I were consigned to boarding school: the Church of England Our Lady's Convent in Abingdon, Berkshire. The girl's section was for ages twelve to sixteen, the boys' serving only as a 'prep school' for nearby Abingdon School, aka Roysses's. Shirley often told me how she was frequently called over by the nuns to comfort her tearful, inconsolable brother. But the kind and lovely Sister Bede became my surrogate mother. Her 'cell' was at the end of my dormitory. One night she left her door slightly ajar. I can still see her taking off her wimple (that snow-white nun's headgear) revealing a shiny, completely bald head. Something of an added frightener for a ten year old!

At the earliest allowable moment I was transferred on to nearby Roysse's and I suppose that is where my growing up process really began. How very quickly one came to understand without protest the intensely hierarchical system within a public school. By the way for those unfamiliar with it, a British public school is actually intensely private as well as being intensely expensive. School rules of behaviour, written or unwritten are absolute. Any kind or hint of rebellion is not to be tolerated - indeed is virtually impossible. And naturally you live on a time watch: out of bed at six a.m., ablutions, breakfast, assembly, classwork, lunch, more classwork or outside sports, evening study in the great hall, dormitory and bed, lights out. Saturdays are free time for study, games or (if good and lucky enough to be selected) sports matches against other schools; or a walk downtown but never, never on pain of cane be found talking to a local boy or girl - especially girl! You attend school chapel without the option twice on a Sunday. My schoolfellows were uniformly Church of England. Church of Rome, church of Telaviv, church of anywhere else - not at Abingdon School!

As a junior incomer one is the lowest of the low, paying lip-service to older boys and being of actual service to senior boys who have the right to punish by cane; of course total deference to masters and housemasters. Headmaster is far away God personified. People often ask me or at least hint about homosexuality in public (boarding) schools. In Abingdon this was indeed the crime that has no name, guaranteed for immediate expulsion without even the delay caused by a ritual public flogging in the gymnasium bent over the vaulting horse. In my time it was never talked about and I neither saw nor heard any evidence of it. Plenty of affection, boy to senior boy and vice versa but never anything physical. The only public flogging and expulsion I witnessed was - almost unbelievably - that of a much admired head boy who it seemed had been caught coming in late at night over the kitchen garden wall with a young lady in tow. I remember his name but will forebear to include it here - you never know, Waterman may still be alive, now a bishop or something.

Talking of that kitchen garden wall, that was where I failed to meet my first love - from up in an apple tree, actually. I never even exchanged a word with her. By way of explanation here's the relevant extract from my narrative verse *Early Stirrings* … oh, sweet Jacqueline …

> *Of course she knew as I know,*
> *sixty four years later, that girls*
> *understand those male glands*
> *from early age, and can see in*
> *the sideways glance of youth,*
> *that boys will die for love of she*
> *so easily, (or love of country*
> *and many, many do): I loved*
> *the pretty girl in the gymslip,*
> *part of the convent crocodile*
> *en route to their hockey field*
> *filing past the garden wall*
> *of Roysse's greystone school.*
> *She must have seen me up*
> *in that fruit laden apple tree,*
> *(Adam and Eve in imagination*
> *oh that snake's reticulation),*
> *may have found my little note;*
> *maybe not - she wasn't there,*
> *later, by Abingdon town hall*
> *or anywhere for evermore,*
> *yet still I see her bouncing curls*
> *her lovely face all shiny clean*
> *pretending I had not been seen*
> *that day, giggling with her friends*
> *as they walk on; oh Jacqueline!*
> *- I hear them say your name -*

> *and you are not the one to blame*
> *for this boy's loud heartbeat*
> *his newfound heat, nor was*
> *the new-swoll breast beneath*
> *your school's embroidered crest.*
> *I guess you made a fine lover*
> *and goodwife and mother,*
> *by now, great grandmother?*
> *You were worth the febrile cost*
> *for all of my love's labours lost.*

However, I have looked back with steadily increasing affection on my days at Abingdon School. Despite my awful after light out, in bed plannings to put an end to the life of one Walter Smith - the man who I was told had taken my mother away from me - I realise now that I learned there far more than English and Science and Mathematics and Latin and Greek. I learned how to live, i.e., to quote Kipling (from memory); how to *meet with triumph and disaster and treat those two imposters just the same*. Also I must claim that, after so reluctant a beginning I actually did well at Abingdon. I was prominent in the under fifteens cricket and rugby teams. However I was somewhat put off the latter after we went away to play against mgnificednt Stowe School. When I tried to tackle low their giant of a winger (as constantly exhorted by our games master), I lost several teeth as his heel came back at me. Woodward was that boy's name. I don't know if he was any forebear of the late England manager. Woodward went on to play for England. In my first novel, the one called More Deaths Than One, I call on those memories ...

> *This match, the one against Stowe, this has been the best. Aberford were a distant second favourite but are now winners; thirty points to their eighteen. They're all larking around in the changing rooms, muddy and high on being victorious, himself and Blake and Simon Reeves-Porter and Ridgeon and the rest of the under-fifteens.*
>
> *Taking part might be good but winning things is much better; whether it's sport like playing Stowe at rugger or winning essay prizes or just beating up Butcher Hammond behind the sight screen for those damned insults with most of the third form watching. Hammond is bigger than him and one form higher but he wasn't so tough. No, not nearly so tough.*
>
> *In the changing room Ridgeon notices the sting marks on Freddie Blake and Freddie tells them about how Thomas and himself had found the*

hornets nest last Sunday. He can't ever keep anything quiet, can he? Freddie says about how the two of them had climbed the willow tree down by the side of the river so they could get a good view of what those two were up to in the long grass and about how the hornets had swarmed out of their nest-hole up there and how the man had heard Freddie's shout and had jumped up with his cock still sticking out and they'd both had to leap out of the tree into the river and swim off to the other side to get away from the man and from the hornets. 'It was damn well worth it, though, seeing the lady's thingie and all that,' Freddie says.

'You absolute bastards,' Simon says, and Freddie says, 'It's no good turning away Simon; we can all see you've got a rise on.'

Thomas stands up. He knows there would have been trouble if they'd had any clothes on, but they won't touch each other naked. Using his new Aberford English voice he says, 'Calm down now, children.' He knows they will and not just because he's the team captain. It's because, for some reason, most often they'll do what he does or what he wants them to do. Especially when he's smiling.

Scholastically I was often somewhere in the middle of the form in ability - other than in English where I excelled. But I did surprise everyone including myself with some outstanding 'School Certificate' results. Honours in six subjects including the hated mathematics and distinctions in English and Art. Soon after sitting for that exam I left - or was withdrawn from school by father. I believe he or Aunt Kay who had been paying most of my fees had run out of money or interest or both. Therefore I sat in my final school classroom at age fourteen years and ten months; it was then 1949.

Many years later father told me that Mr Cobham, Abingdon's headmaster, had subsequently asked to meet him in London. There father was offered a bursary for me to continue through my highers with the expectation that I would then go on to Oxford. Nothing doing. Father refused it. I do not know whether he genuinely had no money at all, which would not have surprised me for by then he had developed a love of racehorses and greyhounds, some of which he came to own. Or possibly his rejection of Cobham's offer was due to injured pride. He may well have seen that bursary as the much hated charity in disguise.

3. Family affairs

Two major domestic events had occurred by the time I left school. Firstly Julia Wicksteed, my father's lover (ex-secretary I believe) had moved in with him / us, and secondly the family home had now been re-located in Newmarket. As for the former, what follows is an extract from my short story 'Thirteen' ...

On the boy's first morning home from school he gets to meet his new mother. He hasn't expected it and definitely does not want to meet her even though his real mother has been gone a long time. 'Ran off with that so-called family friend' according to his father, the implication being that his real mother must therefore be a bad person. The boy does not believe it, in fact doesn't quite know what to believe any more. But he is thirteen years old today and there's the birthday present propped up against the garage door outside to prove it. It's a fine, metallic-silver racing bike with skinny tyres and drop handlebars and he's planning to go on a long ride out into the country with his grandfather's fishing rods tied to the bike's crossbar.

All ready on his back is his grandfather's knapsack. It smells wonderfully of rotten old fish and line grease and ancient adventures and he'd spent hours last evening carefully re-sorting all the tackle in it. The boy has missed his grandfather very much, ever since his father's letter last term telling him grandfather Mason, his mother's father, had 'passed away'. Died, that meant. After lights-out he had cried quietly so no-one would hear, thinking about the times he and the old man had patrolled the riverbank together, very slowly because of the old man's war wounds, talking about fishing and stuff.

Oh yes, he misses his grandfather. Not as much as he misses his mother; differently.

To explain the plan he knocks at his father's bedroom door, opens it without waiting for a response. Alongside his father is this woman. They're sitting up in bed side by side holding cups of tea or coffee - coffee, he can smell it. The woman has biscuit crumbs on the fullness of her red painted lips and has longish light coloured hair all curly-wavy. At first she looks shocked, quite angry, then quickly re-arranges her face into a kind of smile. He can see the breasts with their dark nipples through the sheer material of her nightdress. He's never seen real breasts before, only those in the magazines and the newspapers they pass around at school and on the web of course. He knows his face has flushed. The woman realises what he's looking at and pulls up the bedclothes. 'Hello. You must be David', she says.

The boy's father says, 'David! How many times have I asked you to wait after you knock?'

For 'David' please read 'Bryan'. Other than that ...I was so puzzled and not a little angry about the inclusion into our lives of the woman who was to become my step-mother. But I am not proud of the way I treated her. She was good looking even if something of the brassy blonde, very much an east end of London cockney. As my story indicates, Julia was quite voluptuous of figure without any of the classic beauty of my *real* mother. For a while I would be reluctant, or would even refuse to walk down the road alongside her. But she knew very well her effect on an adolescent male, especially on the occasions when she asked me to rub dry, then comb out her hair after she had bathed or showered.

As I said, that second major event was our family move out from central London to the top storey of Hamilton House in Newmarket. This grand old mansion had been one of Admiral Lord Nelson's many gifts to his mistress (Lady) Emma Hamilton. It was situated on the edge of Newmarket's famous heath, quite close to the Rowley Mile racecourse. During school holidays and early in the mornings I would walk our dog, a cocker spaniel called Ruff, for miles and miles, careful to avoid as far as possible the many strings of exercising racehorses for which Newmarket has long been famed. I found them exquisitely beautiful, totally at odds with the often obscene language of the crude little men perched on their backs.

I remember being home from school on holiday when the classic race, Newmarket's Two Thousand Guineas took place. I walked the mile or so down to the start to watch the horses jockeying for position before the tape went up. Starting stalls had not yet been adopted in nineteen forty eight. One of the horses was ridden by a tall, thin, pasty faced boy who looked about ten but who would have been thirteen or fourteen. (My own age) The other jockeys rode with stirrups long and low but this boy appeared to have them so short he seemed almost to be standing on the horse's back. The older jockeys, some very old, Charlie Smirke amongst them, kept on cursing and swearing at that boy to 'get out the fucking way', or else, (or worse). The boy took no notice. It transpired he was quite deaf and had simply turned off his hearing aid! I cannot be sure but I believe he won that race, the first of his many classics. His name was Lester Piggott. Good for him! You probably know that he went on to become one of the most successful race jockeys of all time.

In pursit of his latest obsession father and Julia used to entertain to dinner local scions of the racing fraternity - trainers, jockeys, and in particular one of Newmarket's handful of professional punters (gamblers). Father told me such pro gamblers worked harder than anyone; out at all early hours on the gallops, timing the runs, recognising all the horses even without a saddle cloth bearing the trainer's initials, estimating the precise mathematical odds for that horse in that race against those others so as to try to gain an advantage over the bookmakers. This man would seem to be strange company for a senior civil servant, but still ... anyway I would listen to their conversation, sitting out of sight on the stairs. One thing has stayed in my mind. He told how he had 'had horse X at three to one' and had hired two men to go with him up to Scotland (Ayr) so that they could all descend on the rail-side bookies at the same time with very large bets, thus allowing the bookies no time to re-adjust downwards their price. But in the event the odds against X started and stayed at only two to one so father's friend and his cohorts took the next train back home without laying on a single bet. *Did X win?* asked father. *Yes*, he replied; *But I had no interest. The odds were wrong.* As dad explained to me later, *It's all about arithmetic, son.* I have to wonder, though: father was brilliant at arithmetic so why did he lose all that money on the gee-gees?

Another two things I heard that would put me off gambling on the horses for life. It was said that you could go into the Red Lion pub on Newmarket High Street on a race day and receive whispered inside information tipping most of the horses competing in any of the races. They couldn't all be winners. The other Newmarket saying; *chicken one day, feathers the next!*

Father had a 'twelve-bore' shotgun and a 'four-ten' - the latter being little more than a ladies gun. He allowed me to go out into the wooded grounds of Hamilton House with the four-ten after pigeons and rabbits. He told me to remember that anything I shot I would have to eat. I saw no pigeons or rabbits but I did shoot a seagull. In a guilty panic I hid the body in the shrubbery. Of course Julia had to find it and promptly tell father, shedding copious tears along the way. Have you any idea how big a heap of feathers comes off a single seagull? Have you any idea how bloody awful it tastes? That is, once you can get your teeth through the tough and scrawny flesh of it! And how the bloody thing smelt in the cooker!

4. Of what use?

My father designed and had built our new home, a chalet bungalow in the grounds of Hamilton House in Newmarket. Having been parachuted early out of school, all through the autumn of 1949 I lay around with no real idea of what could come next. I had a vague thought about becoming a writer, having won Abingdon School's essay prize, a leather bound volume of Edgar Allen Poe's horribly powerful short stories, but how do you get a weekly pay packet out of writing, I wondered? Architecture also appealed but I was soon put off that, having learned that in those days if you loined an architect as trainee / apprentice you actually had to pay him for the privilege! Father constantly urged his son to stop dreaming and start getting myself into gear. But how? Where? At what target?

Running out of patience, that November he announced that he had used his contacts to get me my first job; that of apprentice pharmacist at Boots the Chemist in central Cambridge. So it was that on 1st January 1950 I entrained for Cambridge, twelve miles away, walked through snow the mile or so to the street called Petty Curie and pushed open the big glass doors. Boots the Chemis employed close to one hundred females in that branch and only three much older, even elderly males. As I walked in the girls were dusting off their various counters. It seemed they all stopped to stare at me. Bear in mind that I had had literally zero contact with the opposite sex - other than my sisters or perhaps in my hotly adolescent imagination. I really did not know whether I had strayed into heaven or hell when entering that so very imposing emporium. At first it was the latter; soon enough it became the former.

In the centre of the store was the drugs counter. Of course drugs in those days did not have the connotation the word has today. This was where you went to hand in your doctor's prescription for onward transmission to the pharmacy or to buy some of the many non-prescription medications like aspirin or Beechams Powders or Lantigen B for hayfever or, given that you had sufficient nerve, your rubber contraceptives. I was consigned to the drug room, a kind of cellar beneath the drugs counter containing bulk stores of the commoner chemical preparations, many of them exceedingly dangerous. I remember the high concentration ammonia in huge glass 'carboys', arraigned on one of the shelves behind the door. One morning I breezed in, threw open the door to my dungeon then CRASH - ammonia and broken glass all over the place. I left in a very big hurry on very real pain of death. The whole store had to be evacuated until the fire service could deal with things. The store manager was not one little bit pleased with his new apprentice.

But the thing I remember most about the dungeon was the manually operated little lift that ran from down there up to the drugs counter and dispensary. Why would I remember that? Well, because girls on the drugs counter sometimes came to stand close by the lift hole in the counter floor, affording this nasty little lad the potential for a glimpse of the promised land!

Naturally, (literally I suppose), it wasn't long before I fell for a pretty, plump little dark-haired girl on the cosmetics counter. Her name was Heather Wolfe. I think it was she rather than me who suggested we go over the road in our lunch break to the HMV record shop, there to listen to our selection of music in one of the sound proofed booths. I cannot forget *Pearl Carr and Teddy Johnson's* rendition of *'There's A Small Hotel'*; it was my first experience of the power of romantic music in matters of the heart. Although of course we would not - in any case could not indulge in any canoodling, the booth was very cramped and Heather was well and roundly built. The song went on - *there's a small hotel with a wishing well, I wish that we were there, together ... etc.* And did I ever wish; and did not my wishing turn into fantasia! Eventually I plucked up enough courage to ask Heather to the 'flicks'; (Movies to you youngsters!) I waited outside the cinema for a while but she didn't turn up. Very disappointed I cycled the twelve miles home. When I arrived, father said he had taken a phone call from a young lady who had been waiting for me outside a different picture house. Letting down a lady, he told me, is a very ungentlemanly thing to do. Go back to Cambridge and see if you can find her at the bus station, there to apologise. Twelve more night-time road miles. I was just in time and we were just in time for a quick kiss just before her bus departed. However this affaire had no happy ending. In a later episode I'll tell you why and how.

In Boots, after a few months and despite my above comment (or perhaps to keep me out of the danger zone) I was disinterred from the dungeon and imposed on to the drugs counter. My colleagues up there were three mature ladies and two men, one of them very old. We all had our own tills. One's cash intake each day was a kind of unofficial competition. Although I lost my initial shyness and became better and better at selling stuff over the counter, therefore becoming increasingly competitive, I struggled to avoid the daily wooden spoon and never got near the most consistent winner - you've guessed it - that very old man!

However one day I swelled with pride and the expectation of success, having sold a load of stuff on account to a very professional looking gentleman. Along came the store manager, most surely unimpressed. Unfortunately said gent was a Doctor Someone, his name writ large on the 'no further purchases on account' list. The manager took me back to his office, there to stand in front of his desk accepting the tongue lashing. Then he said; *'Mr Islip. Doctor Somebody has a well known drink problem. He will by now be holding court in the* (local hotel bar). *Go there, take the bill you have allowed him to charge up and ask for payment in cash. Off with you!'* Without doubt this was one of the most difficult, not to say embarrassing tasks of my life. When I arrived at what actually was the first public bar I had ever entered the good Doctor was there all right, surrounded by his drinking friends. I was about to turn and leave empty handed when to his eternal credit he came over, heard my stuttering, whispered request and seemed immediately to understand my problem. He paid up in coin of the realm! (Or rather, in large denomination banknotes.)

By the Summer of nineteen fifty I knew full well that the life of a pharmacist was not for me. I had no idea what I wanted to do or be, except it wasn't and wouldn't be that. Furthermore, father had received notice of his promotion within the Ministry of Works. He was to be posted with Julia, by now his wife, to Singapore. From that point onwards it was clear that my sister Shirley and I were 'Not Wanted On Voyage'. I would soon be seventeen and so would then be eligible for early entry (military) National Service. Much to father's relief I liked the idea of flying; problem solved! I was off to Hornchurch in Essex for aircrew selection. As it happened the lists were closed at the time so I was advised to sign on for National Service then re-apply from the ranks. This I did, as I shall soon relate.

Shirely? She was already eighteen with a job as - guess what? - trainee (unqualified) pharmacist in Boots the Chemist in Newmarket. More of father's contacts I would suppose. Be that as it may, no sooner had daddy dear left these shores than my sister would get herself engaged, then married in something of a hurry to her farmworker boyfriend, Mick Mortlock. Baby John Mortlock very quickly made his appearance.

5. In which we have served

National Service (i.e. 'Military Service') for males aged eighteen finished in or around 1958. I signed up for it in 1951, then aged seventeen. That was when my father and step-mother sold up and went off to work and live in Singapore, myself and my eighteen years old sister Shirley left behind. As I have said, Shirley promptly and disastrously married her farm labourer boyfriend, Mick, and I was propelled early into the Royal Air Force. A touch of any port in a storm, I guess! Not just the statutary two years but signed on for three. So, no problems for father and new mother any more - nor, as it turned out for me because, with my boarding school background I very quickly adapted to military service life.

For some elusive reason I was allocated to the trade of gas turbine fitter (jet engines, that is,) and after initial training at Cardington, Bedfordshire I was posted to St Athans in South Wales for technical training. Three things I remember about St Athans. One was having to embark on a technical workshop exercise over many days armed with a set of hand files and a block of mild steel, and being instructed to replicate, to the nearest, merest micro-fraction, a technical drawing of a matchbox. Sounds simple? It isn't! Another was the theory of jet propulsion - the 'Venturi effect' - and the theory of fixed wing lift. Magical! The third thing I recall is my romance with a young lady I met up with at the nearby seaside fairground and our excursions sometimes with her family over the Welsh hillsides, ostensibly searching for those elusive but so delicious blueberries. Equally magical!

Having completed my technical training I was posted to real-life line duties at R.A.F. Stradishall, there to service the Meteor fighters that always seemed to be crashing in those days. We - even the unfortunate pilots - called them *meat boxes*. In fact one of my first memories is of being one of a line of men equipped with hand torches at night, searching the countryside methodically for the remains of a pair of NF11 (night fighter) pilots - and finding some part of one of them as well. I'll not bother you with the details.

This was where my propensity to dream whilst at work almost cost me my embionic R.A.F. career as well as probably my freedom, as well as, quite possibly, some unfortunate pilot's life. In conducting a pre-flight check on a Rolls Royce engine I had inadvertently left off an oil cap. The control tower stopped the aircraft's take off, having spotted black clouds of smoke in the wake of the taxying fighter plane. They guessed correctly what had happened and informed the military police. I was summoned to the Wing Commander's office and, in a real hurry was given an official reprimand only minutes before the white caps arrived to charge me. Of course they couldn't do so for I had already been 'punished'. I remain convinced that this had something to do with the protective hand of my distant father's Freemasonry connections.

It may well have been something similar in the event that, when I applied for air crew, I was sent back for further aptitude tests at Hornchurch in Essex. I passed and was then posted for aircrew selection to RAF Digby near Sleaford in Norfolk. About twenty of we new hopefuls were marshalled into a cold, dark and empty aircraft hanger at six o clock on that first morning. A spot light shone on a dais in front of us. In came the much beribboned group captain, walking with the aid of a stick. We all knew him (to us, 'the old man') as a WW2 fighter ace. He stood on the dais looking slowly down the line of us, then spoke one sentence that I can never forget: *Step forward any man who does not want to kill the enemy of this country.* Silence. Nobody moved a muscle. But in truth we hadn't thought about killing anybody. We just wanted to jet around in the sky and be heroes, pulling the girls in local pubs aided and abetted by our proudly emblazoned pilot's wings.

My instructor said he thought I had a natural flying ability. Certainly I always felt comfortable at the controls of a Tiger Moth doing the 'circuits and bumps' that would determine whether you went on to officer training as pilot or navigator. Naturally we all wanted the former. I flew solo after eleven hours of instruction, about average. One of our number soloed in five hours!

My most memorable experience in a Tiger Mothcameon on my very first day up aloft. A Tiger Moth is a propeller driven biplane made of wood and canvas with two cockpits, one behind the other. The instructor sits in the one behind. We had already undergone a week of classroom stuff including what are called pre-flight checks. The pilot is required to check everything inside and outside the aircraft, including the tightness of his shoulder straps harness. On take off I confirmed through my headset that all was in order. We were about five hundred feet up when my instructor flipped the plane on to its back! Of course he had seen my shoulder straps were secured but loose. I dropped about three inches that felt more like a hell of a lot more and remember seeing a farmer on a tractor looking up at me as I hung there for a few seconds that felt more like minutes. My instructor righted the plane; *Cockpit checks cadet,* came the terse comment in my earphones. Never again did I forget anything.

6. Flying high: crash landing

1953; and so from Liverpool to the Isle of Man on the good ship King Orry for officer and technical training. RAF Jurby, situated in the sparsely inhabited north of the island, should have been one of the half dozen high points of my life. It turned into one of the opposite, for at the end of my, I think three months there I failed two essential exams: 'Preliminary Calculations' and 'Meteorology'. That was the end of my flying career. I was later offered the opportunity for a Technical commission, but by then all I wanted was to put that bitter disappointment behind me, serve out my three year National Service contract and say goodbye to the Royal Air Force.

How did I manage to flunk those exams? I've often thought about that. I had left school aged fourteen and three quarters - or rather, been withdrawn by father ostensibly due to his lack of funds. But I had secured my School Certificate Matriculation with 'Honours' in Mathematics and General Science as well as 'Passes' in Latin and Greek and 'Distinctions' in English, English Literature and Art. I was aware that father had, afterwards, been invited to meet my Abingdon School headmaster in London and had been offered a bursary so that I could go on to Oxford. Offer refused. Pride? Competing plans? Fringe finance? I don't know. In any event, perhaps I didn't take the classroom stuff at Jurby seriously enough. That, and I have to admit to having developed my own competing spare time interests in Douglas, the Island's capital. More on that in a minute.

But up until those examinations my progress had been, I can honestly claim, well above average. None of us really need much time or vision to know or sense where we stand in the pecking order, do we? I have always been much about imaginative action, often controversial, often of an individual nature. Therefore at Jurby officer training, whenever there was a solo or a leadership role on offer it seemed to be awarded to yours truly. For instance I found myself standing up in front of the entire station, appointed in formal debate to propose the highly unpopular motion that *"Piloted aircraft will become history"*. My proposal was defeated but by a surprisingly small margin considering I was trying to convince more than a hundred professional or hopefully soon to be professional aircrew - including myself! That was when I remembered my grandfather's response to his eight year old grandson's question; *"How can you not be scared, talking to all those people, Grandad?"*. 'The General' had in 1938 spoken to 60,000 Salvationists in the Hollywood Bowl - at that time the world's largest gathering. *"However many are in front of you, Bryan,"* he said, *"Only one pair of ears and one mind can receive what you are saying. Therefore it is only one to one. Those ears and that mind, multiplied many times, will listen to you and may gain something if you have genuine conviction and proper humility."*

Another instance; part of Jurby's officer training program was traditionally the hare and hounds exercise. This involved five cadets being appointed hares and the rest of the station as hounds. I was nominated as one of the hares. I was taken off by myself in a garry, blindfolded and dropped with compass and map at sunset on the Friday. I had no idea where I was, except this was a remote place on the island. My objective was to evade all the 'hounds' and reach a certain reference point without any form of human assistance by sunset on the Sunday. I knew the target could be only a maximum of ten or fifteen miles away, but that first night was pitch black and it soon came on to rain. I decided to lay low under cover of some trees. When came the Saturday dawn, cold and wet but surprisngly untired, I spotted some of the hounds. Noting the direction of their travel I stayed right where I was until late afternoon. That night the moon came out. I must have covered seven or eight rough country miles before laying up in more woodland until daylight on Sunday. By then I had picked up on enough landmarks to establish my position. In spite of some close encounters with parties of exhausted hounds I proved to be the only one of the five hares to reach the objective. Every victory is sweet, however minor it might seem at the time.

I mentioned my 'competing interest' in Douglas. Well, I cannot even remember her name from this distance so I'll just call her Daisy. I recall a sort of cafe / dance hall where each of the tables was equipped with a pole topped by a number, plus a telephone. If you spotted a young lady in a table group across the room and didn't fancy the long walk back after any rejection you simply dialled her number, asked her *('hello, I'm on 22, are you the dark haired one in the red dress?')* for a dance and hey presto! I could write lots about the ensuing Saturday nights but suffice to say that the young lady was very pretty, very lively and a major distraction for this virgin officer cadet. I often told my Joan and then Delia about the final debacle to this romance. Before leaving the island, sitting in the front room of her family home I assured a tearful Daisy that it wasn't the end, I would be back for her. Long story cut short - 'It's not that, Bryan,' she informed me. It seems I had been going out with herself and her twin sister, week and week about. At which point in walks her absolute double! Neither Joan not Delia wholly believed this, but I can tell you now that it is the truth as best I recall it.

So, lovelorn and lost I'm back on the good ship King Orry, bound for Liverpool then Yorkshire. I've been posted back to my 'trade' as gas turbine engine fitter on Meteor fighters at Full Sutton, twelve miles outside the city of York. There, a mere airman first class, in time I was really able to find my feet, regain my confidence and establish a satisfying place in the new pecking order amongst young males of all types and classes. Remember, this was the time of the 'Teddy Boys' with their brothel creeper shoes, draped, and velvet collared jackets that sometimes concealed a length of bicycle chain; those extravagent ducks arse hair styles etc. Ah, those Saturday nights downtown in the garrison town that in those days was York! Drinking and fighting, hunting the girls and dancing. And it was there, in the De Grey Ballroom, that I found my new lady, the girl in the green dress as I have ever since thought of her. And along with Joan Wood came the council house family I cherish and correspond with to this day. Number 123, Tang Hall Lane. I had come the long way home ... rags to riches in everything but money.

Flying? Well, working on the flight line and with my background well known to the young pilots I was offered plenty of passenger trips in the NF11 night fighter Meteors I was servicing. Often, when well clear of any trouble up aloft, I took over the controls. Pangs of regret but fast fading and all gone now. Life no longer about any wings other than the wings of living and of love.

7. The girl in the green dress - R.A.F. ull Sutton

When I met her, Joan Margaret Wood was an eighteen years old dark haired beauty, slight of figure, always immaculately hairstyled and dressed and of excellent intelligence. She had gained the highest school leaving results of any of her family but like almost everyone in those days she'd left school aged fifteen and secured a job on the York telephone exchange. Joan had inherited plenty of Yorkshire fire. She was something of a rebel - just as, I fancy, was yours truly!. A telephone exchange Supervisor called Starke (the girls had nicknamed her 'Spitty') was her sworn enemy. From my R.A.F. base I would often find time to telephone her at work. Private calls to the operators were strictly forbidden of course. Whichever of the operator girls picked up my call would warn me if Spitty was on the lookout before putting me through for a free of charge love chat.

One Saturday I missed the bus into town and found that my precious bike was missing. Because of the sheer size of that airfield all the airmen were issued with bicycles in order to get around. The 'owner's' last three service numbers were painted on the rear mudguards. (I was number 4100031) Undeterred but extremely angry I walked the 12 miles into town, which tended to take the edge of my date with Joan. I caught the last bus back to camp. I was going to be in for it if I couldn't locate the missing R.A.F. property by Monday. If I found out who took it he would be in for it big time! We lived in Nissen huts. On straggling back in the middle of the night it was customary for we 'residents' to gather round the hut's central coke fire, exchanging tales of our Saturday night adventures. The stories always centred around drinking, fights or girls - or all three - and were certainly a great deal more of fiction than fact. However, word had spread around the camp that I (nicknamed 'Fritz' because of my crewcut) was looking for whoever had nicked his bike. By that time I had developed something of a reputation. Everyone knew that 'Fritz' had sparred with Bruce Wells, the All Services - and future British - middleweight champion. The fact that Fritz hadn't been able to see most of the blows coming was neither here nor there! On the Sunday morning word came back. My bike had been taken by a certain aircraftman Ingles, a rather large Glaswegian teddy boy and cook. Ingles was the king of the cooks - cooks for some reason being always at the centre of any nastiness - and was often in some sort of trouble with the military police as well as downtown York authority. In fact it was generally conceded that he was something of a psychopath, much addicted to violence.

My heart did sink but there was no way out. Followed by most of my pals I headed for the cookhouse. 'Fight, fight,' was the declared expectation. My bicycle was parked outside all right and this fellow, Ingles was behind the servery busy dishing out the bacon and eggs. I walked up to him. *You took my bike,* I said. *Yeah,* he sneered, *What you going to do about it?* That's when I noticed a senior NCO watching the procedings and also when discretion proved to be the better part of valour. *You do that again you'll be in a lot of trouble,* I snarled. Ingles laughed his ugly laugh. I turned away and gathered up my bike, my reputation in need of urgent repair.

In July of 1954 I was posted to R.A.F. Valley. But before leaving Yorkshire, to the astonishment of her parents (and the condemnation of my own) I told Joan I would like to marry her. Or should that be that I asked Joan if she would consent to be my wife. It was the 5th of July, her twentieth birthday. I was nineteen, four months her junior. Cutting a long story short she said *Yes, Bryan, when?* I think we should wait 'til you get out of the R.A.F. I told her I hadn't thought that far ahead yet, but I would be demobilised come February. I would then find a job. We would take it from there. I remember in the time honoured way taking Joan's father Ted for a walk along to the Tang Hall Hotel, sitting him down with a pint and asking him for his daughter's hand in marriage. The tough old man could be quite emotional. Tears appeared in his eyes. For a while he said nothing. Then he nodded, drained his pint in one, asked me if I wanted another. I wanted several. Getting back to our table with the replenishments he said almost exactly what Joans mother Triphena would later say; *You'll look after our lass, son, won't you?*

Ted and Triphena and of course Joan agreed to keep our 'engagement' a secret until I was out of the R.A.F. next February. However I couldn't keep it to myself back at R.A.F. Valley. I am sure the secret was soon, in York, no secret any more.

But, as Robert Burns has it, *The best laid plans of mice and men gang all awry*. Back in York on leave from R.A.F. Valley in early January my Yorkshire lass told me she was 'expecting'. Hey, I was to be a father! This was a turn of events completely unanticipated. We named the wedding day; 14th February, the day after my much anticipated demobilisation.

In those days one could not get married without the consent in writing of one's father. My father was in Singapore. I wrote him a letter explaining all. The letter I received in reply was hurtful in the extreme. It included an instruction rather than his advice for me, immediately upon demobilisation to apply to join the police force. However he did include his acceptance of my forthcoming wedding to Joan. The rest of it didn't matter one single jot.

8. How green was my (R.A.F.) Valley.

National service: I had originally signed on for three years instead of the obligatory two. But although I don't recall it, it transpired that in applying for aircrew and a short service commission I had re-signed for four. Anyway I had served two years and a half years when came my posting from Full Sutton to R.A.F. Valley, which is on the Isle of Anglesey (North Wales). Of course I have no idea why my senior aircraftman skills, such as they were, were needed on the Goblin engined, twin boomed Vampire fighters at Valley rather than the Rolls-Royce Merlin engined Meteors at Full Sutton. Perhaps my feud with Ingles the cook and/or my passion for that lovely young lady called Joan had travelled the Masonic line between my R.A.F. commanding officer and my commanding father in distant Singapore. If so they succeeded in killing the problem of Ingles. However my posting to distant parts had merely fanned the flames of young love.

When Joan died after thirty four more years I found in her things a ribbon-tied bundle of the letters I wrote to her from my new quarters at Valley, sometimes two or three a week and invariably on light blue Basildon Bond notepaper. By the way, instead of the traditional R.A.F. Nissen hut, you may imagine my surprise and delight upon finding that Valley boasted a tiny room, hardly bigger than a broom cupboard per each of us, individually. I vividly recall the hours I spent in my 'cabin' writing, reading and re-reading our exchanges of correspondence. And 'cooking' beans on toast on my home made gas ring, too.

Very recently my daughters told me their mother had beern forced to make a choice between me and another boyfriend, apparently an American serviceman called Archibald somebody. My girl must have kept that one very secret, for I was and always have been intensely jealous. I would definitely have fancied my pugilistic chances against anybody called Archibald - especially an American Archibald!

Anyway after Joan died in the nineties I took my letters to her and her letters to me - which I had also kept throughout the years - and burned them in the back garden; not without tears. Smoke gets in your eyes, doesn't it? At any rate I wanted no other eyes to see my turgid, not to say sometimes erotic prose to Joan, nor to see the more practical, definitely less erotic but no less loving phrases that she addressed to me.

I recall that first summer at Valley, much redolent of those Battle of Britain news flashes that sometimes get shown and re-shown on TV. You know, young men in flying kit lounging about, reading or kipping on sunlit grassland waiting for the scramble - the call to arms? For me Valley was idyllic apart from the lack of Joan - and I remedied that by hitch-king or taking several connecting trains to York whenever I could get a forty eight hours pass. And of course there was that never to be forgotten holiday in the Scottish seaside town of Ayr - celebrated on the front cover of this book. More of that later. But we had good quarters, great food, good friends, all-night card gambling sessions, forays into nearby Holyhead, long solo walks along Angelsea's empty beaches, climbing expeditions as a member of the mountain rescue team up Snowdon and, as I say, laying on green grass watching Vampires doing their aerobatic thing way up in the skies.

And then ugly reality. The drone of a Goblin jet engine suddenly stops. We all sit up, look up, saying nothing, just watching. Silence. I hold my breath, remembering the pilot who'd told me, before taking us off on a trip in a dual seater; *this Vamp has the glide path of a bloody house brick. God help us if we have a fucking flame out.* (i.e. engine failure) *because your ejector seat might not.* In a strange and total silence the fighter that lazy afternoon describes a perfect downwards parabola. No sign of any ejector seat. A ridiculously small thud. End of..

That's when I volunteered for the Mountain Rescue. I had been a keen potholer at Full Sutton, relishing the sessions camped out on Derbyshire hillsides, washing in streams and cooking breakfast on kerosene fires before plunging lightly clad into the cold, often very wet bowels of the earth; descending and wriggling through seemingly impossible cracks and crevices deep, deep down. I can still feel the weight of the mountain on my chest. Amazing it is, that sound of one's own fast-beating heart! Although we had a senior NCO in the group I often took the lead. Then there was that time when, after several hours underground we had reached an impasse, the pothole ending in a pool of water shimmering still and black in my head-lamp. *That's it*, said the sergeant. *Back up.* Of course I had to argue the point; *Sarge. I reckon if we duck down under, after a few feet it'll come up the other side.*

That's fucking bollocks, Fritz, was his reasoned response. I don't care to remind myself of what happened next even after all this time. Suffice to say it was the second near-death experience of my young life. And not just mine.

Climbing with the Mountain Rescue was a different thing if in genesis much the same. Anything for adventure. Soon after I joined up, at R.A.F. St Athan, I and my friend would go climbing on so-called sports day afternoons. We were climbing a sea-side cliff in gym shoes and of course without ropes when we came to a very difficult bit. Suddenly his voice, calm and quiet, right alongside me. *I'm going*, he announced. I glanced sideways, saw him peel off, heard him hit the bouldered beach twenty or thirty feet below. Galvanised into action and girded with fear I managed to reach the top. I ran to a farmhouse to raise the alarm. My friend was rescued before the rising tide engulfed him but at least he lived. I visited him in sick quarters, bandaged, much splinted and plaster-cast - but still he managed a grin. Then for me the inevitable stern reprimand from the C.O. Anyway, that experience lived on in me. Forty years later I contrivd to get myself into a position on a Gairloch cliff-face where I could simply go neither up nor down. St Athan was right there in my head. I was literally paralysed with fear. That's when, to my mingled shame and pride, my youngest son Stuart came to the rescue, a fifteen year old scrambling about on the rockface like some young ibex.

Back to R.A.F. Valley's Mountain Rescue and the many climbs in Snowdonia and my night school efforts to learn the basics of journalism. Back to the winning of the cost of my wedding suit in a last game of brag before the appointed day of my discharge (honourable I might add!) from the Royal Air Force. Then the train ride back to York and marriage, money, the lack of it and the gaining of it, eventually to the mortgage and that awful but necessary moderation in all things ... Dull? Well no. I might have lost a family when I was eleven but I had gained one when I was nineteen. And after that I set about making a family of my very own. How very exciting!

9. I'm getting married in the morning!

I have only a vague memory of my wedding day, 14th February (St Valentine's Day, nineteen fifty five. Somewhere I have the photos. They would show a handsome and obviously happy young couple standing outside the church in York flanked by all the members of my new wife's family but none, unfortunately, of my own. Afterwards everybody repaired to a kind of village hall or community centre, there to partake of home made cake and goodies, much lemonade, bottles of beer etcetera. I don't know if my new father-in-Law or anybody else made a speech but I have a kind of snap-shot kaleidoscope vision of a typically emotional Ted with tears in his eyes and my new mother-in-Law, the wonderful Triphena, with no tears - much too tough a Yorkshire lady for that. But before we boarding the train the lady whispered in my ear about being sure to take good care of 'our Joan' before thrusting a hard earned - a very hard earned - fiver into my pocket. That brought our available funds up to a grand total just short of fifteen pounds. We were rich!

My new brothers in law were there throughout: Derek, Peter and fifteen years old Michael, all of course nicely suited and necktied. Also my seventeen year old sister in law, Hazel, with her boyfriend, soon to be husband, Digger. Older brother Derek's future wife Chris would have been there too, together with Peter's future wife, Doris. Obviously young Michael had yet to meet his wife to be, the lovely little Carol.

Ted and Triphena are no longer of this world; neither are Derek and Michael, Joan's older and youngest brother respectively. All of the siblings when newly married themselves bought houses in suburbs of the fine city of York and all of them still occupy them, of course having long since paid off their mortgages. Throughout my adult life the whole Wood family have been welcoming to this strange southerner who had arrived out of the blue (literally, thinking of the R.A.F. uniform) to marry 'our Joan'. And ever since Joan died, all of what I still think of as the 'York Brigade' were uniformly kind to my myself and my second wife, Delia. In fact Dee and I visited York together most years up until the time of Delia's cancer. Great meetings we had, too. They were and are good - in fact very good people.

Joan and I were seen off on the train from York, heading for London with, as I say, very little of the wherewithal but some vague idea of my getting a journalistic type starter job with Aunt Kay's National Magazine Company. Actually the company belonged to American tycoon Radolph Hearst. Kay was but the managing director, a position she had obtained, as darkly hinted at by her brother, my jealous father, because of extra curricular activities.

Being tired after the wedding ceremony we interrupted our journey south at a small town just after Doncaster. The lady on the Railway Hotel reception looked askance at me when I requested a double room. However she lost any need to ask for our marriage certificate. We had left a trail of confetti. I think I have told elsewhere of how a bloody great spider on the bedroom ceiling spoiled things. Just as well Joan was not an arachnophobe like me. We journeyed on the following day and spent a couple of days in London town, having found the cheapest possible hotel there. That was the full extent of our honeymoon. On the third day Joan and I went to see Aunt Kay in her palatial West End offices, having to explain our way past not one but two secretaries, both of them male. She was not unkind about turning down my job application but by now our funds had all but dried up. Leaving that office the future did not look bright, even for an eternal optimist such as myself. We headed for Kings Cross railway station and brought tickets for Newmarket then walked the four miles over the Heath to the village of Moulton. My sister Shirley and her husband Mike were brilliant when we knocked their door, asking for temporary board.

Joan quite quickly obtained a job as cashier at Newmarket swimming pool. I myself borrowed Mike's bicycle and pedalled the fourteen miles into Cambridge. Finding an industrial estate I knocked on all the factory office doors looking for work. I don't know whether State aid was a possibility in those days but, whether or not, the thought of it never entered my mind. There was nothing doing until I came to A W Morlin, Builders Merchant, who offered me a job as warehouseman starting tomorrow. Happily I cycled back to Moulton bearing the good news. The pay was little more than subsistence but so what? I was employed, Joan was emplyed. We were in love..

10. Karen Jane

Throughout the early months of 1955, as I have indicated my new wife already with child, we stayed with my sister Shirley and her husband, sharing their rented farmworkers cottage in the village of Moulton which sits close by the eastern edge of Newmarket Heath. I had soon been able to buy a used bicycle for my daily commute the 14 miles to work in Cambridge and the 14 miles back . Flat country, big winds, hard miles and hard work. It needed all my youthful strength and energy toting lead pipe and sheet, baths and sanitary ware, tiled fire surrounds, asbestos corrugated, copper pipe and fittings etc, etc. But I was learning all the time about being the junior one of a team / hierarchy. I was learning about the serious business of money making. But naturally, being a dreamer I was always dreaming great dreams

On August 31st 1955 I received news that Joan was in labour in the maternity ward of Newmarket General hospital. My boss, (it has to be said with some reluctance), gave me permission to leave early. I pushed myself to the limit riding into a head wind - at one stage beyond the limit in fact, for Joan always told people of how I arrived in the ward just after the birth, hot and sweaty and with trousers out at the knee where I had fallen off my bike. It mattered not, for I was a somewhat bemused - if very proud twenty one years old father to a rather beautiful baby girl. I made our Karen Jane's cot out of an orange box and the remnants of some worn out curtains.

To supplement our diet on early morning weekends and on holidays Joan and I would scour Newmarket Heath for luscious field mushrooms and raid the late summer hedges for blackberries. I downed many a pigeon, using my brother-in-law's twelve bore shotgun. Also sometimes a rabbit. I recall how I would not pull the trigger unless the shot was a dead certainty, for cartridges cost money that I could only afford if the result was a meal for Joan and myself and my sister and brother in law. Of course, on occasion a clucking, strutting cock pheasant or a scuttling partridge would accidentally get in the way of my shot!

This was my introduction to a farming village life now long gone. Everyone seemed to know everyone and therefore everyone else's business . All our foodstuffs were bought at a general store about the size of your living room. That shop together with the church and the village pub were at the centre of our little Suffolk metropolis.

However I was well aware that we were living with my sister on borrowed time in Moulton and that I would soon have to seek our own accomodation. Cambridge was the obvious destination, as close to my place of work as possible. So before the year was out I found and rented us a bedsitter there; Cherryhinton Road. Moving ourselves with all our goods and chattels was no problem; just us and a suitcase full of clothes and a few more bits and pieces along with our happy little baby in her brand new Silver Cross perambulator, a gift from a distant father who on very rare occasions came down from wherever into some kind of contact. Oh, and my Aunt Kay's present of an Olivetti portable typewriter, birthplace of my very first short story.

So we lived in a succession of bedsits and flats in Cambridge. But looking back those fields seem indeed to hve been so very green. Joan and I had nothing but each other and our tiny family, but at no time did I/we feel impoverished. I learned then that it's not about what you 'have' in any material sense, but about the truth in the biblical *'Faith, Hope and Charity (i.e. Love) and the greatest of these is Charity (Love)*. Love for each other and for the human history on which our present is built; for all the mysterious so-called 'arts' and for the world at large and all the life that's in it. I learned that all this is in our gift to love and look after as best we are able. We have to try harder, much harder and much more effectively at that, it seemed and still does seem to me.

But that truly is another story.

11. My parents and their post-traumatic family

At this point I shall break away from my autobiographical narrative and revert to my own, dislocated family. As earlier indicated, when my parents separated and divorced in 1945 that was the end of normal family life for me and also, I strongly suspect, for my three sisters. Christine and Maureen went by Order of the Court with mother into a very bad situation, alluded to later. Myself and sister Shirley were allocated to father initially in the latter war years of bomb-torn London, swiftly from thence into boarding school - Our Lady's Convent, Abingdon, Berkshire.

My sister Tina died many years ago - of substance abuse I was told. Although my youngest sister Maureen is going strong and still makes her way with great resolve, her life has been anything but a bed of roses. Shirley, two years my senior, also endured many problems long before her death by cancer. In her early twenties Shirley had left her baby son with estranged husband Mick in order to 'emigrate' to Hong Kong, but eventually, after yet one more disastrous love affair returned to live by herself for the duration of her life in Milton Keynes Village. I have to say my elder sister seemed a sad and lonely old lady. So I would guess that I have probably had the least destructive fallout from the wartime shenanigans of Mr Edwin Henry Terence Islip and Mrs Marie Islip. I am convinced that my teenage passion for Joan and our consequent marriage, together with my exposure to her York City family was the first of my saving graces. And then of course our emerging family and my burgeoning business career produced an early need to forget history and get on with life. I've been very content so to do, and for the most part happily, and for the most part successfully.

I heard nothing at all from my mother for fifty years. At this point I'll skip ahead … one Saturday afternoon in 1994 the phone rang at home in Lee-on-Solent. A female voice on the other end asked, "Is that you, Bryan" and, you can believe this because it's true; totally unsurprised I answered; "Yes it's Bryan, mother." How did I recognise her voice after forty odd years of total silence / absence? Whoever can tell? Anyway I went to meet her in St Leonards-on-Sea where she had been living in poverty with the latest of her lovers, without knowing it within a long stone's throw of my father. He had moved into his seaside apartment on return from Singapore with his second wife, my stepmother Julia. Through mother, Shirley and I then caught up with Maureen. She and Tina had been consigned to a Salvation Army home for children soon after the family breakup. The place of their confinement - and shameful abuse - was called Strawberry Fields. (Of The Beatles fame). Long since well and truly and so very thankfully closed down.

My previous slice of life blog ended with a comment about my Olivetti portable typewriter, compliment of Auntie Kay, and my very first short story. I do so wish I could have it now. Maureen, in clearing Shirley's house last year apparently has seen a copy. Anyway I remember it was a murder mystery about a jealous husband's attempt to kill his wife by filing a weakness into the breech of his wife's shotgun. When the lady pulled the trigger on a flighting pigeon it blew her head off. Wrong lady! Unfortunately for naughty husband, his wife had lent the gun to her friend, actually her husband's lover. So there!

12. Happy in Bateman Street

So now it's 1955/6, I'm living in a Cambridge bed-sit with new wife Joan and newer baby Karen. I have a job - five pounds ten shillings a week builders merchant warehouseman. I walk to work, suited, collared and necktied in all weathers, dreaming of becoming a writer or, in observing the Jaguars and other cars passing along Cherryhinton Road, perhaps even a wealthy businessman. Whatever, I'm on my way!

That Christmas we had NHS milk and orange juice for our baby girl and a christmas cake from father and a pair of shot pigeons from my sister's husband Mick. That was all but it - three long days before my next payday. No money for cigarettes. No radio. But looking back it didn't seem too difficult and still we at no time felt ourselves impoverished. How odd! Our time was spent pushing the pram about Cambridge's parks and gardens and reading books from the library. That's when I discovered my lifetime passion for the fiction of Ernest Hemingway. I have a clear memory of sitting up in bed reading the final pages of *For Whom The Bell Tolls*, absolutely astonished, much affected by the emotional power of the man's sparse and perfect word construction.

But soon enough came the next implosion. Joan had unfortunately allowed a joint of ham to boil dry in our landlady's saucepan. Much smoke, panic, anger and confusion. So when I got home from work we're on the road again, destination unknown, everything we owned stacked around tiny little Karen trundling along in that lovely Silver Cross pram.

Bateman Street was and still is a long terrace of connected three storied houses with basements, mostly given over to flats or bedsits for American Air Force families in those days. Here was our next home, starting off with a basement flat, then one on the ground floor. I think we progressed to the top floor but cannot be sure about that. However I so vividly remember our neighbours, USAAF airman Richard Lilley, a 20 years old backwoodsman from Washington State and wife Beaulah with their three children (one per year!). I could base several novels or several chapters in this emerging autobiography on these next two or three years. But sufficient to say that Richard and I and Beaulah and Joan became close friends. Richard had a passion for, in descending order, guns of all kinds, his racketty old Dodge motor car, Hank Williams' music and rambling on the lookout for game through the East Anglian countryside. We became Saturday night poachers and Sunday lunch pheasant eaters! I never knew and still do not understand how a man could move so silently through dense, pitch black woodland as did my good friend Richard Lilley.

Meanwhile I secured my very first job promotions - from A W Morlins' warehouse to A W Morlins' trade counter then to junior buyer in the office. At that point my friends in the warehouse used to look up to me at my first floor desk near the window singing *'The working class can't kiss my arse, I've got an office job at last.'.* They meant no unpleasantness. They knew I was and would remain one of them; one of everybody; so I fervently hoped and still I do.

I could go on to tell you about my near death experience on the river Cam, about seeing Richard shoot a swan in full flight - with bow and arrow! - and about how awful it tasted, about smart young salesmen trying to sell stuff to me and watching them drive off in their company cars, me thinking, 'I could be doing that; and oh yes, I could be doing with that Morris Minor - if only I could drive!', about Airman First Class Richard Lilley's repatriation and his scheme to suck gold out of the mud at the base of a certain waterfall high in the Cascade mountains; *'Hey, Bryan. Why don't you guys come out and partner up with me?* Then about Joan becoming pregnant again, inspiring me to begin applying for salesman jobs as advertised in the Telegraph.

Good times. Happy times filled with high promise; enough for now ...

13. Bateman Street resumed

I know I'm skipping about a bit, chronologically speaking, but the more I write and think about those days long-gone, the more milestone events seemed to emerge out of the churning mists of memory and time. It's back, now, to Bateman Street in central Cambridge.

Before that, one final thought about the National Service concept. It may have been of doubtful value to the nation's military capability but its value to the individual male youth of the country, it seems to me, was indeed great. For sure you went in as a boy and came out a man, all strings to the comforts of home well and truly severed. You emerged very much aware of and largely content with your individual place *in* this world and your value *to* this world. Whether or not you had been subject to much or indeed any prior discipline, National Service's military life had instilled in you that essential self-discipline, arguably the most valuable of all the tools each of us has to help us achieve something as we gain maturity then live life beyond.

Post National Service, my three or so years in Bateman Street flats were happy times. Married life and love and parties with friends in adjoining flats and picnics and nappies soaking in the bath tub and walking, walking, walking. That Silver Cross pram must have had a thousand miles on its clock! Of course it was not ideal for Joan to go out to work in a clothing shop or anywhere else but we needed (wanted?) the money. Because of that we had to consign our baby girl to a nursery each morning before going off to our places of work. She didn't like being left and at first we found it very difficult to leave her.

Anyway I knew I had to develop some kind of career, thus manufacture some kind of family security especially when Joan became for the second time pregnant. Our sparsely furnished accomodation may have been OK - just - for we two plus baby Karen, but it was no way suited to an expanding family. Besides, our USAF friends Richard and Beaulah had by then gone home and so my life of adventure had lost most of its lustre. Adventure? Oh yes, but that's a whole story for another time.

Ouch! I've just reminded myself of the giant tsunami that overtook us when we lived in Bateman Street. You see, Joan was heavily pregnant with our second daughter, Julie, when she lost her sight. I mean, without warning she became completely blind! A total shock as her eyesight had always been excellent. She was taken to that famous hospital, Addenbrooke's, where she underwent all kinds of tests including I remember the very uncomfortable spinal tap. For ten days no change and then, as suddenly as she had lost her sight it just came back. No medical explanations were given and, frankly, we were only too relieved for her to get out of the place, so probably didn't ask enough questions. Twelve years later, in 1972 and by then with our total of four lovely offspring Joan developed a series of physical impairments. Her co-ordination and ability to walk were rapidly degrading so we were summoned to a consultant neurologist in Southampton, there told she was suffering from a condition we knew literally nothing about; 'multiple schlerosis' it was called. The consultant gave us the dreadful forward prognosis. Frankly my head was in overload shut-down but Joan just nodded and, as Yorkshire calm and controlled as always she asked him, *How long have I had this, whatever it is?. Well, it was diagnosed when you were in Addenbrookes fourteen years ago,* came the response. Why oh why had nobody seen fit to tell us then? I think of our children. Perhaps they were right, after all.

14. New arrival, new employment

Leaving our babies in the care of a neighbour I rented a Morris Minor and drove for second interview the two hundred odd miles to Lily Cups and Containers (England) Ltd. Joan came with me. Anyone remembering the traffic congestion on the A1 before the opening of the M1 will know the degree of difficulty of such a journey, especially for a virgin driver who had just passed his test at the second attempt. I arrived redfaced, late and in some state of dishevelment. I shall always be grateful to the sales director's secretary who shuffled things around so I could relax before entering the big man's presence. Amazingly I got the job. After training with others in a similar role I would take up duties in selling throughout East Anglia and the northern Home Counties our paper hot and cold drinking cups and containers for ice cream, dairy products, catering outlets etc. No car, so travelling by every known form of public transport. That mattered not - I was on my way!

Pretty little four years old Karen Jane acquired an equally pretty baby sister on 17th July 1959. We were still living in our furnished flat in Bateman Street, Cambridge at the time, but I was undergoing product and sales training in Liverpool with my new employer. Having arrived home for the weekend after a long rail journey our friendly neighbour, who was looking after Karen, told me Joan was in the maternity hospital. I rushed over just in time to greet the new arrival, in almost if not quite as dishevelled a state as as when I'd greeted our first born in Newmarket. Picking up my new daughter I recall, most, the exquisite smell of her, saw with some pride the post natal strain and happiness on the face of my twenty four years old wife. We called our newborn Julie Elaine. She was perfect, not simply in looks but in personality. Always the trace of a smile, so often that happy-making baby gurgle. And, glory of all babytime glories, Julie always slept right through the night!

Living in a furnished rental and now with a wife and two offspring to support I really needed to get my newfound career into fast forward, so I did my best to learn quickly. Having finished the head office / factory training the sales director sent me out on the road with a sequence of territory salesmen. I spent a week each with Ian Rowatt in Scotland, Harry Wilson in Lancashire, Brian Thomas in Yorkshire, George Mercer in London, Jack Snelgrove in the West Country and Bill Davies in the Midland Counties. Fifty four years have gone by since then so I'm genuinely amazed to find I can remember all the names of these new colleagues - as well as much of what they taught me. We all became friends, a single team. The older and the younger, the experienced and the beginner, we were all in it together. I had learned the first rule of any business 'Company': A group with genuine camaraderie becomes a team much greater than its component parts. New company, new products, new markets, new horizons. I felt like Christopher Columbus must have felt on first viewing the promised land.

One conversation I so well recall when during those training weeks: Harry Wilson on our Lancashire territory was a brilliant man and a great salesman. He had been a Royal Marine Commando in the war, landing at Anzio alongside the Americans - for whom he would never hear a bad word. One day we had been on quite a boozy pub lunch with one of his customers. Nothing unusual about that for drinking between supplier and supplied was the order of the day. Our conversation in his car afterwards went something like this ...

Harry: *Bryan, you're not really a drinker, are you?*

Me: (head spinning but not wishing to show it): *Not really Harry*

Harry: *Well, you're just going to have to learn. You have to drink at the same pace as your customer, see? If you don't, you'll make him uncomfortable.*

Me: *Right, Harry.*

Harry: *But never drink at home.*

Me: *Why not?*

Harry: *Because if you lay off the booze those two weekend days you'll never become an alcoholic like so many sales guys and ex-soldiers I know of, right?*

Me: *OK Harry. Thanks.*

For years I followed this advice, aided and abetted by both my wives, neither of whom have cared overmuch for the demon drink.

I have heard it said that a top industrial salesman is born, not made, and during these territorial training weeks I saw both kinds in action - the born and the well made. On the 'born' extreme was Ian Rowatt in Scotland, almost always the winner of our sales competitions as time went by, myself very often a reluctant best of the rest. Like everybody, at the beginning I viewed the prospect of walking into a strange business and its even stranger faces with a certain amount of, I hope well concealed dread. It is not easy, especially for a wet behind the ears tyro. Whatever bullshit they preach about selling things the main driver is always fear: fear of not even being able to get through reception to see the buyer or of being ignored; fear of being asked questions about your products or the use of your products to which you have no answer, fear of being given rude short shrift and, worst of all, the overwhelming fear of failure. To succeed you had to gain the respect of your customer and I learned quickly that you could only gain the necessary respect - that is, respect for your company and your product, not just for yourself - if you truly know what you are doing and truly believe in the benefits of your product. But when you do manage to gain that respect, when you do learn to control or hide your fears and, much, much more importantly, when you receive an order - you don't just exit your new customer, you walk away as if on air. A fantastic feeling. Almost if possibly not quite as good as the proverbially perfect sex!

And talking of respect, there was my area manager, Tom Salisbury, a man who, if he still lives would today be a hundred. Classic salesman, born and bred, always with the juste motte, the light gag, the air of bonhomie. After my tour of the UK and as a part of my indoctrination / training I met up with Tom for a couple of days 'on the road' in my own future territory of Eastern Counties..Those few days stay in my mind. We met on the Monday morning in Norwich just as the seaside resorts along the Norfolk and Suffolk coasts were gearing up for the visitor season ahead. We began our selling in Lowestoft. Of course it had to be raining. A grey and cheerless day for a well-suited, brand new, briefcase toting learner salesman. Tom did the pitching to the seafront whelk and seafood stalls, cafes, amusement arcades with coffee machines, etcetera, me listening and learning. To my surprise, although that first day we (he) only gained a couple of small orders for paper cups, the stallholders, cafe owners etc were welcoming and seemed quite happy to stop and chat. When we'd 'done' Lowestoft's sea front we drove along to Great Yarmouth for more of the same. After parking the car Tom Salisbury turned to me, pointing; 'Righto Bryan, you take all the prospects that way and I'll go this way'. I was once again to fly solo, if considerably more nervous than I was on that day in the old Tiger Moth!

In those days every town had its Commercial Hotels for the travelling sales community. Many such places were really no more than sparsely furnished boarding houses. After Yarmouth (and no, I didn't secure any orders there but several prospects kindly advised me to come back when the season started) Tom drove us back to Norwich, where he had booked us rooms.

My first boss often told the tale of how, when the front door opened to our knocking the most amazingly proportioned, simply gorgeous young lady appeared - and how I had stood there transfixed, he would say, if not quite open-mouthed. She would have been the daughter of the house. This house was one of the last I would come to know where the single breakfast table was occupied accordi9ng to commercial tradition in strict order of seniority, the most senior - that is the most experienced representative / salesman taking precedence, and so on down the table to yours truly - who was not expected to speak much if, indeed, at all. For a bunch of people earning a living through their supposedly silver tongues, meals were strangely silent affairs.

Next time I'll tell you of my first day out selling paper cups on my own in a town called Bury St Edmunds. I shall boast a little of my escalating sales success and of my first promotion to the biggest territory and the acquisition of our first house in Kings Heath, Birmingham. Oh yes, here we go ....

15. Onwards and upwards

1960: then came my first day out as a fully fledged, professional, industrial salesman, the start of that long road. Joan had made sure of my sartorial appearance. She straightened my collar, kissed me goodbye and wished me (us) good luck. Being a Yorkshire lass there were no tears, just a real, well concealed confidence in the young man who had so relatively little of his own. We both knew the importance to our lives of this new beginning.

Armed with a classified telephone book, a briefcase full of samples and price lists and a heart full of fear and hope (in that order) I caught the early train from Cambridge to Bury St Edmunds. There had been some kind of enquiry directed to my company from a brewery called Greene King, so at least I knew a name for whom to ask. In those days breweries often handled the catering arrangements at outside events: point to point racecourses, fetes, folk or jazz festivals, etc. I had rehearsed and rehearsed my opening gambit. No problems. So why did I walk right past that brewery office door - and then back again and then back again? Eventually I took the necessary deep breath and ventured inside. The receptionist looked at my card with ill-concealed scepticism and picked up her phone, but instead of inviting me into his office, the source of the enquiry walked down to see me right there in reception. A sure sign he wanted me out and away as soon as politely possible! Trouble was, he couldn't remember anything about why he'd responded to our advertisement. It was clear he had little or no interest anyway. 'Sorry about that', he said, 'But thanks for coming by.'

'Never let your crest fall', Tommy Salisbury had advised, but mine damn near did at that point. I turned to leave but just in time remembered another of Tommy's dictums; 'It's the bloody sample, Bryan,' he'd told me. 'Get the bastard into his hand. Remember to handle it as you would handle a bar of gold. Bugger won't want it and won't know what to do with it or with you but that thing could be a damn sight more interesting to him than you are.' So I thrust my sample at the buyer, a waxed paper cup made and printed by our principals in the U.S.A. with a rather good contemporary design featuring ears of barley. Bear in mind that in 1960 a disposable drinking cup of any kind was still a virtual unknown. The buyer looked at my sample in silence, turning it this way and that, then, 'Fancy a cup of tea?' he asked. 'Let's go up to the office'. I was in! We sat there chatting for a little while, mostly about the minutae of life and sometimes about business and, right at the end, about my products, my company and the sample. A year later I got my first order - a large one - from that man at Greene King.

All these years later, now that the gates are open the memories come flooding back. Whilst the orders - indeed anything across the wilds of East Anglia didn't ever come easily, steady sales were being made and my confidence grew alongside them. Such progress was made in spite of my having to use only public transport to get around that enormous territory (known throughout commercial UK, by the way, as the 'salesman's graveyard!.) But having been runner-up in a new accounts sales competition (I went into every dentist in Norwich, I recall, selling little pleated water cups) I was clearly being noticed at Head Office. One day on the phone, 'How would you like a Morris Minor?' asked my boss, and before I could tell him I'd like it about as much as would a fish like to swim he added; 'The company has an unused one. We'll rent it you if you like.' At that moment I was phoning in a small new order, standing in a be-puddled phone box with rain and wind-lashed cracked window panes on Clacton-on-sea's sea front. My macintosh was soaked through and through. I tried to appear not overly excited; 'Yes, sounds good to me, Mr Williams,' I mumbled; 'How much a month will it cost me?'

Our flat of course had no telephone so I had to wait til I got home to give Joan the news. As I burst in she was feeding one year old Julie. Now, my Joan Margaret Islip was never easily or overtly excitable. *Will we be able to use the car for other than business then, Bryan?* she asked. I nodded. *Of course, we'll just have to find the petrol money.* She put down toddler Julie, gave me a great big hug and a laughing, promisary kiss. Five years old Karen Jane, sensing the good news, skipped around and around that gas-fire heated, meter fed, tiny little living room. *Take off those wet things and sit yourself down,* said my wife. *Dinner's not started yet so I'm off to get fish and chips. Let's celebrate.*

Let's push out the boat, I said. *Get mushy peas as well, and a large Vimto, OK?* Karen squealed with delight. *All right, I will - Karen, you coming with me? We'll be able to go and see your nan and grandad in York in the car, soon as daddy get's time off.*

Daddy neither wanted nor needed time off although he did albeit grudgingly take some. Guess I was well and truly hooked on this business thing. To my own surprise I proved to be intensely competitive. The more orders I won and the more plaudits I attracted, the more I wanted. Some of my early, East Anglian landmark successes included Campbell's soups - a million small sampling cups, Seaman's Dairy double waxed cups for cream - I remember the buyer was that rarity in my experience, a really, really rude person - and Wicksteed Village theme park - half a million specially printed hot and cold drink cups. It was that last order that won me a sales competition and probably secured my promotion. But my favourite order off that first territory was for fifty thousand of our 'china-coated' hot drink cups at Jack's Hill Cafe, the most well-known transport cafe on the A1 trunk road, a pull-over always busy with trunk drivers and commercials like me. The owner was a classic harridan of a loud, blonde, well-build lady, as famous from south to north as were her all day / all night breakfasts. I went in for my lunch and afterwards sought her out to pitch my case for paper hot and cold drinking cups. She turned me down out of hand but not without kindness. *Our lorry drivers don't want those things, son,* she explained; *Pint china mugs is what they're used to for their tea.*

Sitting outside that café in my Morris Minor I used the crayon set and writing paper that I always carried to create a design based on the Jack's Hill Cafe sign. I cut out my sketch, stuck it on a cup and went back in. I think she had taken something of a shine to this persistent young man, or felt sorry for him - I hope the former. I explained that it wasn't the long distance drivers but the holiday motorists to whom the advertising might work - plus no washing up of course. She ordered fifty thousand hot and twenty thousand cold cups, specially printed. It was my first real understanding of the power and the potential for me and my company of design and print.

Every year Lily Cups held a conference culminating in a grand dinner at Liverpool's Adelphi Hotel. To my utter astonishment and not without some raised eyebrows from my fellow (mostly senior) sales guys I was seated on the top table between DRG Group MD Lloyd Robinson and my own Lily Cups MD Bob Taylor. I well remember two things about that dinner. First, Lloyd Robinson's speech. He stood up. Silence, then, *This is the first time in my life,* he uttered, *that I have turned my back on a naked lady.* More silence, this time of the stunned variety before the penny dropped - behind him stood a marble statue of Venus at her ablutions. The second thing I recall was Bob Taylor's habit of picking out individuals in his speeches, for better, best or worse. During his own speech he turned to look down on me, quoting from Shakespeare's Julius Caesar; *I think young Cassius hath that mean and hungry look'*, he said. I probably did, at barely eleven stones in weight and over six feet in height.

The next day I was offered the company's Midlands territory based in Birmingham. It was the territory with the largest sales revenue, the incumbent Bill Davies having decided to retire into Liverpool head office. The company would use its influence with the Bristol & West Building Society to ensure I got a hundred percent mortgage on a house in that city. Within a month I had 'bought' the semi-detached 121 Yarningale Road, Kings Heath, Birmingham and had moved in. We possessed no furniture. Looking back, stark is the word where you sleep on someone's old mattress on the floor and hang what clothes you have on bamboo sticks resting on picture rails across the corner of the room, but the word coming first to mind about Yarningale Road is 'happy'. We had each other, we were all fit and healthy, we had a bank account with the Midland (more on that later) and we had the real prospect of prosperity. Father even sent me a congratulatory card. Wonder upon wonder!

My first day out on that new territory I drove through the UK's second city up to the top of Dudley Hill. I parked up outside the zoo, got out to gaze around and breathe in air that may have been smoke laden but for me was like wine of the promised land. *My* land. Spread out before me for square miles and miles and miles lay the the heavily industrialised black country. I remember so well the feeling that morning. This was my new territory, my new Kingdom. Mine to conquer not just for myself or ourselves but for Lily Cups and Containers (England) Limited and for the father who had seemed to have forgotten - or not wanted to know about - our existence and for my mother and two sisters who I had not seen or heard of for seventeen and for my sister Shirley, now far away in Hong Kong.

But at that moment none of it mattered as much as this; for this, the industfrial Midlands of England was my Kingdom.

16. Pastures new, things to do

When promoted to Birmingham, the centre of my major new sales territory, I decided that, rather than carry on renting from my employer that vintage Morris Minor I would turn it in and buy myself a new car. With my wife Joan I spent hours poring over the glossy brochures before deciding on a white Ford Anglia; *The car that looks as if it is going fast when standing still* said the memorable advertisement splurge. My cars have always gone fast, so that really did appeal to me!

Returning my rented old Morris up to head office in Liverpool for the final time I have to confess to having had a bit of a lump in my throat. Never since then have I developed any actual affection for a car - or for any machine for that matter, (unless you include boats as machinery), but that car with its orange flip-out indicators had been a part of my personal renaissance. Not just career-wise but also family-wise, for we often travelled in it to Joan's family in the city of York, then used it to explore with Joan's people the wonderful county of Yorkshire, especially its coastline. So far as I recall, we were the first in the extensive Wood family to have a motor car. How many people can you fit into a Morris Minor? Lots and lots! To this day Joan's sister and brothers tell the tale about when we were proceeding speedily to visit Castle Howard. Those in the back included Auntie Margaret with a plastered up broken leg. As we went over a speed bump all of us hit the roof except poor Margaret whose plaster cast was trapped under the seat in front. Everyone but me and Margaret thought it hilarious, and still they do, reminding me whenever we get together - which is most years.

Then there was the time, back in East Anglia, when I had been driving my boss John Williams and his boss, the Sales Director John Gee, from Norwich to Kings Lynn. I was conducting them on a tour of my territorial customers. The straight and level East Anglian roads were empty and I must have been doing about seventy when, fifty yards ahead, a woman with headscarf wheeled her pushbike out from behind a parked lorry straight across the road in front.. She was oblivious to my approach. On my left was a very deep dyke. If I had swerved right I must definitely have killed her so I went left, braking hard but as carefully as I could and came to a stop with the car balanced at forty degrees over the embankment and the water below, having missed a telegraph pole by a matter of inches. My sales manager

John Williams and sales director John Gee were for once stunned into silence. Engine off, quietly I murmured, *John,* (Williams in the passenger seat), *Open your door and climb out. If I get out we'll overbalance and you'll all be in the drink.* Both Johns evacuated the car in something of a silent, although excessively careful hurry, scrambling in their nice suits down into the edge of the dyke and up the grassy embankment on to the roadway. When I got out I went to say some choice words to the headscarved lady but relented when finding she had suffered a broken little finger. My side mirror had just clipped her hand on the handlebar. Strangely there was very little damage to the bike, but six inches either way and 'where the hell's the nearest hospital' would have been the order of the day - for her, or some, or all of us. There were no repercussions, legal or otherwise. But I shall never forget John Williams surveying the scene, shaking his head. *Bryan Islip, do you have any brothers?* he muttered. I took that as a compliment.

Having collected my brand new Ford Anglia from the dealer in Bristol I drove it homewards up the A38, bristling with pride. Reaching the outskirts of Birmingham I stopped to allow a man to cross the road on a beaconed zebra crossing. Five seconds later, bang! Some bastard had driven right into my brand new rear end. Relatively minor damage but my first experience of the hazy, mazy insurance industry. My homecoming was somewhat less than it might have been when Joan and the little girls came out to admire the new car - albeit with its newly bent rear fender and its broken tail lights.

There were much happier associations with that Ford. Besides the aforementioned trips to York we used to pile kiddies and stuff into it for weekend day trips to the seaside. Living close to the dead centre of England we had a choice: east to my old stamping grounds at Lowestoft or Yarmouth, south to the Hampshire / Sussex coast or west to Barmouth in Wales' Cardigan Bay, the closest by road - this was our favourite. Off we would go at crack of dawn on a Sunday, car packed with beach stuff, picnic stuff and little girls squealing with excitement. I remember driving across the Welsh highlands past the Dolgelly mountainsides studded with grazing sheep that Kairen had christened 'woolly maggots'. Isn't it strange how you never remember the rainy days? I can't, anyway. Always the sun shone and always the sea was bitingly, shriekingly, laughingly cold. Sandcastles got built but then so saddeningly dissolved by the incoming tide. Our picnic was shared out and relished. Then at end of day the long, long drive home.

When darkness fell the girls would be asleep in the back. Joan and I would enjoy the silence. I recall that special tiredness and that splendidly uncomfortable sunburn on my back and, for some unknown reason, on my insteps. Our hands would touch and hold as the miles unrolled.

My sales results were climbing at a most satisfactory rate of knots.. By this time I really enjoyed being out on the road. I enjoyed the personal freedom of it and the steady growth of reputation and income. I enjoyed making new customers for my company's machines to churn out product and making new friends on my Midlands territory in the process. Even senior colleagues in the Group's Birmingham office condescended to climb down from Mount Parnassus to take notice of this fresh faced newcomer to their ill-considered Lily Cups offshoot. As we've all heard, success does indeed breed success and the confidence that ensures even greater success. There were no hurdles too high for me to jump, or at least try to jump in those days.

For instance, I recall with affection an elderly businessman by the name of Jimmy Rudge, Catering Officer of the mighty Joseph Lucas Group headquartered in downtown Birmingham. I was determined to crack the large-scale industrial catering market for my company's hot and cold drinking cups. Cutting quite a long story short I learned that (a) Mr Rudge never spoke with salesmen and, (b), he always arrived in his office by eight in the morning, earlier than most. For several intermittent days I waited, sitting in that imposing reception as the man strode in, immaculately suited and hatted with his shiny briefcase. Each time I rose to my feet and each time I received short shrift; just the odd sideways glance, never friendly, never a kindly word. The receptionist, by then familiar with this fruitless routine and patently feeling sorry for me would call him once he had reached his office then put down her phone, shaking her head apologetically. 'On your way', said the headshake and the shrug of her pretty little shoulders. You can guess the rest. One day he stopped to ask the receptionist who the hell I was. That was the beginning of one of our most important company accounts and yet another confirmation that sheer persistence counts most of all..

Next time I'll write about one very hard lesson in commercial finance from a jazz festival organiser and about developing my interests in painting and fishing and opening my first bank account and my newfound friend the manager of the Midland Bank's Shirley branch.

And next time I'll tell you about the fairly dramatic birth of our third child; it's a boy! So great the excitement. And what do you know? this time I could actually afford the cigars!

17. Money matters, so does life

Ever since the year 1500 the firstborn male in my family has been allotted the middle name, Henry, I was told that this explained my own middle name. John Islip had been made Abbot of Westminster on 27 October of that year. The abbot was a close confidant of both Henry VII and Henry VIII, and therefore a Privy Councillor. Abbott Islip was also responsible for the building of large parts of the Abbey, including his very own Islip chapel. I have fine copies of his funeral roll here, well mounted and framed and displayed on the upstairs wall of Kirkhill House.

Anyway Robert Henry Islip was born in number 121, Yarningale Road, Kings Heath, Birmingham on a snow-bound January 5th, 1963. Because Joan had potential childbirth problems the other three of our children were born in hospitals. (chronologically: Newmarket, Cambridge and Solihull), but Bob was a homebirth and don't I know it, for I assisted - albeit at a distance - whereas with the others I kept or was kept well away from the action. As I say, the snow lay deep and crisp and even for the birth of my firstborn son when Joan's time at last arrived. I called the midwife. A couple of hours later that brave lady made it to our house, having several times had to call for assistance in digging her car out of the snow - and having had to park a couple of roads away. By this time Joan was making the most agonised of sounds, poor girl, and yours truly was in serious need of alcohol. Fortunately I didn't have any in the house! I say fortunately because the midwife instructed me to go to her car and bring back a cylinder of oxygen. I slipped and slid through the drifts and falling snow, finally finding her car and struggling back with the cylinder, exhausted. At that I was told, *No, not that one. That's the air cylinder. Take it back and bring the other one - the oxygen.* Joan then increased her weeping and wailing, adding a few choice epithets as regards her stupid husband!

But soon enough the midwife called me from upstairs. *It's a boy, Bryan. Come up and meet your son.* And so I did, taking with me our two little girls, six years old Karen and two years old Julie. It's a wonder all the noise and kerfuffle didn't put them off child bearing for life - but in fact they've between them had seven of their own offspring

At this time of my life I had bedun to paint pictures in my spare time, often working by artificial light long after the rest of the family were fast asleep. At school, thirteen years before, 'art' had been one of my best and most enjoyable subjects. I had now become obsessed with the French Impressionists, using artbooks borrowed from the local library to copy, in oils on Dalerboard, well known masterpieces from Renoir, Cezanne, Van Gogh, Degas etc. Then I progressed forward to Picasso and Braque and backwards in time to the old Dutch and Italian masters such as the 'Fall of Rome' by, I think, Carravagio; a copy only recently rediscovered after many 'lost' years in a corner of our attic...

And then came my own first original. A still life with fruit in a glass bowl. It hangs to this day on the wall in Kirkhill House. I recall the bananas becoming blacker and blacker as my painting days (or nights) progressed...

Soon after moving from Cambridge into Birmingham I opened my first bank account with a small branch of The Midland in the adjacent suburb of Shirley. The manager was a keen golfer. I believe I was his only client in a position to take the occasional time off work to accompany him for a midweek round. I should explain that a new friend, Ron Amos, a sales executive with DRG Group based in Birmingham, had urged me on to the Coxmoor links and taught me the rudiments of the game. Being something of an obsessive I soon became well and truly hooked. Crazy! In fact I can remember going out on the course by myself one wintery day when my ill-afforded golf balls, well-driven, just disappeared - white into white! My bank manager's name was Norman Windebank. Quite appropriate, for although we became regular golfing buddies, age difference notwithstanding, the relationship enabled my very flexible overdraft to become much, much too flexible!

It wasn't until just before we moved away from the area that I learned about this typical suburban bank manager's wartime exploits. Norman had been a pilot on Mosquito fighter-bombers. He was one of those unbelievably brave souls who went to bomb German's heavy water plant in Norway, knowing they could not carry sufficient fuel to get them all the way home. He duly ditched in the cold North Sea and was picked up. The target was essential to Germany's efforts to construct what would have been the world's first atomic bomb. You can imagine, 'what if ...' Norman and his like had failed ...

By this time the company's sales were regularly outstripping its production. Many times I had little or nothing to sell anyone! So one workday morning I called head office and asked if there was anything I could do to help out in the factory. John Williams was quite horrified. *Listen*, he urged, Don't be daft. *You play golf, don't you? Just get out there and improve your handicap.* I needed no second bidding.

Then came the hardest lesson in a business career; the lesson that says it's all about money, cash and cash flow; you know, real coin of the realm! I had obtained a large order from a well-spoken young guy in the entertainment industry. He was organising a giant jazz festival out at Earlswood Lakes. He had a nice office, big car, Oxfordian accent; in short, a solid gold new account. Or so I thought. The Saturday dawned sultry hot so Joan and I took our brood out to the festival. We sat on the grass, listened to the music, ate our hot dogs from 'my' paper plates, drank beer or lemonade out of 'my' paper cups. Brilliant. Free entry for us of course. On Monday my home phone rang. My finance director. The well promised Earlswood money had not been paid over, would I go see the man and obtain it; like, now!

I was just and only just in time when I literally burst into his office where I surprised him busily counting a huge pile of silver coins. Suffice to say I walked away with his invoice fully paid and a very heavy briefcase. Later on, I believe from a piece in the Birmingham Post I learned he had defaulted here, there and everywhere - including many of the poor jazz bands themselves. Clearly a well orchestrated fraud.

One day in 1963 I was summoned to Liverpool head office and there promoted to area sales manager for the Midlands, Wales and South West. New title, new responsibilities, new motor car and, very soon a new home. Oh, the giddying heights! But always there seemed to be a dark side of the moon as I learned how colleagues and friends can be frustratedly jealous rivals. I also learned all about the divisions of rank, unwelcome as they were gto me.

Anyway, to celebrate I brought home a fish and chips supper - just like Cambridge!

18. 1963: thrills and spills

1963: a solo summons to Head Office could mean only one of two things; I'm either getting fired or promoted. As I have said, fortunately it was the latter. As I have also indicated, the company was going through hard times because of its inability to manufacture anything close to its rated potential, meaning that we salesmen had to spend much of our efforts, having taken orders in all good faith, explaining short deliveries. Industrial buyer/seller relationships were extremely hard won and therefore very valuable assets in those pre-internet days. The commercial and personal damage could be permanent. Like everyone else I had to be aware of the possibility of undeserved redundancy. On the other hand, both as salesman and area manager my work had almost always found favour with the management.

At a stroke, for me promotion meant that life changed, and I don't mean just business life. I can understand why large companies often have policies to prevent one from a group of colleagues being promoted in situ over the other members of same group. Especially in a solidly results oriented team and especially when the selected one is junior in years and in experience to the others. Some time later I asked my boss how come the finger had pointed at me? Finger is a quite appropriate word. At one of the preceding sales conferences John Williams had invited all his sales guys to prepare a short talk on any subject of our choice. We were to congregate in a hotel conference room to watch in a separate room, as each of us presented our efforts to a revolutionary new closed circuit TV camera. The thing is, I had just read a book about the South American policeman who'd discovered and developed the universally adopted finger printing technology. That book and a few of my homespun illustrations and an earnest look into the eye of the TV camera had done the trick!

It took me a while as area manager to find the essential ground between being overly authoritarian and overly egalitarian with my team. In this I was assisted by being seconded on to several junior management training courses at the Bristol head office. In that way I got to know others of my ilk in the Group - plus the nightlife and pub life of Bristol! I remember that one such training course was all about speaking to a large audience. For a week we junior managers would be taught the rudiments of standing up and saying stuff hopefully worth listening to. On the final afternoon of that week we would each deliver a ten minute address, on any subject we chose, to the Group Chairman, Sir John Foster Robinson. 'Piece of cake'!!! For goodness sake, weren't all we eager young managers expert with words? But unfortunately, despite the emphasis on preparation we spent far too much time in Bristol's clubs and pubs and little if any time on that essential evening homework. When Friday's presentation time came around, one by one we made a bloody silly fool of ourselves. Thus I found out the hard way that ten minutes is one hell of a long time to talk about anything to an audience and quite impossible in the absence of specific preparation, even rehearsal. As I recall, when the last of us had huffed and blundered his way through his speech, probably with many an embarrassing silence, Sir John - an immaculkate public speajker himself - stalked off, saying ne'er a goodbye to anyone!

Several things have remained fixed in my memory about our family times in Yarningale Road, mostly good things. For a start we were very, very happy there. But of course not always; I remember the tears as we learned on November 22, 1963, via our rented TV, that President Kennedy had been shot and killed. How, I wondered then, (and still do), could such a remote politician (even as we now know one as much flawed) evoke such a depth of love? But we did love the man. He was our symbol of hope for the future. At the time, expectations in his aftermath were a perfect, much worrying void. Anything, nothing; possibly even that horribly anticipated nuclear disaster.

And, from major to minor, I remember my best ever figure painting - maybe my best ever painting, period. Ready for bed in a blue nightie little Julie had fallen asleep on the settee. Stupidly I sent the resultant oil painting to my father in Hastings. I thought it might inspire him to take some kind of interest in us, especially since we had named our second daughter after his wife, my stepmother Julia. I know he received the painting but when I asked after it years later he denied having had it. One for the rubbish tip I suppose. Thanks once again for nothing, father!

Then there was that awful morning when, driving eight years old Karen and her little friend to school, upon said friend getting out a car came hurtling down the pavement, smashing her into the open rear door. The poor girl had a piece as large as half an orange gouged out of her thigh. The out of control vehicle ended up against a crumpled street light. At the inquest I learned the elderly driver had been dead at the wheel from a heart attack. What a rotten, rotten way to leave this world I thought, and still do think.

In view of our expanded family Joan and I decided to sell our semi and buy a larger newbuild detached in nearby, upmarket Solihull. (Onwards and upwards, yipee!!) My home-made 'for sale' board had not been up outside our home in Yarningale Road more than a day or two before a young Asian gentleman came calling. It was the oddest house sale of the five I've made since then. This man hardly looked round the rooms before making a bee-line for the garage. After detailed inspection of that he signified his approval and we rep[aired to the kitchen where he opened his attache case and counted out the full asking price - in banknotes! Of course the Bristol & West Building Society took the vast majority of it but not before I had paid it into my depleted bank account by counting it out on to my somewhat taken aback bank manager friend's desk. Oh, temporary wealth!

Our new home was one of the first completions on the gigantic Damsonwood Estate, situated alongside 'the Rovers' (British Leyland) test track. We furnished the house mainly on the good old HP and added a warm water fish tank to the lounge. At the rear of our back garden I created a goldfish pond, (something I did in every subsequent new house purchase). With much ceremony.Karen planted a number of acorns and introduced Sammy the tortoise, who lived happily there until our next door neighbour's lovely little dog killed and ate much of him! So many tears!

For the first time I was now to spend much of my working week staying away from home in hotels, therefore fully exposed to all the temptations of the expense account flesh. Life's focus was inexorably shifting to the heady excitement of my burgeoning career. And of course like any reasonably nice looking, well dressed young business executive I was beginning to notice that most heady of wonders - i.e. that strange young women were beginning to notice me! Unwanted potential diversions for a young man married to his one and, so far, the only lady he had ever known.

19. Camping, fishing, prospering

In 1961 I invested in a tent and all the necessary camping kit for our holidays. In our brand new two tone Ford Cortina Estate we tried it out early in the year - too early actually, for it rained and it rained. We had difficulty locating a farmer in West Wales good enough to let us pitch in his field. Erecting the thing in the rainy darkness and sorting ourselves out for the night should have put us off camping for ever. We were not happy bunnies at the time. But it didn't deter, for from then until about 1968 camping was our holiday, most often in West Wales at a place called Shell Island. I understand it is now a recognised and fully equipped camping ground but in those days we were one of a very few of farmer Workman's 'guests'. You could get there across a causeway only at low tide. (One trip across we noticed a great big salmon trapped in a tidal pool. One for the pot after a good deal of splashing and crashing around with a bait digging fork.) When you knocked on the farmhouse door and checked in we would go to our usual corner of a certain field, pitch up, then dig our sanitary hole (pitching the special little latrine tent around it). Looking back, we seemed always to arrive with very little money but very high hopes for the bass fishing and with a lot of happiness in anticipation of joining up with the same group of families each summer.

Oh, those beach parties! We would take it in turns to tend the fire and turn over it on a spit a small pig or lamb - and/or the bass and mullet we had seine netted from the edge of the sea! Glorious. One of our good companions was a Professor Mike somebody from Aston University and his family, and then there was the unforgettable Norman Bush with his family of two. 'Bush' was right. He had the biggest, most luxurious growth I'd encountered up to then. I don't know what Norman did for a living but, sitting around the beach fire, kiddies fast falling asleep, his pretty wife singing folk songs for us … wonderful! She had, literally, the voice of an angel (or Joan Baez).. You know how it is when you experience a form of sublimity close up at first hand something so perfect, so fine that it stands the hairs up on the nape of your neck?

As a little boy and all the way up to my first job at Boots the Chemists I had been obsessive about angling, both freshwater and sea. Now a well married family man aged twenty eight, the opportunity and the obsession re-emerged. Perhaps selfishly, for Joan had only limited interest in it, fishing went along with camping as the thing we did on all those family holidays. There was a spot on the beach at Shell Island at the end of a range of rocks uncovered by each night-time rising tide where the bass would patrol. They couldn't resist the clam bait we dug out of the estuary mud. I can tell you one thing - for me, barbequed bass is much tastier than barbequed mullet or any fishy restaurant offering with the possible exception of pan-fried Dover sole. One summer holiday we were locally given the use of a small speedboat. It was totally unsuited to angling but what the hell. From it I caught a forty pound tope (small shark) which we tried to barbeque but which proved a disastrous waste of a very fine animal. Pride can be a false master. I should have let it go.

Our second son and the last of our children, Stuart Graham, arrived on the 29th of December, 1965 , in a Solihull maternity hospital. We used to leave him in the living room in his carry cot parked close up to the new tropical fish tank. For hours he would follow the multi-coloured fishes' peregrinations around and around their glass ocean. Perhaps that is why Stu might as well have been born with a fishing rod in his hand. We took him, Robert, Julie and Karen to Shell Island many times until the girls decided there were more important and/or more comfortable things than camping. I remember the friends with whom we caught up each year used to call baby Stu 'Me-og' (his baby version of 'my rod') because that was his constant refrain as he toddled around looking for his miniature fishing rod. He would stand on the pebbled beach casting his line with stone attached into six inches of seawater, gazing with total conviction in hopes of a catch.

I remember with great affection the wonderful sound of rain on canvas as you're snuggled together in your sleeping bag. And I recall chiselling our family name into a boulder close by 'our' site that rock must still be there). I remember being up to my fully clothed chest in the sea, spreading the seine net, feeling the fish hits and dragging in to the beach to the accompaniment of much shouting and splashing; I so vividly recall that first cup of tea in bed; the barefoot excitement of children running around on rain-soaked grass; the simple freedom and the sense of adventure that went with it; seeking and finding seabirds eggs - and letting them be - and of course all those barbeques beneath the stars. All of it truly wonderful, no less for the backward look.

There were other holidays of course; I remember South Wales and Pendine beach and Cornwall's Bude where my feet got so sunburned I could hardly bear to drive the car home; and Mevagissey, fishing the end of the pier in company with others of my angling obsession. There, the taste of pasties and salty lugworm fingers, smoking Hamlet small cigars for evermore, for me, associated with Jacques Loussiere's *Air on a G-string*. Meanwhile my career was developing as fast as my family, but with two girls and now two boys we decided to call a halt. Enough was enough of wee babies, however enchanting. Our girls were promising to develop into fine young ladies and the boys were progressing from squeaky infants into angel-faced little nursery primary or nursery schoolboys.

In late 1967 I was promoted from area sales manager to national sales manager. This entailed another house move, from Solihull in the Midlands to Formby near Liverpool head office in the north.

So now the whole of the U.K; tomorrow Europe; after that the world ... why not? thought I.

20. Toils and spoils, work and play

1967. As if being promoted above my peers to area manager hadn't been difficult enough, being now promoted from area manager above the other two area managers to national sales manager was even more so. Both Tom Salisbury and Brian Thomas were my friends, especially Tommy who had been my first boss in East Anglia when I'd started with the company six years earlier. The three of us had become used to meeting up here and there to compare notes every now and then. Of course such get togethers had invariably involved a round of golf and a lunch or supper with plenty of liquid refreshment. Before the drink driving laws - remember that? No more after this final promotion. It was neither possible nor desirable to maintain the same relationships when I was now the one not being questioned but questioning the use of the sales force's time and expenses money! ... Something about gamekeepers and poachers …

I have a photograph of myself with my twenty strong sales team at the first of our annual sales conferences. I had come up with the somewhat theatrical idea of importing a formula three racing car into our Buxton hotel. *Let's go fast*, was the message. I am second left with my foot on the car. My first boss Tommy Salisbury is in the driving seat and the pretty young lady sitting on the bonnet is Mrs Sandy Ferguson, second in command of our design studio. Forty five years after I left the company I remember all their names. This was a truly great team. Trouble is, the 'company' car had little petrol and was badly in need of a good servicing - i.e. we could never produce enough product of good enough quality to meet our sales.

My boss, John Williams had been promoted to the Board. I was now expected, as national sales manager, to spend most of my days at head office in Fazakerley, Liverpool 9. That is why I had moved residence once again, this time from Solihull to a rather nice detached house in Formby, Lancashir. It was about a twenty minutes daily commute. Although Joan and the family did not protest and our new home was lovely, I knew that we had all been more than happy where we were, and moving schools is never easy for children, especially Karen who had won her way to the most prestigious school in Solihull. However by this time my career had taken me over, big time - had probably even taken precedence over family. In seven years we had gone from a furnished bed sitter to a four bedroomed detached house in a 'nice' suburb. I was told - in confidence of course- that my next move would not be long and would see me ensconced in that Dickinson Robinson Group tower block in Redcliffe Street, Bristol.

I had become pretty good on Birmingham's parkland golf courses but I was in for a rude awakening when I tried out the ancient championship links up and down Lancashire's sandy coastline. I have a vivid memory of driving the ball over some mighty dune, hopefully towards a totally unseen green only to find it (if I was lucky enough to find my ball at all) buried into the sand or into the whispy marran grass. And the sheer length of the courses! It wasn't long before Joan's oft repeated question; *Bryan, your family or your golf - which is it to be?* was answered with a sigh. *You, dear, you. I'm giving up the game.* But in truth I now knew full well that I could never be a contender at that wonderful, exasperating, humiliating game. From now on spectator sport would be my thing. Especially boxing but always golf and over time many others - in fact I had an ongoing interest in almost all other sports.

When I did travel away from base anywhere in the UK it would always be to accompany a sales representative in helping to sort out some tricky customer problem - or do my best to help make a breakthrough sales contract. But the ship called Lily Cups and Containers (England) Ltd was beginning to spring leaks in a quite alarming fashion. It was the old problem; lack of in-plant morale leading to production inefficiency leading to constant short deliveries - or non-deliveries - and finally to the anguish of my poor old customers. At times I would almost dread getting to the office in anticipation of the irate phone calls. So this indeed was my real baptism of executive fire. I reasoned to myself, *so this is why they pay me so well?*

Our problem was the unions - or rather the company's relationship with the unions. Lily Cups' first managing director, the imposing Bob Taylor, an ex-WW2 British army colonel, had a special way with the shop floor. I had seen him grabbing a machine operator by the lapels in anger and lifting him off his feet. But the workers really loved the guy. More importantly they respected him and would strive to help the company out of trouble. Now we had a new M.D. in one Graham Corner who was an absolute martinet, all too often idiosynchratic, all too bloody distant. He seemed to do anything possible to get on the wrong side of those tough and obdurate Liverpool workers - and not just the workers, the office staff as well. It was he who instituted a 'directors lunch'. Although not a director I was included, I have to say against all my instincts. The six or seven of us 'leaders' would assenble in a specially built dining room, there to select our wine and our menu and talk about anything and everything for two hours plus - except, it seemed, the business that was paying each of us a handsome salary each month. Corner had begun his tenure of office by getting in early one day and sweeping all the papers on every desk into the waste bins. In future we had to deal with everything on our desks before going home at night, irrespective of whether or not we had had time to properly research the problems and find solutions. This led to short cvuts and yet more customer alienation. I shuddered as production fell even more and the inevitable air of discontent further eroded morale. Our losses rapidly escalated.

The one positive thing about Mr Corner - although trivial in the context - was his insistence on all the sales guys driving company cars with automatic gearing. They had to arrive at customers as fresh as possible, he instructed. None of us liked automatics. They were for old ladies, we thought. But ever since then I have driven automatic cars except when abroad when hired geared cars were more obtainable. Yes, the b\d M.D. had been quite right!

I reckon I must have been a pain in the proverbial to the directors of the company. Time and again I would warn them of the impending catastrophy although nobody seemed overly bothered. One morning John Williams said he wanted me to go develop some export sales. *Where?* I asked. *Wherever the hell in Europe you like*, came the answer. *Try Switzerland for a start.* This was my first time out of the country and how I liked the new adventure. I disembarked from the plane in Zurich's Kloten airport with the list of possible sales targets I'd obtained from the British Embassy in London and a bagful of samples, took a taxi to the city centre, found myself a good (very good) hotel and spent the evening walking the streets, trying out the odd bar and a restaurant. Marvellous food. This solo stroll was a habit I have since then maintained when arriving on my own in a new city.

I travelled all over Switzerland by train and rented car, very seldom having trouble with the language as everyone seemed to speak English. Berne was my favourite place but Geneva ranked high and, of all the high places, Davos. And of course Zurich and the beautiful little town named Zug that overlooked lake Zurichsee. I obtained some good orders on that initial sales mission and later, on return visits - even though we couldn't supply all of them - and made some good business friends. Suddenly my international goals seemed not only closer but also highly attainable. The only trouble was that bloody factory - or rather, my bloody bosses who didn't seem able to run it properly. By then the infamous lady leader of the local print union had well and truly dug in her heels. It was my very first exposure to the real power of the Trades Unions.

Back home the girls and boys were fast growing up. Formby for us was such a lot of fun. Our home on Longcliffe Drive led into a beach-side woodland with red squirrels everywhere and then on to that immense, flat, sandy beach. When the tide ebbed it must have extended out the best part of a mile and when it started to flow, if you were out at the edge of the water you had to walk back in something of a hurry just to keep your feet dry. Then there were the great sand dunes, populated by a whole, nationally protected tribe of natterjack toads. I recall one evening, returning home after taking Joan out for a meal when we tiptoed in the dark into the front porch only to tread on something squishy. I switched on the light. Everywhere there were these fat and knobbly amphibians shuffling and hopping about, except the one that would never see another dawn. They'd been captured and imprisoned by Robert and Stuart. It was after midnight before I caught them all (but one) and returned them to their natural homeland.

Trouble was, I was once again spending more and more time, and I guess I have to say more attention, away from home. Yet I was never overmuch afraid of my business life damaging my marriage. Having been subjected in my early life to the shock and trauma of my parents' split, I never wanted anyone or anything else than Joan and the children. But my lovely Joan - the lady with whom I had shared so very much - had begun to show signs of rebellion at my absences. And correspondingly I had started to rebel at work. Rank and money notwithstanding it was no longer plain sailing in either department of my life.

21. Breaking up, breaking out

By 1970 on the surface everything for me and my tribe was on the up and up. But underneath, on the business front, I was becoming increasingly worried, believing the company needed drastic remedial action if it were not to exhaust the Group's patience as well as its available funding. I fully realised that one of the prime responsibilities of leadership consists of engendering positivism amongst the troops, even when things are patently negative, nevertheless I was becoming mighty tired of warming my own and everybody else's hands in front of out of control fires.

The Lily Cups tipping point came first thing one cold winter's morning. I had just been telephoned by some poor coffee bar owner in London, emotionally much disturbed, shouting and swearing about how, because of bloody Lily Cups he had nothing to sell in the way of hot drinks after one broken delivery promise after another. At that point in walked my Director - I have to say my mentor and my friend, John Williams. He was all fired up because he'd heard one of my salesmen talking to sales administration ... *from his fucking home, Bryan! Get the bastard out on the road,'* he shouted. I then did something that I might and should have lived to regret. Instead of biting the bullet and thinking of job, wife, fifteen and eleven year old daughters and eight and five year old sons, not to mention the mortgage and the overdraft (in that order); not to mention either my reputation for cool headedness in an emergency, I responded with cold silence, picked up my coat and drove my very nice company car, homewards bound, my head in a flat spin.

After getting home and revealing all to an astonished, understandably concerned Joan I sat down and wrote an eight page handwritten letter to Sir John Foster Robinson, Group Chairman. How often and with such yearning have I wished I had retained a copy of that letter. Although I say it myself, it was probably my masterpiece! That took me two hours. Immediately it was finished and enveloped I walked across the road, bought a stamp, stuck it on and slipped the envelope into the letter box. Oh yes, now I could smell the bridges burning! I had whistle blown full blast knowing well that the upper ranks must at once close against me. Criticism of my colleagues' professional conduct would be construed at a kind of treason. Less than a week later the company chauffeur arrived to collect the firm's car. (Yes, the near bankrupted company's *chauffeur*, for God's sake!) I remember him muttering something supportive as he surreptitiously slipped me a note from my pal the personnel director enclosing a cutting from that very day's jobs pages in the Daily Telegraph. (More on that later). In fact the sender broke ranks to come around to see me that evening. He told me privately that the Board had convened three days after I had vacated the premises. They were to work out the correct strategy to bring me without loss of anyone's face back into the fold. It seems they had been expecting me to walk back in of my own volition, full of apologies which would then be generously accepted. Normal service would be resumed. Unfortunately it seemed that meeting was interrupted by a phone call from the Chairman and the Group M.D. Lloyd Robinson. The call was taken in private by my local MD so I shall never know what was 'discussed'! Whatever, Robinson failed to take any or enough action. Lily Cups and Containers (England) Limited lasted just over three more years before it closed its doors, letting go all those few still remaining. I genuinely took then, and I take now, no satisfaction in reporting this fact. On the contrary I could damn near have cried about it at the time. Ten years of my life - and a good life for me and my career and my family and my team - unnecessarily gone to hell and damnation. Five years or so later when I was staying overnight in Liverpool I was driven out to the old Lily Cups industrial site by my local guy Alec Matthewson. Nobody stopped us entering because the factory / office gates were hanging off. All was overgrown with weeds, littered with broken glass and rubble. There was some choice graphitti on the factory building walls and on the inside and outside walls of that damned directors' dining room. What a bloody awful end of what should have been a damn good story. One I would never let myself forget.

Earlier I mentioned a certain message and jobs cutting fed to me by a friend. I always had the feeling that few if any of my contacts in the trade or my new colleagues ever believed I had *not* been head hunted before I walked away from Lily Cups. But I wasn't! That Telegraph cutting advertising a sales manager position was in fact pure co-incidence! The job vacancy was for sales manager of a non-existent company that was planning to produce plastic and paper cups 'somewhere in England'! Apply to Sir Julian Salmon, Jermyn Street, London W.1.. Within a week of leaving Lily I entrained to London to be interviewed in his dauntingly upmarket office by Sir Julian Salmon of the immensely wealthy J.Lyons Group family. Within another week I had (a) had a long telephone conversation with Sir Julian's partner and friend in America - President of Maryland Cup Corporation, Mr Henry Shapiro. (b) I had endured exhaustive two day medical / psychological tests in London and Lancashire, and (c) been offered the job at a higher salary than the one I had abandoned, plus top of the range Ford Zodiac, etc. The following week I was on the plane to Baltimore, USA. Something called their 'College of Product Knowledge' beckoned. Very American. More next time on that. I was up and on my way again.

Even more of an Americanism thean their College of Product Knowledge was the name chosen for the new UK venture; "Sweetheart Plastics." When I put down the phone on my 'acceptance speech' Joan was ecstatic. *What's the company to be called?* she finally asked. *Sweetheart Plastics* I responded. She hesitated for a moment, then; *How very embarrassing. Thank God you've joined in time to change it.* But I wouldn't attempt to change the name. *What stays in the mind first and best*, I asked myself and told my wife; *Sweetheart Plastics or Gosport Plastics?* (Gosport being the Hampshire south coast town where would be born our business.)

At any rate I spent the next month in the States, learning and getting to know the half-parent organisation's products and people. The sheer scale of everything Stateside for me was breathtaking. My excitement ratchetted up. By the time I returned home Lily Cups and Containers (England) Ltd was but a distant and actually quite an irrelevant memory. I felt like a bright and shining new star. Whether or not I actually was - that remained to be seen!

22. Going to America

When I alighted from my cross Atlantic flight at Baltimore I walked straight into the salesman's dreamland that is The United States of America. For me, it was a bit like Alice must have felt after falling down that rabbit hole.

Maryland Cup's Marketing Director - with his wife - met me at the airport. *Mr Bryan Islip please go to Information,* bellowed the public address; *Dick Folkoff is waiting for you.* The word Folkoff sounded somewhat like I wasn't too welcome! Not at all; Dick and his lady wife were perfect business hosts. I remembered they took me straight out of the airport to a swanky restaurant. The starter - seemingly without the option - was the local delicacy, a bucket of steaming clams. Lovely but about three parts of a bucket too much for me. *What kinda steak would you like? I was then asked* Already full to bursting but for politeness, *I'll have the fillet, please,* say I, fillet was the smallest by weight on offer. Visibly worried by this, Dick whispered, *Hey, Bryan, the fillet's for ladies. Take the rump if you can't handle the T-bone, yeah?* That was my first lesson in American business life; the bigger the appetite the better. Nobody - definitely no salesperson ate fillet steak! Which must explain the average size of the guys with whom I was to attend Sweetheart Cup's College of Product Knowledge.

Actually it was misnamed because the College of Product Knowledge was really a sales school, and a very good one. i.e. It was twenty percent what the product actually is and eighty percent what the product will do for you, Mr/Mrs customer. That is in terms of incoming good old US dollars; more of them for you. Mr/Mrs customer and of course more of them for we successful salesmen!

At first I felt a bit out of place - or should that be out of rank? My 'learner class' consisted of young males, newly recruited from all over the States. I was thirty six years old and had already worked my way up the career sales ladder. I thought I knew most of what there was to know about paper cups and selling the things. But to those Americans no Brit could be a serious contender - too polite with all their pleases and thankyous and always excusing themselves. Plus many of my new compatriots knew little about Great Britain and, frankly my dear, could not care less. In the States, competition is totally what life and especially business life is all about. All our sessions were very serious and very competitive. To illustrate, with the first session assembled, seated and raucous, in walked the course tutor who stilled all conversation by pulling out what appeared to be a cowboy six-shooter and firing a shot (blank, I hope!) into the ceiling. Total silence!

But individually these Yanks proved to be great fun. To me they were excessively welcoming but - *just don't get in between me and my next buck, buddy*, was the subliminal message. A tough old guy called Maury Fiterman was the lead sales manager. From his sales territory in New York State Maury was said to have earned a million dollars, plus, each year for the past several years. Yes, the salesman was king of the heap there, and I was just a little bit impressed! One instance of their drive for the next sale will give you the picture. I should first explain that one of the less prominent Sweetheart USA products was a toothpick made from a very small-bore plastic 'straw'. Our class was seated in a hotel restaurant for the end of course dinner when our leader at head of table jumped up to inform us that *there are no toothpicks here, guys! Two hundred bucks to the first man getting an order from this hotel for a case of toothpicks*, he announced. It was like the Yukon gold rush, everyone vacating the table to find a manager with ordering authority. I went straight to hotel reception, explained the situation and presented the guy with enough dollars to buy a case of toothpicks, asking him just to give me a handwritten order for same. Now, please!!! *Hey, no problem, Bryan*. Consequently I was first back at the table, handed in my 'order' and, when all were re-assembled, received two hundred dollars plus fulsome praise from Mr Fiterman. I was learning fast. The whys and wherefores were of little or no consequence. Results were everything. When in Rome do as the Romans do, right?

It was by no means all work and no play. I and my band of learner brothers got to know downtown Baltimore pretty well of an evening. It was, for me, all larger than life. I recall one night when several of us repaired to a bar with the memorable name of Queenie Macsteve's. You sat up on high stools to a large horseshoe shaped bar whilst one of the barmaids, clad in little more than her high heels, stepped around on top of it in time with the rock music. The fellow seated beside me, not one of us, was making very rude comments and issuing invitations of a most ungentlemanly nature to the lady. She 'accidentally' trod on the back of his hand. When she withdrew the spiky heel I swear blood jumped two inches into the air. Everyone except the bleeding fellow thought it hilarious.

I have mentioned before that the joint founders of Sweetheart UK were Sir Julian Salmon of the UK's J Lyons family and Henry Shapiro, multi-millionaire lead shareholder of Maryland Cup / Sweetheart Cup in the USA. Fortunately I got on well with them both, especially the latter. Henry ran his section of the American business from an office situated slap bang in the middle of a million square foot factory in Chicago. It was really weird, walking out of the high decibel clatter of that massive array of machinery and bustle of people into the quiet of Henry's soundproofed, oak panelled, coal fire heated 'study'. To see this huge expanse of factory roof from the outside, with just the one smoking chimney in the middle of it, was also quite surreal. Not a piece of paper in sight. After my course at the College in Baltimore finished I was invited to visit him in his factory 'eyrie'. He showed me around in his golf buggy. I remember at one point he stopped and pointed to a machine belching out at high speed a certain paper cup. *What's that, Bryan?* he asked. Thinking he was testing my new found product knowledge I answered with some pride, *That's a hot cup 2107*. Henry looked at me intently; *That machine*, he announced, *Is making nothing but money*. This must have been one of his stock philosophies for he said precisely the same thing in our Gosport UK plant a couple of years later.

It seems odd, looking back, how a relatively young English gentile could get on so well with an elderly Jewish-American multi-millionaire. And with his rather beautiful lady wife, Sorretta. Their apartment in Chicago's prestigious Lakeshore Drive was something to behold: original works by Degas and Picasso, the very finest of wines, discreet security all over the building, etcetera.

Over the next seventeen years whenever Henry came over to my domain in England he would stay at The Connaught hotel in London. Often I would be invited to breakfast with him; Oh those quails egg dishes with asparagus and bits of bacon! Or for lunch at nearby La Gavroche. Of course he would question me about the health and the prospects for his UK investment, and he was as hard bitten a businessman as you might expect, but right up to the time when he and his brothers sold out, whilst the UK's four successive managing directors, three production directors and three finance directors came and went, I remained in place as sales director. In between MD's I once asked Mort Gilden, another US director, why I hadn't been invited to occupy the newly vacant top chair. *Because you're great at turning on the lights* came the answer; we *needed someone to turnthem off,* thus implying they didn't trust my financial control discipline. What a calumny! Mort was the man who never carried papers. At one Board meeting he interrupted the discussion by announcing disgustedly, *You guys are just shuffling smoke,* before wandering away, puffing on his usual giant, aromatic cigar.

My first exposure to business life in the USA culminated with two weeks out in some of the midwest sales territories with the resident salesmen, then two memorable days and nights in New York City before flying home. Back in the UK I was allowed a whole weekend off before driving down in my new company car, a Ford Zodiac, to spend my weekdays planning the business with my new colleagues in Sir Julian's Jermyn Street, central London offices. But that first weekend at home was one of the best. We picnicked in the sunshine on the sand dunes between the red squirrel populated woodland and Formby's sandy beach. All the kids were doing OK at home and at school. One lovely wife - very happy, if understandably a touch nervous at what next could lie ahead for us all.

How lucky can you get? I asked myself, but how relatively soon can contentment threaten to sink beneath a sea of troubles; the slings and arrows of (William Shakespeare's) outrageous fortune.

23. At the foot of the mountain

1970: having returned from the States and after that idyllic weekend with Joan and the children* on the beach at Formby I came down to earth, driving down from Lancashire to London in my brand new bench seated, column gear change Ford Zodiac. I was to meet with my newly recruited future colleagues, assembled for the first time in Sir Julian's Jermyn Street offices: managing director Alan Watchman, ex-Unilever - he had been their youngest yet MD; Don McNab, our production manager, ex-ditto of the giant Ever-Ready Batteries in the northeast of England and Richard Seaman, our hugely qualified young finance manager. Richard was very cultured and very clever in equal measure - one of the very best of his genre in my experience.

Alan would 'leave without the option' three years later to be replaced in succession at several year intervals by three other managing directors during my seventeen years with the company. Of all of them, Alan was by far the best at managing and directing a manufacturing company. None of them or for that matter any other director colleagues left us of their own volition. Donald on production would last a little longer but would be replaced by a chain of three 'imports', mostly American. Two finance directors would follow Richard in quicj succession. They had all become my friends. They had all fallen out with the company or the company with them. Please never talk to me about industrial growing pains and its appallingly remote over-management! Like doctors with poison in place of medication.

That first get-together in Sir Julian's Jermyn Street office was something almost surreal. We had the investing partners' couple of million dollars in our bank account but no products, no machines, no factory and no employees! They were all looking at me. Alan asked, *Which is to be our market, food service (disposable cups etc) or dairy packaging (ice cream, yogurt cops etc)?*, an understandable question if a trifle late in the day. I was the only one present with any first hand knowledge of the highly specific cups and containers industries. Cutting quickly here to my long-winded, well-rehearsed response; *Plastic dairy packaging* I advised. I knew I would have to generate very quick and very high volume sales income if we were not to rack up massive and long extended start up costs and I knew the handful of UK dairies were where such prospective sales were possibly to be had.

I had brought back from America drawings of Sweetheart Plastics Inc's magnificent, own design extrusion and thermoforming line. I unrolled it on to the Board table. *How much will that cost?* was the next question. *A quarter of a million dollars complete with the tooling for a single product. Second and ongoing product toolings at around fifty thousand a go.* Those present appeared a wee bitty shaken. *What product then, and how much of it will this line turn out, Bryan?* asked Don. I said, a*t standard rating, a million units of a fluted 4 oz mousse or ice cream container a day.* Gasps all around. *Who the hell's going to buy that kind of volume?* Richard asked. *There are three companies in the UK who could each buy at least fifteen millions a year of these particular* *containers: Walls Ice Cream in Gloucester, Lyons Maid Ice Cream in London and Liverpool and Ross Foods in Hull. We will have to get contracts out of at least two out of those three.* Don and Richard looked at me and at each other, shaking their heads. Expressionless, Alan's fingers drummed the table top.

They did right to shake their heads. That machinery, loaded on to us by the Shapiro brothers had been developed for America's gigantic, highly mature markets. Sure it would give us the lowest cost base in Europe, (provided Don could inspire his team to get to know how to operate the thing!) but to what avail if we couldn't secure sufficient of the right kind of orders? So, this was gamble number one of the many, many risks to be taken by Sweetheart Plastics, soon to be renamed Sweetheart International as the years rolled by. All industrial, manufacturing start-ups have to take risks. Big ones. With machinery, with products, with people, and overall with their investment money. And the riskiest of these factors are always the people.

Sitting in that Jermyn Street office I shall not forget Alan Watchman's next comment, calm and quiet as always; *Then we'd best get busy finding ourselves somewhere to put this machinery. I have here four bundles of agents' factory details. Don, you''ll look at those to the north, I'll take the south coast bundle, you'll take the east of England Richard and Bryan, you know the Midlands best, so you'd best cover this lot.* He grinned. *And by God after that you'd better get to selling something.* He handed me a file of six industrial properties. *Re-assemble here a week today to compare notes and make the decision. Right now I think we all need a drink.* And so we did, at Joule's (very expensive) Wine Bar just around the corner. The following morning we were out on the road factory hunting. A week later we re-assembled, discussed our results and Alan made his decision. There was this empty, ex-steel stockholding building down on the edge of Portsmouth harbour in a town called Gosport. Don looked at me and winked. By then we all knew Alan's passion for sail boats!

That decided, we drove separately down to Gosport, re-assembling in Alan's choice of factory. The vast, dirty, empty space echoed to our shocked voices. It smelled powerfully of rusty metal amongst other rotten things and such 'offices' as there were were totally derelict - uninhabitable. *Don't worry about that,* advised Mr Watchman, *I've rented some nice offices for us up in Fareham.* Fareham was four miles away. *Don, you'll need to get contract cleaners in here, pronto.*

Of course we would all have to move our homes. This, it became crystal clear was not going to be any nine to five, nor any five or even six days a week proposition. I spent the rest of that week exploring the area for schools and houses, phoning Joan at home up in Lancashire at frequent intervals to seek her counsel. I discovered that Gosport was a Royal Navy town. It was and still is a kind of blunt, south pointing peninsula, on its eastern side Portsmouth harbour, to its south and west the Solent. Four miles away across the water you could see Ryde church steeple on the Isle of Wight.

In number forty five Raynes Road, Lee-on-Solent I found our new home. A couple of hundred yards from the beach it was / is a modern, four bedroomed detached with nice garage and a big enough back garden complete with empty swimming pool in much need of attention. At ten thousand pounds it was probably ten to twenty percent above the going rate for that locality but for that I cared little. Having signed up I went back to my Bellevue Hotel room to call home. On the phone I spoke to Joan and all the children about it, one by one in order of descending age. In spite of their all being happy and so comparatively recently well settled in Formby there was much - and positive - excitement. *Can we have a boat, Dad?* Robert asked. Little did any of us realise how much of our lives would come to revolve around that question and its answer, together with the almighty sea. *When should we think of moving down?* Joan asked. I took a deep breath; *Two weeks today, whether or not we've sold Longcliffe Drive*, I told her.

After dinner in the Bellevue Hotel that evening I walked across the road and down on to the pebbled beach. It was a beautiful moonlit, starlit sky over the calmest of seas. The lights of a tanker were heading slowly up the Solent into Southampton. Over on the Island I could see the pinprick twinkle of Ryde and Cowes. To my left the city of Portsmouth cast its sodium orange all across the skyline. I sat down on the shingle, lit a cigarette and breathed in deep to catch the lovely, intermingled scent of brine and fish and seaweed that would come to excite me and my family so much.

I had fallen in with some of the hardest, shrewdest, premier division industrialists and financiers in the world. It seemed I was now holding their newest baby. God help me if I dropped it. More importantly I was holding in my hands the lives, or at least the wellbeing of Joan and my four children. Close in to shore came the swirl and splash of a night-hunting sea bass. At thirty six my life probably wasn't even half way through. What a great adventure it had been! What great adventures were yet to be!

By the way, 'kids' for me are young goats; they are not *children - or at least not my children.*

24. Pausing for thoughts

February 2015: I began these reminiscences at the suggestion of my son Stuart. Writing them has now become a habit, quite a therapeutic one. In disinterring things long consigned to the furthest recesses of my mind I have not tried or wanted deliberately to obfuscate the facts. There's really no point in doing this thing without truth. However I have found that the truth, the whole truth and nothing but the truth is near impossible. In speaking or writing of oneself there are lies by omission as well as by distortion of truth, and furthermore that 'truth' which is believed by oneself may not always be the truth as known or believed by others. Also, like love, truth can hurt. As I have said before, nobody wants to be hurt, especially me!

Having in this discourse reached almost half way through the days of my fairly unremarkable life I am determined to carry on. That said, the only question is; should I 'publish' the ongoing memorabilia or should I leave these chapters from age thirty seven to eighty on my PC for someone else, some time in the future, to make that decision? Or, more likely leave them to disappear into cyber space and/or the waste disposal when this hard drive of mine goes the way of all things? Obviously I am talking real life and real people. Not only will many of those real people be with us still, but they have a perfect as well as a perfectly legal right not to have someone like me raking over the ashes of their lives along with his own. Don't misunderstand me, this is not to assume that more than a handful of folk have or will ever get to read my thoughts, however marvellously infinite and sans frontiere may be the might internet.

Having elected to carry on, I shall not consider publishing what I write until after an interval of time. And whether I publish here or not I will not over-sanitise my best memory of historical reality - not even where there is an obvious failure of character or failure of achievement. Such there is in all of our lives, I would suppose, of course leaving aside the lives of the saints! Those like me not saintly are taught from birth that failure of character, short of criminality, should best be gloss-painted over and forgotten and that failure of achievement is somehow shameful, therefore to be avoided in healthy communication. Bollocks that may be but perhaps it is the unhealthy reality. I have right now to put myself back into the mind and experience of that thirty six year old man sitting on the night-time shingle beach outside the Bellevue Hotel in Lee-on-Solent inhat, at that point had he concluded about life in general and his own in particular? And what at that point did he actually want?

I shall here be detailing my thoughts on such as ambition and money, on love and sex and marriage, on one's last and one's next generation, on fairness and justice, on pleasures and tribulation, of history and race, of war and peace, of the spiritual v the material v the arts - and of what I would want engraved on my theoretical headstone, (theoretical because I desire cremation rather than burial.) I'll begin with the latter.

I had once sat up at a bar in a public house with some business friends when one of them out of the blue asked each of us to write down on a paper napkin the words he wished to have engraved on his headstone. I believe Robert Burns scratched something like the following on the window of a pub in Scotland …

    HERE LIES, DEAD, A MAN, WHO LIVED

That's good enough for me, too..

25. 1970: love and marriage

This 37 year old husband and father of four, the newly recruited sales manager of a company with as yet no product to sell is sitting by himself in the dark on the beach at Lee-on Solent, smoking a cigarette, watching the ships and the lights. Sounds like he was on a cushy number, doesn't it, but to him it seems exactly the opposite. Never mind about all that, Bryan Islip, he thinks, what do you make of it so far?

Thoughts come a-tumbling one over the next. Mostly good ones for the world has not yet turned in any serious way against our family unit. Of course there have been difficulties but we've managed to deflect most of them and I am / we are not in a bad position now. Some would say in a very good one. My main worry is about Joan, my wife, the mother of our four offspring. About how worried she has become, not just since my change of employment but for a year or two before that when I had been forced, and had enjoyed, increasingly working away from home. I know she's been feeling more detached from my life and/or life in general - and more questioning about the value of her own. As Joan's favourite song has it; *You flying high in the air and me on the ground.* Yes indeed; and here's another song; *Things ain't what they used to be.*

Perhaps, as our family has grown and flourished Joan's life has turned inwards whereas mine has turned outwards towards my career. I thought back to 1953, the City of York's De Grey Ballroom and that heart-stoppingly beautiful dancing-queen, the one in the green dress. I flick the stub-end of my cigarette in a parabolic shower of sparks down the beach. It's not that there is any possibility or the faintest liklihood of a split. The recent arguments had always been quickly and easily terminated in a reaffirmation of love. We had been through a lot together. We loved each other. The more you go through and the more you share, the tighter the bond. I thought back even further to my eleventh year, after my mother and father had split in a welter of acrimony. I'm lying in that boarding school bed after lights out night after night, possessed by such sadness, such anger, such awful thoughts. Never, under any circumstances would that happen to our children - or once more to myself.

I'm wondering how and why the divorce rate in my country has escalated so wildly. For me, when you make a promise, especially the one about marriage, then you stick to it 'til death really doth part or whatever else might occur. That is what I had been taught during my adolescence at Abingdon School. I believed and still at 37 do believe that the whole of civilised life, the entire fabric of human society ancient and modern depended on keeping one's word! *In the beginning was the Word - and the Word was with God - and the Word was God.* I am in no way conventionally 'religious' but I believe fervently that what promises mankind has made, let mo man put asunder.

Once upon a time in my teens and on holiday from school, my father had excused himself and the breakdown of his own family by referring to the cruelty of his father, my grandfather, who, he told me, had been less than happily married to my grandmother. *But, father,* I said, *They lived and died together, didn't they? They always seemed happy to me.* He agreed. Yes they had, but it had been something of a sham. With evident satisfaction he went on to tell me that, at grandfather's funeral service had appeared the proverbial strange lady in black. *Turned out the old bugger had been all his life maintaining two families. Ours and a secret one in London.* I thought about this, about the grandfather with whom I had spent so many of my summer holidays in Hastings, the grandfather who had given me the key to his fishing tackle locker on the pier. I looked up at my father; *Grandfather Islip was a good man, then,* I said; *He kept his word.* I don't think father was best pleased with that.

I stood up, brushed myself down, crossed the road and went into the hotel bar for a nightcap. The place was buzzing as such places always were before the drink driving laws. Sitting on a bar stool with my glass of beer I glanced left and right, in the process catching the eye of a young woman, part of a group. She nodded and smiled.

26. 1970: The world around

1970: Looking backwards as a 37 years old at life, fairness and justice it seems to me that, broadly speaking each of us gets roughly that which each of us deserves - i.e. that which our individual mix of talents, looks, applied energies, genetic parentage, upbringing and basic 'character' has warranted. Of course I'm not here talking necessarily about money. Whether or not we want to admit it I think we all realise that there are many rewards in this life other than the financial. I suppose I'm talking about reward equalling or perhaps not equalling some kind of natural justice.

I know all about the genii who live in anonymity and/or penury producing truly earth-moving works. For such people their genius is the reward all by itself. It is enough. Personal comfort to the *truly* gifted means little or nothing. Read up on your Socrates and to do so you need to read up on his pupil, Plato, for Socrates didn't leave the written word and Plato did. I love the interchange at Socrates' trial, as reported by Plato, between himself and his prosecutor. Asked whether he considered his seditious advice to the young was because he thought himself wise, the octogenarian philosopher said that, yes, he had indeed consulted the Oracle. *What did it tell you?* asked the prosecutor. *I asked it if I was indeed the most knowedgeable, the wisest, in all Athens. It said that I was, for I was the only one wise enough to know I knew nothing.*

Natural justice! It seems to me that the prime exception to prove the rule is not the individual but Mankind as a whole. In the sacred name of money and that which we are taught must come with it - comfort, security, happiness - mankind is constantly seeking ways to take out, or attempt to take out of planet Earth more than it can possibly offer or afford. Yes, it's that classic guy up a tree sitting out on the branch whilst busily cutting off. There is only one outcome; natural justice indeed.

Such thoughts have loomed large in my mind since reading Dr Rachel Carson's seminal work *The Silent Spring*. This is a book about the effects of the US led post-WW2 DDT fixation. In summary, if an insect eats 'our' food then let's kill it. Never mind or think about all else that depends on it - including all that which in the end we depend on ourselves. All for the sake of what? The next dollar bill! I'm not sure if it was Plato who declared that those whom the Gods wish to destroy they first make mad. True enough.

I went on to borrow from the library Dr Carson's wonderful trilogy *Under the Sea Wind, The Sea Around Us* and *The Edge of the Sea*. The content of these seminal works have not and never will leave me.

So how do I reconcile such thoughts to my new position as promoter and promulgator in chief of these dreaded manmade hydrocarbon plastics? Well, I cannot, so I don't! Like everybody else I am trying my damnedest to earn a living; i.e. to accumulate (and spend) as many pound notes as possible. I have four offspring to bring to maturity and twenty five years of mortgage payments to make. My mind goes back to that party in distant Solihull, the one where a bright young Indian guy, sensing my innate radicalism, told me the only way anyone could ever change things without recourse to mass weaponry was from the very top of the heap. *Work within all the rules, Bryan. Then when you get to the top, if you have enough energy left you can change the rules.* I have a very long and rugged climb ahead of me. The odds against are long indeed. Long enough to divert me from my mission? Probably. Thinking won't do it. There are things, actually many things to do.

I drained the last of my pint of beer, bade a goodnight to the barman, nodded to the young woman, and her friends and retired to bed.

27. The world around

Our house in Formby had sold as quickly as the Lee-on Solent house had been purchased with the aide of Bristol & West Building Society, but unfortunately the lawyers hadn't kept up. When I moved my family - including our Burmese cat - south from Lancashire to Hampshire we had to take up temporary residence in the Bellevue Hotel whilst awaiting 'completion'. After a few days of this and with the imminent arrival of our furniture van I borrowed the keys to 45 Raynes Road from the estate agent and without further ado we all moved in to our new home. Word quickly spread back to the seller, the solicitor and the agent; huge consternation all around! However, illegal possession really proved to be nine tenths of the law. It's amazing how our nation's legal machinery can grind into fast forward when it sees no reasonable option!

So, within three weeks of first seeing Raynes Road we were fully ensconced in our new home and all the children had 'signed up' at their new schools. Karen would then have been fifteen, Julie eleven or twelve, Robert nine and Stuart six years old.

Joan was talking about getting some sort of part time job. As with many women who've been a number of years out of circulation bringing up their families, and even though she was extremely capable my lady wife was nervous about the prospect of going back into the big wide world. However what she lacked in confidence she made up for in good old Yorkshire grit. It wouldn't be long before she was doing the rounds of housing estates selling freezer meals on commission. How was I feeling about that? Not very good, I'm afraid. Not entirely supportive. I saw no need for her to work other than at the arduous task of running our household and the lives of all who lived in it. Also we had decided that our new abode should be seriously upgraded. As I was away for much of the time I thought the work would need close supervision. Upgraded? For a start we wanted an open fireplace and that entailed running a chimney flue up from the living room right through the middle of the house then chimneyed out through the roof. Then there was the little matter of the derelict swimming pool at the bottom of the garden. And so on ... As I've indicated I had to give way on the issue of Joan's employment but circumstances would soon enough cruelly conspire to scupper her ambitions.

Meanwhile we were moving into our new offices at 26 High Street, Fareham. Mine was the second best / biggest office after Alan's, the managing direcor's, on account of I would be the one entertaining our visiting / hoped for 'customers'. That wasn't bad, considering we hadn't yet acquired any customers! Nevertheless I interviewed and hired a secretary, a rather high personality girl named Irene Smith, and began the task of planning our first trade exhibition at London's Alexander Palace. I was also finding and recruiting a pair of salesmen, one for the north of the UK and the other for the south. Enter Alex Matthewson and Ted Pool, respectively. Both were a few years my junior in age and both would be with me and Sweetheart International for the next seventeen years. They proved to be top class industrial salesmen and company men. They were also my friends and I still correspond on occasion with Alex and with Ted's widow, Jane. Straight away I sent them to follow in my footsteps at Sweetheart U.S.'s Baltimore College of Product Knowledge. After a while I phoned the boss there in the States to ask how they were doing. There was a pause then, not without humour I trust; *Hey Bryan, is this your idea of revenge for our GI invasion?* Lively lads they certainly were.

I had begun making field sales contacts, some of whom I knew from my past at Lily Cups and some who'd never heard of me or this weird sounding new 'Sweetheart Plastics' potential supplier of packaging. That's when I and my colleagues suffered our first major shock. It transpired that Henry Shapiro, before investing his money with Sir Julian, had met in the States with the UK's Walls Ice Cream head buyer, a very bright man named Vic Jones. He (Henry) had assured me that an order for many millions of our initial product - the fluted mousse cup - was just awaiting my first visit to their immense new ice cream factory in Gloucester. When I arrived in Vic's office I was informed to the contrary. There was no such bloody order! Thanks a bundle Henry!

(To try to explain the company's commercial situation I've just written but have nowdecided to eliminate a summary of the history of Sweetheart and the world's cups and containers industries. It is marginally relevant and a truly fascinating story but one for another time - probably another voice.)

So, at our first Board meeting I was confronted with having to tell Henry Shapiro and the rest that, if their venture had been based on a great big Walls Ice Cream order, forget it. *Vic Jones has told me there had been no such agreement, verbal or otherwise.* Some misunderstanding! We now had a factory and an office, skeleton staffing, heavy machinery on its way over the Atlantic complete with said mousse cup tooling, all the associated costs but no orders therefore no revenues. To their eternal credit neither Henry nor Sir Julian walked away, switching off the lights and closing the door behind them. These multi-millionaire businessman, neither of them any longer of this world, were made of sterner stuff. After something of a pregnant silence, Henry said, *OK, so how you going to tackle the situation, Bryan?* At that I have to say I made one of the best presentations of my life, including a complete digest of the UK dairy and ice cream industries and the parts of its weak underbelly that I thought we could profitably exploit.

Henry always hosted dinner for the Gosport management and Board at one of the better local restaurants when he came to the UK in between stays at his home from home at London's Connaught Hotel. On that first local dinner the food was deemed excellent and expensive wine flowed freely as ourkey sponsor / shareholder told us about his father Joe Shapiro, a Russian Jew emigre arriving in the States during the 1930's, penniless and without a word of English either spoken or written. He had obtained a job making ice wafer cream cones by cooking the mix on flatplates before rolling them by hand. For years he saved every penny whilst designing a machine to do the job much faster and with no hand blisters! Rather than sell his invention he rented a tiny factory. The rest is, as they say, typically American history. After he'd finished Henry looked around the table. *You guys have it easy,* he said. *It's all out there for you. Go get it.* He also said something else that I can never forget. It may well be the fundamental secret of American business success over the rest of the world. *Remember this, he told us;*

everything inside this company's office and factory creates nothing but costs. It's your job to manage those costs, sure, but the name of the game is profit and all profit comes from outside; from the customers who pays our bills.

Two months after switching on that first extrusion - thermoforming line we had forty - yes, **forty million** unsold 4 ounce fluted mousse containers FM100 stacked up in a specially leased warehouse! For me that was a time of nightmares as that damned great machine churned out the buggers at the rate of half to one million per twenty four hour day. And then *at last* I secured our first sale - a million of those cups to Lyons Maid in Liverpool.

We were finally up and, if not exactly running, at least staggering to our feet and forward.

28. Lift off: new frontiers

1971: Sweetheart had lift off. After that initial Lyons Maid order came another from Walls Ice Cream and yet another from Ross Foods. The old saying - you wait ages for a bus to come along then three arrive one behind the other. Then we got our first order for many millions of printed yogurt cups from Unigate in Somerset. Printing on curved surfaces was yet another new technology so we had need to employ more specialised, highly skilled incomers. Of course as our range increased the company's orders for costly product tooling were flowing across to the States faster than UK customer orders were coming in. In other words money out more than money in. No problem; we would soon enough be reversing that trend, or so I had to constantly reassure the Board. By that time I had been promoted from sales manager to sales director. I still have the letter of appointment from Chairman Sir Julian Salmon.

The major part of our monthly Board meetings consisted of my report on sales and our prospects in the markets. I had spent ten thousand pounds on our first exhibition. A lot of money then, but it had succeeded in putting the company fair and square in front of all the major dairies, most of whom I then invited to come see our new operation in Gosport. In addition my 'lieutenants' Ted and Alex were beavering about, making themselves and Sweetheart known to the buyers. And also, less welcome, to our competition who were spending much time and energy talking down this brash newcomer called Sweetheart Plastics / International. There was much customer entertaining in between all the serious stuff for, in the days before the net, relationships and the build-up of trust between industrial sellers and buyers were absolutely key. These days I am told that buying and selling is more about bids and offers on-line. How very dull tht seems to me! Is it a nett gain to anybody?

The girls were doing well at their schools, especially sixteen year old Karen who had been quick to make her mark at Bay House Grammar and had many friends amongst the youth of Lee-on-Solent and Gosport. She was quite irritated when she heard they referred to her as 'the princess'. Julie was also popular, a bubbly and beautiful little girl, like her sister with a love of animals but especially the horses or ponies which she learned to ride at nearby Charque Farm. One Saturday our whole family went to watch little Julie in her first gymkhana. She really looked the picture as she rode up to that first jump before the pony stopped and our little lady didn't! tearfully unhurt but highly mortified. Oh, how true that pride does come before a fall! Throughout her pre and early teens Julie had an imaginary pony of her very own. She called it Crystal Ball as I recall.

The boys at their new schools were a different kettle of fish. Literally. Perhaps they had inherited too much of my love of fishing and my old disdain for conventional education, I don't know. I hope not. Joan and I knew they were both bright enough, it was just that they seemed to prefer adventure (sometimes misadventure) to competitive school work. Robert especially was a worry. The other day I read through some of the eleven.year old's school reports. Dark shadows were already evident. At that stage and ongoing, fish and fishing dominated the lives of my sons. I have to say also my own life outside of the company..

Living close by the sea and by Lee-on-the-Solent's yacht club slipway it wasn't long before I gave in to the boys entreaties and bought an old boat with which to fish, out on the Solent. 'Culash' we named her, which is phonetic gaelic for 'little fly'. Culash was no ordinary boat. She was really out of time and out of place; a very traditional seventeen foot larch on oak clinker built double-ender. I had one of the engineers at work make me a trailer which we promptly hitched to the back of my company Zodiac and journeyed all seven hundred miles north for a holiday in Applecross. This was my / our first taste of the Highlands of Scotland, and what a taste. When we arrived at the foot of Belach na Ba (the pass of the cattle) and saw the wavy thread of a road even daredevil Stuart wanted to get out and walk up. No way. But how I got that car and boat around those unguarded one in four gradient S-bends, sheer drop-offs to our left, I shall never know. These days I service a couple of customers in Applecross, going up that pass in so doing. I never fail to think back to that first ascent. One of my fifty six landscape paintings features Applecross Bay and the card that bears it also carries the following verse. Each of my paintings have an associated verse, spmething I think about as I size up, sketch out and/or actually paint the picturte. Hence 'Pictures and Poems' as a trade name for that whci I have been doing since moving north ….

a'Chromraich (Applecross)

Breathtaking, truly,
when you climb the twisting heights
of Belach na Ba (Pass of the Cattle)
first see the drop down into Applecross
look over the sea to Raasay, Skye
and think of Saint Maelrubha,
Irish monk, coming here by oar and sail
thirteen hundred turning years ago
with holy messages for Pict and Gael

'a'Chromraich' the Gaels called this place
'The Sanctuary' to me and you
and that is what it is, Applecross,
this lovely shelter from the storm,
from life's hard race
a race from where to where who knows?
who knows of where went
St Maelrubha's saving grace?

But what a holiday that was! We had used the boat as our camping trailer. After unloading it and pitching our tent we introduced ourselves to the only other campers on that remote, near seaside field. Between us we gathered firewood and soon had a nice blaze going to cook our supper and deter our very first experience of those perishing midges. I recall that the boys and I had ventured into an adjacent stand of trees when a mighty, well-antlered shape reared out of the darkness, sailed majestically over a high fence and was gone; renewed silence. Unforgettable! Especially for we soft southerners whose only exposure to wilderness had been the flat, well-trodden acres of the New Forest.

We had trouble launching Culash without a proper slipway but an old man - a very old man named Donal who spoke only the Gaelic - put us all to shame with his strength and agility. He took a real shine to Culash and to our lads, drawing a diagram in the sand showing how such craft had been equipped with slanted mast and square lugsail in the old days. (A visit to the Nautical Museum in London bore it out, so the next year I rigged our Culash in like manner.) The boys and Donal developed a great sign language relationship throughout our ten days in Applecross. We fished and explored that ragged coastline every day from our boat. A long and wonderful way from anything any of us had known before.

Can you fall in love with a piece of land? Perhaps 'in thrall' was a better term for how we felt in leaving at the close of our holiday about the Scottish Highlands. We would return time and time again, then one day and many adventures later I would come permanently to live a beautiful life in this beautiful place.

29. Glimpses of damnation and salvation

1973 was a year of massive shocks for me and mine. What I am going to write here is very difficult. If any family member does not wish to read on I would most surely understand.

Those who have followed this bio-blog from the beginning will remember that, in 1957, Joan had become temporarily, inexplicably blind. She was given many tests at Cambridge's prestigious Addenbrooke hospital but whilst there her sight had - equally inexplicably - returned in full. As I say, the medical staff had no explanation, or so they told us, so she left hospital and we carried on with our lives, forgetting all about it. In addition to Karen, as the years rolled by and our prosperity increased.we brought Julie, Robert and Stuart to join us in our mostly happy little world. However, even before moving south from Lancashire I had known that something was really amiss. There was - at times but not all the time - an unpredictability about Joan's behaviour. For instance, one night I arrived home quite late to find all the children fast asleep but no sign of my wife. I had the bedroom telephone in my hand to call police, hospitals etc when she burst out of the wardrobe, quite frighteningly wild-eyed and hostile. And then, soon after the move to Lee she started to walk with a slight limp - again, for no apparent reason and without any kind of pain. After many visits to our local doctor she was referred to Southampton General Hospital. I should have known that some kind of a bombshell was about to burst over her, over me and over our whole family life, for she had been referred to something called the neurology department. A quarter of an hour after walking into the consultant's office we walked out in a stunned silence, knowing now that her problem (and mine and the children's) was the dreaded multiple schlerosis. We also learned that it had been diagnosed or at least suspected back in Addenbrookes, Cambridge, twelve years or so previously. Above all we were made to understand that there was no cure as such. It would, said the consultant, possibly / probably regress in irregular stages through the need for a walking frame then a wheelchair and then ... ? ... well, nobody could tell.

Our discussion in the car whilst driving home was strangely calm and collected, at least from Joan's side. All she wanted to talk about was how difficult and then unbearable would or could become the lives of our children. They were at the time aged about seventeen, (Karen) fourteen, (Julie) eleven (Robert) and eight (Stuart). She asked me to stop the car somewhere. I did so. Again and again she insisted I make her a solemn promise to the effect that, if and when her illness reached a certain stage I would help her to terminate things. I made her that promise, refusing to believe that such a stage could or would ever be reached. An ostrich with head in sand comes now to mind. (When that time came I did not / could not keep my promise. Joan never truly forgave me for that.)

But as they say, what cannot be cured must be endured, and that is what we tried our best to do; with as much good grace and making as few concessions to MS as we possibly could. Of course Joan had to give up her thoughts of gainful employment. Soon enough she would need the help of a walking frame. At least on the surface our daughters and sons took the situation in their stride but I was of course never to know what actually went on deep down in their minds. As for me, on the one hand to all appearances I seemed to 'have it made' but on the other I knew how finely balanced was our wellbeing. I had all the usual mortgage and bank indebtedness to service and although I was earning a top salary I knew very well that everything would collapse should I lose my job - or be forced to give up work altogether in order to look after my wife, our family and our home. This had to be a real possibility when the MS reached the point where, in effect, twenty four hour nursing would become essential.

We (Sweetheart International) had invited our local Member of Parliament Peter Viggers, (yes, he of the duckhouse expenses fiasco!) to join the Board in a non-executive capacity. I spoke to Viggers in private, asking if there was any system of financial support for live-in nursing for cases such as my own. He came back to me later, having, he said, spoken with The Minister. The answer was a brick wall; 'No, sorrry'. I was on my own.

Well, not altogether alone and not for long. I spotted this rather lovely young lady walking along the harbourside road with her two little boys, holding one with each of her hands. I recognised her as the divorcee barmaid in a local pub, *The Jolly Roger*. Her name was Delia Perry. One day she would be Delia Islip.

30. Pleasures and pressures

By the time of our annual holiday in the May of 1973 Joan's multiple sclerosis had become obvious to all, for she had exchanged her walking stick for a zimmer frame. Nevertheless we decided to go back to the Highlands of Scotland, this time even a little further north, to a place called Gairloch. The girls were now of an age not necessarily to want the rigours of a twelve or sixteen hour car journey or of being tossed about on the ocean in a small boat for ten days. We trusted them to stay and look after our home. (When we returned we found our household had increased by one small kitten, but that's another story!) Joan herself liked the sea fishing and with two increasingly strong young boys alongside me I knew we could get her in and out of boat, car or anything else. We pitched our tent at Big Sand, overlooking the Sound between there and Longa Island. It was in that

Sound, that magical holiday, that we had great catches of plaice, dabs and haddock amongst other species, and where Robert caught his British record dab (limanda limanda). Two pounds, twelve ounces and two drams!

I phoned to register the record and was asked to take the fish as quickly as possible to the Glasgow Museum of Natural History for validation. Yes, it was the record and it has stood (as featured in the Guinness Book of Records) for more than twenty five years. It won us several prizes including a two week family holiday on the West Coast of Ireland, so that October we towed *Culash* up to Liverpool, were ferried across to Dublin then drove across Ireland to lovely Trallee. A second great holiday. But nothing is easy, is it? On the way back, whilst heading for our ferry on the Saturday night the wheel bearing on our boat trailer gave up. We were immobilised just off the famous O'Connell Street. 'The Troubles' being at that time in full spate I was more than a little concerned. Nevertheless a fellow dressed up for his night out offered to help. He drove Stuart and I to his home in the suburbs, leaving Robert in charge of my incapacitated wife and incapacitated transport. The man was kindness personified. He botched up a piece of galvanised iron pipe and, with a handful of glutinous grease we were up and running, at least as far as the ferryboat and into a Liverpool garage the next day. Furthermore our benefactor would accept no compensation. Reminds me of when a fellow did me an unsolicited kindness here in the Highlands. Again I offered to pay; *Bryan,* he told me, *Up here you have to learn how to take.*

The early 70's were pretty wild years at Sweetheart International. We needed to hit three quarters of a million pounds a month in invoiced sales, and quickly; otherwise the owners would lose patience. Already Sir Julian had baled out, selling his fifty percent to Malcolm Bates' London City-based Spey Investments. Most importantly our sales had to be at prices that (a) produced the necessary gross margins of profit and (b) did not destroy the industry norms. Setting low-ball prices would only serve to prolong the loss-making agony. We all know how easy it is to drop your price and how difficult to increase it. Nevertheless at a board meeting in 1974 Henry Shapiro, tired of pressure from his Board back in the USA instructed us to increase all prices by a substantial - and set - percentage. I gathered together my sales guys, Alex and Ted. They were in agreement that Henry's dictat was impossible, we would lose all our hard won sales. I said it wasn't impossible but in truth had difficulty believing my own message. That evening I remember we three got quite well drunk, not a first! Then over the succeeding months, lo and behold we actually did make the price increases stick and without losing much sales momentum! It was a lesson well learned; sales without profits in a manufacturing company mean precisely zero other than in the interests of temporary job security.

If anyone thought Sir Julian Salmon a hard taskmaster Mister Malcolm Bates very soon disillusioned them. His Spey Investments were financiers, pure and simple, with palatial offices in the City of London. They had latched on to one astonishingly simple moneybag fact concerning the investment of industrial pension funds, especially the giant pot of gold owned by the nation's postal workers - all one hundred and twenty thousand of them plus lord alone knows how many others in retirement. The truly massive fund's senior manager was at that time paid not much more than me! Bates and his bright-boy entourage certainly knew how to woo him into trusting them with their particular pot of gold!

But, never content simply to invest, like many such genre Spey believed they could and should actually run the manufacturing industry in which they had placed the pensioners' money. God-like in their City towers of ivory, they totally believed themselves better able and/or more intelligent than the incumbent managers. So one of the first things Bates did was to fire my boss, managing director Alan Watchman, by some way the best managing director I have ever worked under. He then summoned we three remaining directors to his City eyrie and 'interviewed' us one at a time. I was first in. The interview was very short, beginning with but a single statement and linked question; *'I've just dismissed Watchman. Do you think I've done the right thing for the company?'* He glared at me across an ocean of polished walnut table. It was obvious that any prevarication would lead straight to the exit door. In spite of my being totally convinced he'd made the wrong move I said in effect, *Yes, good move*, whilst telling myself the lie was in the best interests of the company (by leaving me in place). In fact it was in the interests primarily of myself and my recently disadvantaged family. Feet of clay? I was and am to this day actually ashamed of that 'yes' response. Alan Watchman was a good man. His dismissal probably cost the shareholders millions in lost profits.

Going back a bit in time, when Henry Shapiro and Sir Julian made their joint green field investment in the UK he and his Maryland Cup Board had bought a family owned paper cup manufacturer operating out of the small town of Groenlo in Holland. They re-named it Sweetheart Holland. But (and the following happened before Sir Julian sold out to Spey and therefore before Alan Watchman got himself fired,) Henry had been made aware of certain, let us say doubtful financial practices on the part of Groenlo's Dutch managing director. That is why Alan Watchman and I found ourselves on a Sunday flight out, then knocking on said managing director's door at 08.00 hours Monday morning. The guy had worked there almost man and boy and was something of a popular village luminary to boot. Our meeting with him was short and not at all sweet. At the end of it he was out, summarily dismissed. Alan Watchman returned to Gosport and I was left in position as stand in managing director. I had a special remit to dig as deeply as possible into the company, its practices and its finances. I was there in Groenlo for a little over a month conducting forensic investigations by interview with the staff and its suppliers and by an in-depth study of the company's historic accounts. In submitting my report to the owners I was all too well aware of how much compensation money my researches had probably saved them. No court of law ever needed to be involved. But when I stood to speak at the appropriate meeting of our Board I made two basic points. First, such 'malpractice' as I had uncovered was not necessarily unusual in Holland. Second, the man had been a very fair long time leader of the company.

For me, this whole business of hiring and firing top managers is ridiculous. It says that either the company had been built on sand in the first place and could never have prospered with the manager they had put in charge. Therefore the person (Chairman usually) making the appointment was himself incompetent, his judgement suspect. But who fires the Chairman?

Early the next year Bates offered me the position of managing director of a substantial paint manufacturer near Leeds that they had acquired. I discussed it in depth with my disabled Yorkshire lass. We thought about the logistics and of course the children and their education. Seventeen years old Karen had by then left school and obtained student nurse employment in the geriatrics ward of a mental hospital. Julie was happy at school and with all her friends, the boys were not doing so well at their studies and showed little enthusiasm for them but would have hated to leave the sea and all the fishing. They certainly did not need yet another move. And yes, I thought about Delia, the secret part of my life that made bearable all that would have been unbearable.

So I turned down Bates and his henchmen. It was the first of three - possibly four head hunter approaches over the succeeding years, two of them from the USA and all of them refused. I knew I could therefore never hope to reach the heights at which, according to that Indian party-guy all those years before in Solihull, I could actually change things for the better and for everybody. But my philosophy held good. Still does. *You don't deal yourself the cards, you just play the ones you're dealt as best you can.*

31. 74-79-the troubled years

These were for me a very strange dichotomy: life at home and life at work. The episode I am about to write is about the former.

Home life was itself divided into two parts - or three, actually. Possibly even four if I include all the sea fishing, so important a therapy. The first and most important part was of course Joan's multiple schlerosis, which wasn't showing any signs of stabilising. On the contrary her progression from walking sticks to walking frame to wheel chair was relatively rapid. Soon enough she was unable to carry on with much or any of her domestic housekeeping role, meaning that whoever happened to be home - nurse, me or any of our children - needed to cook, clean and tidy for ourselves and/or the rest. Sounds like chaos? Well, yes I suppose it might have been. And soon enough somebody always needed to help my lady get dressed, lift her into and out of bed, on and off the toilet, etc. For such a fastidious woman, so justly proud of her appearance this was a source of extreme sadness that too readily merged into bitterness. To make matters worse, that 'somebody' (at home) was all too often our youngest son. Stuart, or our youngest daughter, Julie.

Of course it wasn't all so downbeat. In spite of knowing all too well how and why our family unit was beginning to splinter we generally managed to put a good face on things. Joan had always had a dry, very Yorkshire sense of humour and it did not desert her through those painful years. By the way don't ever let anyone tell you, as so many unthinking people, including medical professionals, told Joan and I; that MS is debilitating but not physically painful. In order to alleviate extreme pain my wife underwent several operations to sever certain pain-producing tendons including those behind her knees. Of course that meant we had to give up on any hope of some new 'cure' being discovered, for she could never, after that, have regained the ability to walk. And the ops may have reduced but certainly did not terminate the pain with which she had to live by night and by day for all her remaining years. She and I became completely fed up with medical professionals telling us; *The pain isn't real. It's just your nerves sending out wrong signals.* I yearned to tell them, *this lady's pain is real, doctors, she isn't bloody wrong! It's you who are wrong!* But, as carefully well modulated as ever I for ever kept my own counsel.

Whenever my job did not take me away overnight I used to drive home from the office, see to the family's evening meal and then, at Joan's insistence, lift her into the passenger seat of the car. We would talk about the family situation whilst touring the district, often parking by the Solent where we could see the ships' lights and the lights of distant Ryde on the Isle of Wight. I would wind down the windows so that she could smell the weedy brine and listen to the shushing, calming sounds of waves on shingle. The sea did indeed give her great comfort. But once on such an occasions she quietly referred me to the promise I had made on driving back in 1973 from Southampton General Hospital after the MS diagnosois / prognosis; the promise that, as I have related, I knew by then that I would / could never keep. Parked on a slipway by Haslar seawall she asked me to release the handbrake. *An accident,* she said; *You'll be able to get out when the car sinks. I won't.* I drove home in a bitter silence. Twice she ended up in St Mary's Hospital in Portsmouth having attempted to end things by herself, Stuart having had to call the emergency services. They had a special ward there, seemingly for attempted suicides. Sympathy, as I recall, was well rationed, the implication always being that if someone really wanted to take their own life then they would, thus needing the undertaker and leaving the medics to concentrate on those grateful ones who actually wanted to carry on living. That suicide ward was a ghastly and miserable place on several levels.

Adding to the pain of all this was the effect on our teenaged children. As I said, our family was beginning to splinter. Karen had put Bay

House School well behind her at age seventeen, albeit with good leaving certificates, preferring to find work in the local mental hospital's geriatric ward. But it wasn't long before she left there and left home to enroll as a student nurse at the Middlesex hospital in central London. Then she abandoned that in favour of a brief spell in the Metropolitan Police Force. This in turn ended when my twenty year old daughter was told to confront the deranged wife of one of the infamous Kray brothers down in a subterranean ladies toilet. All the while Karen, now having re-spelt her name Kairen, was with Roger, her boyfriend from school days. They came home to get married in '77; a joyous and for me highly emotional occasion and a marriage that, in North London, has withstood so very well the test of time. We measure our lives to some extent by the lives and the happiness of our children. Standing to deliver my fatherly speech at the wedding reception I spoke of how I had read Tennison and other poets over pre-school breakfast to our ten year old first-born, and had made this rather beautiful baby's first cot out of an orange box and an old curtain. A good lesson in how to embarrass your daughter - if not quite as good as when I had taken her at age fifteen out of the company of her friends (including Roger, I seem to remember,) from a local pub - by the elbow and without the option. It was past ten o clock, you see. Oh, how very stupid I was ... but in 1979 Kairen and Roger presented us with Ella, our first grandchild.

At the time of Kairen's marriage Julie would have been eighteen. The four years of age difference sometimes felt like much more, for Julie was always the bubbly, extrovert teenager whereas Kairen seemed the more seriously 'grown up' of the sisters. Besides, we all know how great is a gulf of four years to those undergoing their teenage. I may be wrong but perhaps Julie always did feel in the shadow of her big sister, the sister who always got good school reports, knew exactly what she was doing, where she was going, etc, and made few if any obvious mistakes. For Julie life really was just a bowl of cherries ready for the eating and she was therefore much more open to the making of said mistakes. I seem to remember that, like Karen, Julie had one main boyfriend in those Lee-on-Solent days. His name was Boyd, a real young smoothy, the one no father could have entrusted with their darling daughter! As you've gathered I didn't particularly take to Boyd, which may not have helped matters. Looking back, how wrong I was! A fine young man emerged, as so often is the case. Julie too left school at sixteen. From then on she lived sometimes home with us and sometimes away with her grandparents in York. I remember comparing her with that line in the *Sound of Music*, 'How do you solve a problem like Maria? / How do you catch a cloud and pin it down? / How do you find a word that means Maria? / A flibbertigibbet! A will-o'-the wisp! A clown! // Many a thing you know you'd like to tell her / Many a thing she ought to understand / But how do you make her stay / And listen to all you say / How do you keep a wave upon the sand? / Oh, how do you solve a problem like Maria? / How do you hold a moonbeam in your hand?

Robert was our main concern as the 70's progressed. His school work - and I do mean work, not just the results of it - went into terminal decline along with his general behaviour. In retrospect it began in '75 on our last holiday in Gairloch. We should have known - or perhaps we knew but could not admit it even to ourselves - that something was fundamentally wrong when he began to imagine all sorts of catastrophies if and when we took the boat out fishing. Our obsessive fisherboy resolutely refused to board Culash, so we sailed off without him for the day. I can still see the lonely figure awaiting our return, standing still on the end of the harbour pier. I knew this wasn't - couldn't be - any kind of normal teenage angst. Suffice to say Bob's problems eventually involved the law court after a confrontation with another boy, himself locally a well known trouble maker, and then the hospital for Stuart who he, Robert, had shot in the bum with his airgun. The friction between Bob and myself eventually even led to a physical confrontation during which I was forced to accept the humiliation of my eldest son's superior strength and aggression. One day I came home from work to find him missing. That came much later. The telephone rang. It was fifteen years old Robert informing us that he had now left school, had hitch-hiked the two hundred miles to Grimsby, had enrolled himself into the deep sea fisherman's course and was living in the Seaman's Mission. Taking Stuart and I think Julie with me I got into the car and drove up to Grimsby, of course planning to bring Robert home. We arrived there at close to midnight. The Seaman's Mission at Grimsby is not any place for the faint hearted or for those of a nervous disposition. Certainly no place for my introspective fifteen years old son. But no words of mine or his younger brother or older sister would change Robert's mind. We drove all the way home without him, mostly in a worried silence (mine, not Stu's). Joan of course was in great distress about this, yet to my delight Robert finished his course and immediately got himself signed on as a 'learner deckie' on the immense trawler *Ross Cougar*. Ten stormy days in the Barents Sea followed during which my son could never take off his 'yellows' and during which a senior member of the crew ran amok with an axe, trying to reach another crewman who had locked himself in the cabin out of harm's way. Something to do with one of their wives, apparently! Anyway, by the end of the decade Robert was back home and working in a local metal working company. We did not know it but the worst was yet to come...

Both Robert and Stuart were physically very strong, fine looking, intelligent boys. But neither of them liked going to school and neither liked school work and neither of them liked the school teachers. And of course the school did not like them in return! Why should it? Yes, without doubt, Robert became something of a role model for Stuart. Looking back, I didn't help matters by spending every spare home-time moment with my sons in our lovely old wooden fishing boat, *Culash* (by now a fully rigged lug-sailer). There were so many problems on shore but once afloat ... I remember, in the middle of winter one night racing home from London, wheeling *Culash* on her trailer down to the slipway, then the three of us being out there 'til after midnight on a windy, pitch-black Solent fishing for cod. No way for them to be ready for their next school-day, I see that now. In due course Stu would follow in his brother's footsteps by running away from school and from home, this time to Penzance in Cornwall rather than Grimsby, but that's another story. Right now, in 1979, he changed life for the better for all of us, and for me in particular over the next thirty years. How? All my fourteen years old son Stuart wanted that Christmas was a dog. Not just any dog now ...

So by 1979 Kairen was in London with husband Rog and had made us proud grandparents, Julie was increasingly home and away, Robert was at home but not behaving in any way normally and Stuart was acting housekeeper - and wanting a dog ....

32. 1980 and Delia

In 1980 my life at home was (1) family and housekeeping, (2) nursing, (3) boats and sea fishing, (4) dogs.

My life at work was the (1) the company, (2) my customers (3) my job.(4) my sales and sales administration team.

And, in between these, my life since the early seventies was and had been Delia. A segment small in time but massive in meaning. It is no exaggeration to say that, whether or not she was conscious of it, Delia saved my way of life if not my life itself. I do not want here to sound a note of self-excuse for seeking and finding a lover whilst my wife, who I had loved and still loved, was permanently disabled. But I simply cannot conceive of how I might have fared through these deeply troubled times without her and those necessarily brief moments of respite that we were able to share. Dee was, when I first met her, a 28 years old divorcee and mother of two young boys living in rented accommodation close by her place of employment as a barmaid in Gosport's *Jolly Roger* pub. From the beginning we shared a physical attraction. We shared much else as well; our love of books, writers and writing for one instance. Who is there amongst us, I wonder, who can understand and chart the origins of their own behaviour, who is there who consistently behaves against their own instinct, exactly in accord with the human definition of what is 'right' and what is 'wrong'? These are no excuses, just genuine questions.

By 1980 I had begun to scribble lines of poetry on my travels, then had started to take this versification more seriously. In the mid nineties I wrote a very long narrative poem entitled *'A Walk Downtown'*. It relates the thoughts of a lonely, somewhat drunken young man walking back to his cold bedsit after a Saturday night out in Dublin ... included in the forty or so verses, this one where he is considering his affair with the wife of a very dangerous friend ...

> *What purpose has that urge that blots all other things,*
> *And drains your mind of all except a certain she?*
> *That has you risk what's safe to find that old glory,*
> *That grows, a fresh pink rose in thorny secrecy*
> *To prick you, have you bleed no matter what you give?*
> *This agony, it moves from just a thing of glands?*
> *'Forsaking all others'? But a rose that's not your own,*
> *Is a fire by which you, cold and lost, may warm your hands?*
> *Questions like your shadow leap ahead across the way.*
> *The answers dancing, swirling in unread shades of grey.*

At any rate what started out for me as a brief encounter soon morphed as if by itself into a way of life at once calming and exciting that had overcome any agony of conscience. Dee was my shelter from the storm. And there was born that so mysterious thing that we call 'love' between man and woman; the thing that transcends, uplifts, indeed is the sole ennoblement of our act of lust. Again in the mid-nineties, whilst staying with an American business friend and his wife in Al-Khobar, Saudi Arabia, I was asked a question. The enquirer was their daughter, a young, female US Army officer. Over dinner with the family it became obvious that this lady was suffering a severe bout of lost love, or lover, or both. Her question to me went, shockingly simple ... *'What the hell is love, Bryan?'* I said that nobody could answer that other than by illustration of some personal, real-life example, adding that poets, writers and artists had since time began addressed the very same question without finding solutions other than by example. *You might,* | I told her, *Just as well be asking me, what is light? All I do know it that real, unimagined, two way love is heaven rather than hell.* Then on the way back to my hotel, three hundred monotonous cross-desert kilometres away I wrote this and e-mailed it that evening to her parents, for the attention of their daughter Cindy ...

A Question of Love

"I want to know what love it," starts the song
And then goes on, "I want you to tell me,"
But the answer may in history only be;
With just the question's echo left so some
Feel cold the vacuum when replies don't come.
"Come live with me and be my love," he wrote
Went on; "And we shall all the pleasures prove:"
Four hundred years ago that poet's love
He saw reflected in his lovers eyes
The truth, pure love, now with the poet lies.

But there are many kinds of love; "Ask not,"
He said, "What my country does for me, just
Ask, my country, that I love, what I must
Do for thee?" Golden words that burn so hot -
What greater than for love, to die and rot?
"I love (whatever,)" some car windows say
Thus take that truth of brightest human light

> *Dim and de-value it, thus make it trite:*
> *Without true love can we the pain defray*
> *Of nothing at the dying of the day?*
>
> *"And He so loved the world..." It tells of blood,*
> *(That Book), and of the life that's here on earth*
> *It's only we who're blessed to know from birth*
> *The joy, the strength of love so fine and good,*
> *Able thus to reach, to touch the face of God.*
> *"I want to know what love is," still you ask:*
> *And yes, it could be all that you can feel*
> *Or need to feel or all of life that's real*
> *Or nought for you or once just now and gone,*
> *Or yours to have and hold from this day on.*

By 1980 Delia ('Dee') was as much a part of my life as was I of hers. I had no idea where we were going with this so-called 'affair' but I knew she had become that essential balance on my dangerous tight-rope between past and future. And, as I shall relate, the time would come when Dee would choose to walk out of the shadows and become, with her boys, a solid and enduring part of all of our lives.

This is another poem I composed, in 1980, for Delia's St Valentine's Day ...

> *A sonnet for Delia*
>
> *My mind's eye sees her as I saw her first*
> *And still she thrills me as those years ago*
> *When Nature's breathless clamour did its worst*
> *And best when deathless love began to grow.*
> *So easily she found my heart, my mind,*
> *And calmed me without over-tenderness;*
> *She uncomplaining led me from behind,*
> *Shared failure's pain, shared joy in my success.*
> *This day of Valentine I feel you still,*
> *And closer are you, Delia, to me;*
> *My crowded mind knows that I ever will*
> *As from my heart and soul I reach for thee.*
>
> *Mysterious love shall be our saving grace*

Through time beyond this ever-loving place.

33. A dog called Seth

For Christmas 1978 the only present our youngest son Stuart wanted was a dog. I have remarked before how persistent he had become with this. We decided to buy him a really comprehensive dog breed encyclopaedia as a Christmas present. His birthday falls on 29th of December. Our challenge to our thirteen year old - *study the book and tell us which three breeds of dog you would most like, and why.* Back he came with (a) Doberman Pinscher. We eliminated that one, not liking their reputation for fighting and biting, (b) Pyrrenean Mountain Dog. Again eliminated - massive so would need huge quantities of food besides being very, very hairy. (c) A splendid looking short haired animal called a Hungarian Vizsla. We had never heard of it. That breed was in those days a rarity in the UK. However we told Stu we'd go with this vizsla selection provided we could find a UK breeder with puppies for sale. It turned out that there were only two Vizsla breeders in the country, one up north and the other Mrs Gay Gottlieb of St John's Wood in central London. I called Mrs Gottlieb to make an enquiry. She had a litter of puppies 'on the way'. Would you like to come up to town to see them in March?

On that first of January (1979) our first grandchild was born to Kairen and Roger in London, a beautiful baby girl to be called Ella. So much excitement for the whole family. Joan in particular took to the idea of grandparenthood especially well. Perhaps baby Ella took her mind somewhat off that insidious multiple schlerosis. So Joan and I had become grandparents. A very strange feeling for a pair of forty four year olds!

At Sweetheart International the times were definitely a-changing and not necessarily for the better. Following the infamous 1979 'winter of discontent' including its government enforced three day factory working week, demand for packaging plateaued and then fell back. I had that difficult choice to make, especially as we were not yet ten years old as a manufacturing company but had already grown sales to some three quarters of a million pounds a month. My choice was (a) to hold our price levels and thereby endure a fall in sales, protecting gross margins of profit - because the competition would surely be lowering their own prices, or (b) reduce prices and endure (at least, try to endure) a reduced profitability. I chose the former. Falling sales meant that we had to lay people off in the factory I took my sales force to shake the hands of the workers as they left with their final wage packets. It was not an easy thing to do. None of us can forget it but the experience toughened us mentally, made us try even harder to re-grow our sales. In addition I would talk at specially convened meetings with all three factory shifts (yes, the midnight one included!) to try to bring understanding of what it was all about to those employed 'inside' - and of course to receive any ideas the factory and office people - and the rest of the Board for that matter had to offer. Overall, as hard as it was, I like to think our business grew into an even more effective unit after it was over than before the great national recession.

One Sunday in March 1979 I drove Joan and Stuart up to London, to visit Gay Gottlieb's ultra expensive residence in St John's Wood. The lady welcomed us into her kitchen. On the way through the big house we couldn't help observing a group of well known figures having themselves a fine old Sunday afternoon drinks party. I recognised Peter Cook and Jonathan Miller amongst the merry throng. When Gay closed the kitchen door and opened the scullery door a veritable stream of voluble, light reddish-brown dogs surged out at us. This was mother bitch Russetmantle (kennel name) Sophie and her eight puppies. When things calmed down we were taken to see the father dog outside in his garden cage. Russetmantle Troy had won umpteen show and field trial awards. he was an amazing animal, an outstanding example of the national dog of Hungary, the product of a thousand years of strict gundog breeding. Stuart was totally struck dumb. How he wanted one of those vizsla puppy - and how did we, his mother and father, for that matter. I had an instinct that such an animal could do my family nothing but good in any number of ways. Back in the kitchen Gay enquired as to whether I would be shooting over our vizsla, should she agree to let us have one. I shook my head. *So you'll want to show him or her, then?* she asked. I looked at my son and he at me and again I shook my head. *Oh, I'm so very sorry,* she said, *but these dogs are not just family pets. I'm afraid I've wasted your time.* We drove back to Lee-on-Solent in a virtual silence.

Two weeks later the call came. It was Gay Gottlieb; it seemed an American puppy buyer had defaulted. Were we still interested? Hastily she added that it would be the runt of the litter, a male called

Russetmantle Seth. *Unfortunately not suitable for showing or for field work.* The next day Seth was ours (Stuart's) at home, and our family life had changed for ever and had changed infinitely for the better. Seth was eight weeks old when I carried him into our home.

Seth and Stu became inseparable over the months ahead. By that July he was three parts grown. One day I looked at the breed standard Gottlieb had given us and compared it with this Russetmantle Seth anumal. Even to a non-doggie person he was clearly a near perfect specimen of his breed. I made another Sunday appointment with Gay Gottlieb. I shall not forget the look on Gay's face when she opened her front door to the three of us - plus the nearly full grown dog. I'd swear her face went white. She could not take her eyes off him. I'll not forget, either, what she then said. *I've bred eight hundred hungarian vizslas looking for this one, and now I've given him away.* Not exactly *given*, I wanted to respond, (but didn't) *as I paid you four hundred pounds for him!* Anyway she took us out to her back garden and asked Stu to walk him up and down. *He's perfect,* she breathed, *just perfect. Stuart, you simply have to learn how to show him - or leave him back here with me!* Stu's face said forget that. Like most fourteen years old boys, Stu didn't relish the idea of 'poncing up and down in front of judges' but he was eventually persuaded to attend the local ringcraft lessons. Gay sent me an entry form for the next Championship Dog Show which happened to be in Leeds. I filled it in, in my ignorance entering Stu and his dog Seth in all the listed classes, not knowing it was customary to enter a dog in only one of the five age-based groups. Then there was the Open where all of the class winners were adjudged side by side to arrive at the best of gender. The top dog would compete against the top bitch to arrive at best of breed. Also unknown by me, it was very rare for a mere boy to be showing a dog at these big Championship Shows. They are a very serious business indeed for breeders and expert fanciers, certainly not suitable for participation by any amateur youth.

Stu had to have Seth in the designated ring at Leeds by 09.30 which meant an 04.00 start for the drive north. Even then we were running late. I could not believe the buzz when we got there. More than ten thousand animals entered with all the people and cars that this suggests! I dropped Stuart and Seth at the car park gate. By the time I'd found a space, got Joan into her wheelchair and (eventually) found our way to the appropriate show ring I could hardly see what was happening through the surrounding crowds. I asked a lady if she knew

101

what was actually going on. She said, *it's fantastic, that boy's dog has won every class. He's now in with Gay Gottlieb and Show Champion Troy for best of breed.*

34. Invincible Macdonalds

In 1982 the return of HMS Invincible from the Falklands War afforded me an opportunity to assemble all our major customers for a unique 'entertainment'. Buyers from Kraft Foods, Lyons Maid, Walls, Unigate, Express Dairies amongst a dozen or so others stayed overnight in Gosport prior to making their way in the morning to Camper & Nicolson's Sailing Club premises. The club overlooks the entrance to Portsmouth Harbour. I had hired it for the day. None present - certainly not myself, will ever forget the sight of that great, grey, rust-streaked warship looming out of the early morning Solent mists, slowly entering the harbour surrounded by a massive flotilla of small vessels of every kind and accompanied by a cacophany of hooting from land and sea. Her crew were lined up in traditional Royal Navy fashion along her decks. Whatever you might have felt about the rights and wrongs of Margaret Thatcher's carefully orchestrated campaign, I personally had never felt more proud of my country. And I could tell by the looks and emotion on the faces of my business friends that I was not alone. The moment had struck some kind of a nationalist nerve deep within us all, not least the two ladies alongside me - there on a business occasion for the first time - Delia and her ex-WREN mother, Wynne Boulter.

By thar time we had recovered the company's sales and profits momentum and I had a full complement of field and office sales staff covering the UK markets in depth. I was also managing fully staffed offices in Stockholm and Paris and was working closely with agents in Northern Ireland, Eire, Switzerland and Norway. In addition I was a frequent visitor to our sister company in Holland, (the company of which I had in the early seventies been appointed caretaker managing director). There was also our subsidiary plant near Bristol, specialising in the manufacture of drinking straws and, after the start-up of Macdonalds in the UK, the paper cups that complemented Gosport's plastic equivalents. In fact several of the people key to these operations including my friend Ray Gaskell were recruited as a direct result of my own 'previous life' in the by then defunct Lily Cups and Containers of Liverpool.

Macdonalds! Now there was a name to conjure with! One day, over a drink with Henry and Sorretta Shapiro in their Connaught Hotel suite I was told the story that had underpinned some of Maryland Cup's latterday success in the USA. As I recall, a certain fifty something years old L.A. commercial kitchen equipment salesman by the name of Ray Kroc had bought into an L.A. barbeque restaurant and given it the name of Macdonalds. He had come up with the basic idea of hamburgers in a hurry and turned the M of Macdonalds into those famous golden arches. Kroc approached Henry for extended credit on the disposable paper food and drinks packaging. Henry agreed and even secured preferred shares in Kroc's company. The rest, as they say, is history. By the time of his death in his eighties Mr Kroc was the wealthiest person in the USA and Henry's shares had multiplied in value many thousands of times over.

It was around this time that Macdonalds commissioned a market research covering the possibility of opening up in the UK. The net answer; *don't touch it with a bargepole. Brits will never consent to drink out of paper cups or munch big-time into fast service burgers.* Mr Krok said the researchers were wrong. He threw out the researchers, found a licensee in the States who shared his views in the UK potential and opened up the first franchised UK Mcdonalds store in Tottenham Court Road. Henry Shapiro and I went there during that first week of their operations. Unbelievably, customers were queuing down the road! We sat having our burger lunch with the Chicagoan franchisee - I forget his name. I could hardly believe it when kids came up with requests for the Americans to sign menu cards! A bright prospect for packaging sales had opened up for my company. This was clearly going to be a good bit more important than another new venture in people feeding. It was going to be a sea-change in the British way of life. Whether you like, love or would leave alone Mcdonalds and all it stands for, the way and the sheer speed with which they opened up the whole of the UK and European markets was one of the world's foremost example of mass marketing in brilliant action. And they took Sweetheart with them.

Back at the ranch house (as the saying goes) things were not getting any easier. I'll be writing next about the three, perhaps unlikely new directions in which our family life was turning: Julie and her snooker ambitions; Stuart / Seth and the dog shows; Robert and the commercial fishing boat I was prevailed upon to buy for him!

35. MFV Kerry Jane

You may remember that my oldest son Robert had literally run away from school and home, aged fifteen, to enrol himself into a commercial fishing course at Grimsby. You may also remember that he had an traumatic initial first trip out on the giant trawler *Ross Cougar* after which he came back home to a job in a metal galvanising plant. But all he really wanted to do was to skipper his own small boat and fish the waters of the Solent for money. He and his mother worked on me for some time before I gave in. I went to see my long-suffering bank manager and secured the loan to buy a twenty eight foot metal hulled converted lifeboat. Why did I do it when I knew my son was not always entirely 'balanced' in his mind? Head in sand stupidity I guess. Looking for solutions where in all reality there were none?

There is an oyster fishery in the waters around Southampton, between the mainland and the Isle of Wight. Anybody with a suitable boat could go out - from November to, I think, February - to dredge the gravel beds for their high grade 'Belon' oysters. Later on, the fishery became a fully licensed closed shop for the benefit of that band of local, well established fishermen, none of whom were overly pleased to see the arrival of my (that is, Robert's) boat with its young crew. I had bought *Kerry Jane* from a guy in Langstone harbour. Robert and his brother went over there to take her out to sea and bring her round on to her new moorings in adjacent Portsmouth harbour. I waited dockside for their arrival, heart in mouth, but had no need to worry. Both young men were very good at boat handling - even a boat as unsuitable / difficult to handle as that weary old *Kerry Jane*. Looking back, I think it's called being sold a pup! We had a lot of work to do on the boat before the season opened. Amongst other things I myself needed to learn the arts and crafts of steel welding in order to fabricate and install a gantry and sorting tray apparatus!

The oyster fishery season opens on the stroke of midnight. By then every boat with a winch is milling around in the darkness, in ultra close proximity one to the others over the gravel beds off Calshott, all ready to drop their dredges. Dangerous stuff, much accompanied by bluff, counter-bluff and profanity! I still have two oyster shells at home. The smaller one is the very first oyster dredged up by Robert's *Kerry Jane* on that first midnight. It cost, I used to say, slightly over ten thousand pounds sterling. The large one is a perfect example of a mature Belon (Atlantic) oyster - much better eating than the gnarled and twisted Pacific oysters that are mostly what you get these days in British restaurants. I helped crew the boat when I could. Robert would be skippering with Stu on the winches and me sorting out the legally sized oysters from all the undersized ones and the stones and rubble that come up in the wire mesh dredges. It was serious fun whilst it lasted. Great satisfaction when you put into Portsmouth Docks to unload and sell your catch - until you realised that for every bag of oysters you had, some of the real old pro's had managed to get two or three. When the oyster season ended I financed the acquisition of trawl and long lining gear. Trawl net for catching plaice and sole, long lines for bass. In spite of all our efforts, for two full years we ran the boat at a loss.

When the boys were out in Kerry Jane without me, when I got home from work I used to go down to the sea front with my binoculars, watching and waiting, hoping and praying that they had met with success. There were low points and high points. Perhaps the former was when the boat's engine gave up the ghost and she had to be towed in the early hours into Cowes for repairs. *Kerry Jane* was never anything but marginally seaworthy. Not good when you understood the risk to the life and limb of my young sons and their friends who would form her crew. And another low when Robert (and/or I?) was taken to court and fined for landing undersized oysters. High point? Definitely when I went to the harbour to see the boys landing a massive catch of long-lined bass. Mother lode at last? No, just another swallow that that never did make a summer.

Hard times indeed, even though full of hope - mostly unrealised. I remain convinced that the pressures of that old Kerry Jane and my need to get some kind of a return from her operations contributed to Robert's increasing mental illness. Because we were 'commercial', for tax reasons I had to form a company. I called it 'KJ Fisheries'. And because a company needs to keep proper accounts I prevailed upon a reluctant Delia to study accounting at night school. To her own surprise she secured her O Level. I further prevailed on her to go on to study for her A Level but all she got was a second O! Never mind, she took the burden of doing the boat's books off me and her knowledge came in very handy when I left Sweetheart to form my own consultancy, and again when we started our micro business in cards etc up here in the Highlands of Scotland.

For a further couple of years, *Kerry Jane* lay on her moorings without being mechanically sound enoiugh - or her skipper being mentally well enough - to earn her keep. Eventually I called the boat salvagers in Southampton, glad enough to let them tow her away free of charge to be broken up. End of that chapter. As I say, it had not been altogether an unhappy one but I was glad to be rid of the worry of the boat at a time when I had plenty of other worries. Amongst others, the experience had left my son Robert unwell and adrift. Joan and I were by now very, very concerned for him and for his future.

In ending my previous bio-blog I said I would be writing about *Julie and her snooker ambitions; Stuart / Seth and the dog shows and Robert and the commercial fishing boat*. However, this blog being quite long enough, Julie and snooker and Stu and Seth will have to await the next episode! One thing to say though; never a dull moment!

36. Games of life

Probably through the Pot Black TV series and the exploits of the so-called Ginger Magician (young Steve Davis), in the late seventies, I'd become interested in playing and watching the game of snooker. With a couple of work colleagues I joined the 147 snooker club in downtown Gosport. Then Stuart told me he'd like to learn how to play the game so I enrolled him into the club's Saturday morning instruction course. Hearing about this, our twenty year old daughter Julie, home again after a lengthy stay with Joan's people in York, decided to make a personal stand against sexism. She wanted to learn to play snooker as well! In vain I told her that snooker clubs were not necessarily a suitable world for attractive young ladies, so one Saturday morning in 1979 there she was, alongside Stu, under instruction in front of a crowd of more than interested club members. She loved the attention and furthermore displayed a degree of natural ability to actually play the game - play it better than Stuart, I might add.

From there on Julie got herself into snooker big time. She became ultra focussed on it, constantly playing matches against good male amateurs and other top ladies in social clubs, political clubs and working men's clubs all around the country. Having said that, I remember that many of the working men's clubs and Conservative clubs in those days (maybe still today) had rules prohibiting a woman from playing on their snooker tables - and in some cases even from entering the club at all! Notwithstanding that, in common with a handful of other young women our Julie 'turned pro' and acquired a manager. I think it would have been in 1980 or 81 when her big opportunity arrived. She was to partner Tony Meo, one of the top male players in a doubles match against world champion Steve Davis and the then world ladies champion, whose name I cannot right now bring to mind. The match was televised live on ITV from a large sports hall in Clacton just prior to that year's football Cup Final. Joan and I went to watch the mjatch live. Julie looked so beautiful in her black and white man's type evening suit and frilly shirt. How proud we were to see her pot the first ever televised snooker ball by a female. (But then of course Steve took over and cleared the table, as was his wont in those days.) After the match Joan and I were introduced to Barry Hearn, well known sports promoter and Steve Davis's manager and friend. *The first woman able to play and win against these top men,* he pronounced, *will be an overnight millionaire.*

I could understand that, especially as snooker's massive TV audiences were at least fifty percent female. There seemed no physical reason why a female exponent of the game should not emerge but the fact is that it didn't happen then and hasn't happened since. My own theory is that the ladies just do not have the necessary focus - that mysterious winning drive / mind-set - to apply themselves either on the table or for the necessarily boring hours and hours and hours of daily practice. Perhaps it is that Mother Nature equips we males to hunt and compete and fight and equips the female of our species to attract, procreate and defend. If that's sexist (whatever sexist is) I'm sorry, but if you have a better explanation please do let me know. Please - no guff about 'opportunity'. We all - of both genders - have the opportunity to do with our lives what we will, then to try again and again even when our ultimate failure becomes depressingly obvious or our goal gets to seem ridiculously irrelevant.

Julie went on to marry an ex-Royal Navy man, a highly rated snooker amateur; a bright enough guy but one always on the lookout for money making schemes requiring as little as possible actual work input! They managed to buy a snooker club in Nottingham but sold that in favour of another one in the East Anglian town of Swaffham, providing us in the meantime with two more grandsons to add, by then, to Kairen and Roger's three girls and a boy. Fortunately Kairen's marriage was as happy and solid as Julie's was the exact opposite.

Back at home, Stu and his lovely vizsla dog Seth continued to provide Joan and I with a much needed antidote to her slowly degrading MS. Although she was permanently wheelchair bound I managed to take her with boy and dog to major dog shows all over the country: Leeds, Peterborough, Builth Wells, Bath, Birmingham and even as far north as Edinburgh, amongst others. Oh, and Crufts of course, at Earls Court in London and then the NEC in Birmingham. But perhaps my own favourite memory is of Stu/Seth coming reserve best in show at Southampton. I still have the clipping from Dog World ... *This combination of Russetmantle Seth and his young handler has to be seen to be believed,* it reads. When Stu eventually left home to go commercial fishing down in Cornwall I opted to show the dog myself at what turned out to be his final Crufts. What a let down! Seth moped around the ring, unresponsive and disinterested. He wanted Stuart on the other end of his lead! End of that dog show chapter of my life.

I want to end this particular blog with a record, as near verbatim as I can manage, of a telephone conversation that took place one Saturday afternoon in our house at 45 Raynes Road, Lee-on-Solent. I picked up the call. Before I could say anything came a female voice; *Hello Bryan.* At once and without thinking I responded, *Hello, mother.* Somehow - goodness knows how - I had recognised the voice of my mother, Marie, last seen and heard from when I was eleven years old, all of forty two years previously! Yes, this is the unadorned truth, like all else in these memoirs There are some truths in my life that I shall never write about, but the ones I do write about are indeed the truth as best I recall them! More about mother (and father) later.

p.s. Apropos the latter, someone asked me why I do these blogs, after all the life of a non-celebrity is of truly minimal interest. I referred them to Ernest Hemingway's response when a budding young author asked him for his advice. Hemingway said, simply; So you are a writer? So bloody well write!

37. Family affairs

I closed the previous episode with an account of how, one Saturday afternoon in, I think, 1982, I instantly recognised my mother's unintroduced voice on the telephone - having last heard it in 1944 when I was aged just ten! I have tried to keep these memoirs as closely as possible to their chronological order but here I'm going to fast forward for a moment to 1993, when mother lay dying in a Milton Keynes hospital and I was returning from another trip to the USA. I remember that flight, one of those 'red-eyes' from Chicago that discharge you into a mostly deserted, often rainy Heathrow with most of the UK happy to be still fast asleep. I remember it because, with all the aircraft lights turned low and the sound only of the drone of engines and sleeping people, I wrote my very first small verse since leaving school. This is it ... so far as I know seen until now only by mother and the other folk in her hospital ward ...

To my mother

So many fine things, fine mornings.
Long evenings, beauty, new things
And the many kinds of earthly love
That through our trials live on
Now and forever in the stars above
And never from my memory truly gone.

With everything
Your son, Bryan
21 April 1993.

My beautiful mother Marie was the daughter of General of the Salvation Army, Albert Osborn and Captain of the Salvation Army, Evalina. I *think* Evalina was my grandmother but cannot be quite certain for the General had three wives, (consecutively I should add!), outliving them all. Albert and Evalina's daughter Marie had six or seven siblings. I don't know just how many. My father Eddie Islip had also been born into a strongly Salvationist family although these, my paternal grandparents, were unpaid Salvationists. In 1932 my sister Shirley was born to Marie and Eddie, followed by myself in 1934 and then my sisters Tina and Maureen. Later on, in my early teens, Father told me that although I, Shirley and Maureen were 'his', my sister Tina was not his. An unnecessarily hurtful revelation. I retain two versions of my parents life together before and during WW2; the version with which I grew up as told by my father and the version as told in female confidence mainly to my wives Joan and later to Dee by my mother. We would all like to re-write parts of our history, would we not? (Please note I'm trying my best not so to do right here!) According to father my mother was a bit of a spendthrift, well addicted to a fast social life and men in general. According to mother my father was a tyrant and a bully, partial to masochistic sex, the result of being brought up alongside his two sisters by a subserviant mother and a father who frequently made him stand for hours, for the most minor of offences in the corner of the room facing the walls. However, it seems that father as a young man was presented by grandfather Islip (who had made large profits through building works in WW1) with his own building business, which unfortunately went into liquidation in the late 30's. According to father, his partner had defaulted and defected with all the loot. How strange a co-incidence! At any rate, father was not forgiven for losing the family money.

When grandfather Islip lay on his Hastings deathbed (he had lung cancer) his doctor summoned all three of his children. The last will and testament was read out. My aunties Kay and Peggy were to split the estate between them and father got - nothing! He had, so my grandfather declared, already had wasted his share! Afterwards the doctor urged the three of them to say their goodbyes then go wait in the living room. Ten minutes later doctor brought them back. Grandfather was dead. Very soon afterwards grandmother Islip also left this mortal coil. I am quite prepared to believe not without proper medical help.

But looking back it does seem odd to me that their three children, brought up in such a strongly moralistic tradition, each had to suffer at least one divorce. And I do mean suffer. As I have said before, divorce must rank as one of the most painful of self-inflicted wounds.

Britain declared war on Germany in 1939. Probably my very first memory at five years of age is of all the family sitting around the radio in our Chigwell home in the northern suburbs of London. I can hear still the sadly sonorous voice of Prime Minister Chamberlain as he related how he had sent Herr Hitler an ultimatum: ... *No such response has been received,* our prime minister told us, *and therefore this country is at war with Germany* ... This sounds like a lot of guns and jolly good fun, thought this five year old at the time.

By then, father had used his masonic contacts to secure a position as a quantity surveyor in Whitehall's 'Ministry ' (of War, as it became). He was therefore exempt from military service, being required to help manage the building of wartime airfields and encampments. One of his sites was Burtonwood in Lancashire and it was to this area, in nearby Walton-le-Dale, that the family migrated soon after the outbreak of the war proper. I don't think mother appreciated the move away from the bright lights of London town, but at any rate her relationship with father soon descended into that well-remembered, emotionally disturbing shouting v silence match. I have said before how my mother eventually embarked on an affair with one Walter Smith, a plumber and sergeant in the platoon of Home Guards commanded by father. I remember this man very well, for after doing some work in our attic he curried favour with this particular nine year old by presenting him with the most beautiful object I had ever seen in my short life; the egg of a starling in the purest of azure blue. The beginning of a lifelong interest in wild birds (and their eggs as a boy, before birds nesting was made illegal.)

Late in 1944 came the split. Mother went off with Mr Smith, taking Tina and Maureen with her by rule of the courts which had allocated my elder sister Shirley and myself to the care of father. So my sister and I, a bewildered duo, were entrained, unaccompanied, to London. My final memory for the following forty odd years of a beautiful mother adored by her son and who loved me was of her waving and weeping on the platform as the train pulled away from Preston railway station. Father had a house in Pimlico opposite the famous / infamous Dolphin Square on the banks of the river Thames, but Shirley and I were at once sent off to our respective prep (boarding) schools in Abingdon, Berkshire. I have no idea whether father had already begun his own love affair with one of the Ministry typists, Julia Wicksteed. I suspect that was the case. In any event Julia became my stepmother. I became aquainted with her in a quite traumatic fashion - as recorded in one of my fictional short stories ... the thirteen years old is home from school ...

To explain the plan he knocks at his father's bedroom door, opens it without waiting for a response. Alongside his father is a woman. They're sitting up in bed side by side holding cups of tea or coffee - coffee, he can smell it. The woman has biscuit crumbs on her lips and has longish light coloured hair all curly-wavy. At first she looks shocked, quite angry, then quickly re-arranges her face into a smile. He can see the breasts with their dark nipples through the sheer material of her nightdress. He's never seen real breasts before, only those in the magazines and the newspapers they pass around at school and on the web of course. He knows his face has flushed red; very red. The woman realises what he's looking at and pulls up the bedclothes. 'Hello. You must be David', she says.

Regrettably I could never find it in myself to do very much more than tolerate Julia's presence, especially throughout my troubled teens. She died in in her seventies in a Hastings Nursing Home.

I am not about to allocate blame for this chaotic dissolution of a family but I most surely can advocate the state of lifetime monogamy ... In my own, deeply held view the sins of the fathers etc should never be visited upon their progeny, whatever happens outside of their marriage. Perhaps these views - yes, very much unpopular according to latter day lore - can at least in part be attributed to my paternal grandfather. According to father the family only discovered after his death that *their* father had for many years supported a second, secret, family throughout most of his adult life. Yet grandmother and grandfather lived and died together - it seemed to me quite responsibly and even happily - well into their eighties. *How about your own conduct?* you may well be thinking. I can only respond that I honoured and would always have honoured my marriage vows, come what may, 'til death did part either one of us from the other. As indeed it was to do.

As I say, in or around 1982 mother made a truly shocking contact with me and mine and afterwards I arranged to go to see her. To my (and father's) amazement it turned out that she had been living, albeit in very reduced circumstance within half a mile of father's sea-front apartment. He had been living there for some twenty years with his second wife, Julia. I tried, perhaps half heartedly, to bring about a rapprochement between my parents but, predictably, that didn't work. You do try to stay away from fire once you have suffered a burning, do you not? But I am glad that my children had the chance of a contact, even if only a scant one, with their grandmother - and ditto with a grandfather who could find it in himself to give them so little of his time and interest as they grew into adulthood.

38. Anyone for libel?

Meanwhile, back in the ranch house ... by 1982 Sweetheart International had made a good, profitable recovery from the country's financial trials and tribulations. In fact all was going swimmingly apart from the seemingly constant changes in ownership and managing directorate.

As I have previously written, Sir Julian Salmon had years ago sold out his initial fifty percent to Malcolm Bates, a prime City of London predator specialising in buying and 'turning around' small and medium sized privately owned companies like ours using cash-laden industrial pension fund money so to do. I parenthesised - and now italicise *turning around* because all too often the only beneficiary turned out to be the sleight of hand *turning arounder*! Those other two stakeholders, namely the company's customers and its employees, were always of minimal interest, so often emerging the worse for such 'buyouts'. Bates's second in command was one Alan Mathewman, who gave me a copy of his just published book aptly entitled *The Genghis Khan Way of Business*. He it was who dropped me like the proverbial hot brick after I said no to his attempts to parachute me as managing director into a struggling Yorkshire paint company. A refusal that may be difficult to comprehend in these job-hopping days, I know. Insufficiency of personal ambition? Perhaps, but I had my very disabled wife and my very able Delia to consider. Besides, having spent ten high pressure years building a manufacturing business from a green field start, and by now being the only surviving founder director, (apart from Henry Shapiro in the USA), I had developed a certain love for and a great deal of pride in 'my' company and its growing assembly of employees, most notably those in sales and marketing. Finally, in spite of all its problems my family and I had settled well into life in Lee-on-Solent. I didn't fancy exchanging it for a life in industrial Yorkshire, even though Joan was still very much my Yorkshire lass.

Nevertheless, having turned down that head-hunter approach (amongst others) I knew I had to forget about any ambition of becoming what my friend Ted Pool sarcastically enquired of me; *Bryan, what the hell you want to be; Chief Executive of the Western World or something?* Nevertheless, to paraphrase Marlon Brando in *On The Waterfront*, I had always felt that *I could have been a contender*. Misplaced self-egrandisement? Probably.

My original MD, Alan Watchman, had been fired by Bates and replaced by Lionel Klackan, ex of Lyons Maid, the ice cream company. I asked the visiting Americans why they had not put me in charge, for I was generally seen as deputy to the incumbent managing director. Mort Gilden gave me a response, at first enigmatic; *We wanted someone to come behind you turning off the lights, Bryan.* The implication being that I had been coming up with new ideas and that mysterious element called leadership but that I was not sufficiently reliable at controlling the costs arising. Totally unjustified of course! Anyway I got on very well with Lionel, an extremely clever man even if one who never became emotionally attached to the company and one who never did move domestically to the Gosport area, preferring his veritable mansion on St George's Hill in Weybridge. Perhaps he sensed that the occupants of this Sweetheart International seat would always have a limited shelf-life. Certainly I saw a veritable succession of manufacturing and financial directors come and go as well as these overall bosses. I will though, say this; having worked in close quarters with everybody inside and connected to the company since its inception, the original directorate, had it been allowed to stay together, would have resulted in a much bigger and better and more profitable company than the one I finally left - or who finally left me - in 1987. As sizeable and as profitable as it was at that time.

This all-too-destructive hire and fire philosophy succeeded in implanting in me serious doubts about my nation's Thatcher-inspired industrial destruction in favour of her soon to be de-regulated City of London. How, I wondered, could anyone, greengrocer's daughter or not, fail to see that the only long term source of Great Britain's financial wellbeing lay - past, present and future - in the invention and manufacturing of things? Instead she handed over the keys of the nation's treasury to the sharp-suited 'City of London' and then spent the rest of her tortured life (and ours to date) wondering why they wanted to rob us blind with impunity. This was the beginning of my slowly hardening conviction that both Westminster and The City were (and very much still are) in urgent need of radical long term reform.

Anyway it was now Lionel's turn to be parachuted out of Sweetheart International. The man coming in as MD was one Mike Townsend, previously head buyer of one of our larger customers, Express Dairies. This appointment made zero sense to me or, I suspect, to anyone else bar Mr Bates and Mr Townsend. I'm not going to dwell on this. Mike was a perfectly good man but one without the necessary abilities to lead and direct the operations of a company now well into eight figures of sales and seven figures of profit, a company that had built itself a beautiful new factory in Gosport together with extensive new offices and warehousing. Mike had never been anywhere this close to the industrial pit-face. Suffice to say that when the City powers-to-be decided his time was up they made a special journey to his hospital bedside in order to 'let him go'. He was suffering an agony of spinal pain at the time. Nice people!

By the mid-eighties the Wall Street vultures were circling over everything in sight, even over the Shapiro brothers' mighty Maryland Cup Corporation, by then a publicly owned U.S. Corporation and still the owner of half of my Sweetheart International Limited. One had a distinct sense that the roof was about to fall in on fifteen years and all the fears and tears of our Gosport endeavour. Although I do not remember feeling it too much at the time, looking back I must have been under a great deal of stress. In spite of my high earnings my bank account was for ever in the red and Joan's condition was deteriorating steadily, now requiring round the clock care. That placed a great strain on the rest of the family - both those still (on and off) at home and those now living their own family lives away from Gosport. To add to the generally surrounding unease Bates sold out to another and even bloodier financial entity headed by one Bill Fieldhouse with his deputy - who immediately became yet one more brand new MD, the accursed Roberto Gasparini, a man of nil morality and a business intelligence straight out of Harvard and Pampers. He/they should have stayed in baby nappies and kept out of my and the company's sight.

One day I asked to meet Chairman Fieldhouse and went up to the City so to do. That was a lunch which might have been orchestrated by Salvador Dali. My host started off on a long and rambling yarn about how he, as a teenager in backstreet Manchester, used to see his mother unlocking the front room door whenever visitors appeared. The room had one of those picture rails running all around, on it rows of ceramic plates. *Mother, why put all tha plates on t' picture rail,* asked Bill, verbalising what the guests were thinking, he told me. *Why, son? Because it gives folk summut t' think about,* responded mother. Bewildered but unbowed I moved on to the reason for my request for the meeting but the man's answers were so vague, so arrogant, so uncaring and so convoluted that I might as well have been addressing him in the secure ward of a mental hospital. Nevertheless he can't have been as stupid as he had sounded for when we returned to his elegant offices I could not help noticing the four original Lowry paintings of the industrial north, each of them with their scurrying stick figures. I knew them each to be worth six figures and up.

In 1985 Maryland Cup Corp, together with all we little fishes, was bought out in the States first by the tissue paper company, Fort Howard. All too soon after that Fort Howard itself together with its eccentric founder, Paul Schirl fell to a pair of financial whizz kids operating under the wing of that thrice accursed merchant bank, Morgan Stanley. I had a great admiration for Schirl, who was said to have dropped out of Yale in order to create Fort Howard of Green Bay, Wisconsin. The multi-millionaire came to the UK at least twice, on both occasions turning up at a Gosport Board meeting without any papers, open-necked shirted, wearing jeans and with feet encased in gym shoes. In the next episode I'll tell you about this, and about The Last Supper - one that all present will never forget.

Oh yes, anyone for libel?

39. Golden lobsters

In the late '70s and the 1980's I held monthly sales meetings. All the individuals in my sales and marketing* team were required to write up on the whiteboard their own territorial sales results for the previous month and year to date. I did the same myself because I had the overall responsibility for all sales including our very important key accounts. This results exposure could be at the same time both a painful experience and a heavy incentive for every individual. After all, nobody wants to self-proclaim him/herself to the rest of the team as its weakest link. I also took the opportunity to provide a necessary update on the company's overall technical and financial fortunes. The monthly meetings were held in head office or in hotels locally to

Gosport or in hotels all around the UK. I reasoned that the cost of them, including travel, meals and hotel expenses would be similar wherever we assembled, whether it be in London, Edinburgh, Belfast, Cardiff, or any other easy to reach point in the UK - and sometimes outside it, in Europe.

Motivation ; now there's a word to cover a multitude of business costs as well as massive business benefits. My sales meetings were unashamedly motivational. A chance for one of the finest industrial sales teams in the UK to become re-fired in the company's interests and, frankly, to have some fun, entirely necessary in my opinion for guys out there working on their own if they were ever to be a proper team working to peak efficiency. As we all know a true team always exceeds in performance the sum total of its parts. Although I would never have admitted it, my model was the high-living, high flying Spitfire and Hurricane pilots of the Battle of Britain. A poor comparison I know, but people who take it to the required limit are never going to be the ones sitting at home of an evening reading a newspaper. So when the very serious business of the meeting had been concluded we would relax over dinner and whatever else the evening and/or the night might bring. I know for a fact that none of us will forget those sales meetings. Whenever I meet with my ex-colleagues su7ch get-togethers invariably come into the conversation. Amongst my personal favourite memories was the one in Amsterdam's Kraznapolski Hotel. Late in the evening Peter Bright, who played and had brought along his trumpet, led a crocodile of us across the city centre, marching to an oft-repeated Colonel Bogey. *'Bollocks, and the same to you'*, we sang ... No doubt the good Dutch people crossed the streets to avoid these madmen and no doubt the bars to which we adjourned were grateful for our largesse, even tolerating our harmless musical self-entertainment. Some amongst our number did not get much in the way of sleep; but nobody, ever, was late for breakfast and all were expected to play their full part in the following day's business proceedings. (Just as in major key those boy pilots at Biggin Hill in '41 would come back to base much the worse for wear but still take off at crack of dawn to meet the enemy on high, perhaps to live another day, perhaps to die.)

I said nobody (would be late), but I'm now thinking to refute my own statement, for our sales office manager, Mike Medland, after a heavy night did once turn up very late for the next day's sales meeting. After that meeting we were to embark by private coach to visit our sister company in Holland. I was furious with Mike, who was a very good friend, one of my very first appointments in fact. I remember how I had asked him in those very early days to join myself and Ted Pool to entertain Albert Sherman, the venerable and highly respected Express Dairies head buyer, to a light lunch in Fareham's Red Lion hotel. Mr Sherman was not noted for his sense of humour, nor for taking fools lightly, so the lunch had been pretty restrained until, all of a sudden Mike, who up until then had been silent, whether as a nervous reaction or as the result of too much wine leaned over the table and uttered the immortal words; *night porter, send up another woman; this one's split.* I thought, in despair, well there goes the biggest dairy account in the UK but to my astonishment Mike's risky out of the blue joke broke all the ice. I cannot claim it influenced everything or anything but we were very soon 'in' at Express. Anyway after Mike Medland's late arrival to that sales meeting I invited him into my office and instructed him to give me one good reason why he should be allowed to come along with us to Holland. *Because I've got the ferry boat tickets*, was his response. Of course after that I had to forgive him. That excursion is quite another story, featuring crates of brown ale being emptied before we even got to Harwich for the boat crossing and Roger Berry distinguishing himself at the hotel in Groenlo with his favourite bar-room stunt whereby he finished his drink then ate a part of the glass! Yes, bit into it, crunched it up and swallowed the shards. No illusion, I promise you. Along with a handful of others I saw him doing it - and later, on more than one occasion. By the by, I understand Roger is now managing director of a substantial company and good luck to him. He was one of the brightest and the best.

Then there was the meeting in Edinburgh's Great Northern Hotel, the meeting where one of our number registered a particularly poor result on the whiteboard which I promptly marked with a scribbled asterisk and a stern, silent look into the eyes of each and everyone around. This was at a time when, for various reasons to do with yet another change in ownership and its ridiculous new policies, the company's production was continually falling short of sales / customer needs. Morale amongst the team was correspondingly low. Then, *why have you given Mark's figures the golden lobster?* enquired Alex Matthewson, to some general hilarity. Indeed my asterisk did look somewhat like a lobster and yes, I had used the yellow marker pen. *Because lobsters can cut off your balls*, I responded. *So he who props up the monthly table will from now on get the golden lobster.* Of course nobody wanted one of these mythical accolades. Avoiding getting one of them got to be quite a sales incentive all by itself. In 1987 after I was made redundant (fired) I took the company to an Industrial Tribunal. One of the 'witnesses' for the company - one who had not been invited to attend any of my sales meetings - told the tribunal how I had made a special award of a gold lobster brooch to the very worst performer in sales and marketing. Much all around hilarity. Even the three judges had to laugh at the sheer improbability of the statement. As you will see later on, I was awarded maximum damages. I have to partly thank my asterisk for them!

There is a fine line between business expenses that are, to quote H.M. Revenue, 'wholly and necessarily incurred in the execution of the claimant's duties', (well, something like that) and expenses that are primarily incurred for one's private satisfaction. It's all about the difference between what is customer entertainment, what is self-entertainment and what is business subsistence. Having signed off my managing directors' and many dozens of other employees' expenses for some seventeen years I reckoned I could most often spot the differences! As for my own expense claims, they were never challenged even though my annual expenses often exceeded my annual salary. So looking back, were they always 'wholly and necessarily' incurred? No, sometimes only in part . So were they ever pure, unadulterated fiction? No again. Looking back I am convinced that I actually under-recovered the money I took out of my own bank account in the interests of the business. And furthermore I am convinced this was nobody's fault but my own.

There are many more than fifty shades of grey in this whole area of business expenses, simply because at a certain level or in certain areas in the business the claimant really is expected to be involved in the life of the company to the detriment of everything else, even his domestic life. His/her time thus belongs to the business quite possibly to an unhealthy extent. Whether the business then or now can ever return or ever repay such devotion is a matter of considerable doubt, as time here will tell. And by the way both sales and profits continued to proper throughout those early and middle 80's.

Golden lobsters played their part, no doubt.

*Industrial sales, that is, face to face promotional contact with a buyer - versus industrial marketing, that is all the non-person to buyer ground between advertising, public relations, brand awareness etc - what ever is the difference? I accept that now, in the age of the internet, the pound spent on marketing has more value than that spent on selling but back then sales, sales influence on the product and the maintenance of good relationships with a company's individual customers had by far the greater bearing on the company's 'money-in' numbers.

40. Home life and money

I guess I was never very good at that old 'money in versus money out' equation when it came to our family finances. I suppose I had the feeling of a true born optimist that my earnings would simply continue to grow as they had in the past. And besides, the bank always seemed anxious to lend me whatever I needed. (I still possess their gold credit card with its £10,000 limit, and unbelievably it is still fully active in spite of my having slight visible means of support!) . So what the hell, no worries? Well, just a few. Having invested in Robert's loss-making oyster dredger, *MFV Kerry Jane (*Funny that - *Kerry Jane* rhymes with *money drain),* there was always the personal danger factor that comes with a commercial fishing enterprise. And of course there was the need to pay for Joan's around the clock care whenever I was required to be abroad on business and her day care when I was at work. But as to the latter it is at the same time fair and unfair to say that our daughter Julie and Stuart, our youngest and the last one left full time at home, took on board overmuch of the burden, the latter never knowing quite what would await him when coming home from school. On one occasion, sadly it was his mother's self-made blood on the floor.

There were quite a few capital costs at that time, for whatever Robert wanted Robert had to have, at least according to Joan - and agreed to by myself in the false hope of a 'cure' as well as in the interests of the quiet life. We financed him not just to that fishing boat, its moorings and equipment, but to a motorcycle and then a car, both written off in very short order, and even a caravan when our eldest son decided to leave home and live with his rather lovely girlfriend. He promptly parked that caravan by the empty swimming pool at the bottom of our garden. We turned our usual blind eye to the intrusion and the happy couple's ongoing need for provisions. Nevertheless that adventure ended when Joan told me with considerable relief and some pride that Robert and his lassie were now into self-sufficiency, for had they not started to grow tomatoes in our empty swimming pool? Yes, you've probably guessed it. For tomato plants please read 'weed'!

I do not think that my wife Joan loved Robert any more than she loved our other three. She loved, even if to an often restrained extreme Karen and Julie and Stuart as well. But I guess a mother will always incline to devote an unfair portion of her time and attention to the weakest of her brood. Looking back with dispassion - and no pride at all - I realise, whether we knew it or not then, that we were in a way trying to 'buy off' Robert's incipient mental illness. In spite of his obvious intelligence, his needs seemed always to be greater than those of the others, just as his mind was in regions where neither we, his parents nor they, his siblings could ever go. And the others always seemed better able than Bob to cope with things. At any rate by the mid-eighties Kairen and Julie were both married ladies with homes and children of their own. Even Stuart, who by then was often getting himself into scrapes, always seemed quite capable of getting himself out of them!

However, in spite of all, I can say in truth that family life in 45 Raynes Road, Lee-on-Solent was not by any means all doom and gloom over the fifteen years of our occupation. Quite the opposite. For instance by the mid seventies the swimming pool was in good order. I can see the children and their friends disporting themselves with much splashing and screaming down there at the bottom of the garden, Stuart climbing on to the next door neighbours' garage roof in order so dangerously to dive bomb the others. I can see the henhouse I built out of old pallets and the half dozen chickens at home in it. (the morning gathering of fresh eggs was a joy for all of us). And I can see Julie's pet buck rabbit, a surprisingly active creature that I had to secretly dispatch early one morning before anyone else had arisen. Why? Because he was not content with playing out his sexual fantasies on the legs of anyone coming into range, but also he had fallen deeply in love with one of our chickens. That poor bird had consequently lost all of her back feathers, a great worry for the girls, even more so when I had to announce that their furry friend had escaped and had probably gone to live happily with his bunny cousins over on the Browndown wild land.

Then there was that Christmastide when Joan's parents came down from York to stay with us and I myself volunteered to cook the Christmas Day lunch starter. Before the usual main course of turkey and as a really special treat came Robert's *Kerry Jane*-caught oysters, 'angels-on-horseback' style. By the time The Queen put in her customary TV appearance there seemed to be something pretty noxious in the air. By early evening everyone seemed unduly tired, clutching tummies, needing to retire early. And then all that long, long Christmas night one could hear the flushing of the toilets and inadequately choked back moans and groans. Never again will most if not all (except me) eat an oyster, and never again would I fail to cleanse these or any other shellfish for days at a time in buckets of water thickened with oat flakes.

If my father and/or my stepmother Julia ever ventured out of Hastings along the south coast to see us at Lee-on-Solent I cannot remember it but Joan's mother, Triphena, and her father, Ted, came south to stay on holiday with us a few times. Ted was a real character. Nobody in the family knew quite where he had come from or how or why but to judge by his accent it had to be somewhere in East Anglia. He had met Triphena when, in her early twenties when she was 'in service' at a grand house in deepest Yorkshire. The feeling was that he had been something to do with horses and the countryside for he was always studying the racing form and visiting the local bookie's and whenever we took him out on a country drive there seemed little he didn't know about the wildife, especially the parts of it that you can eat. Perhaps he had run away from a gypsy encampment having offended Romany law? But his wife Triphena, Joan's mother, was a genuinely strong and silent Yorkshire classic who, like her daughter, was not without an often macabre sense of humour. It could never have been easy for that lady bringing up four children in a three bedroom council house virtually single handed, children who all developed into upstanding property-owning citizens of the realm. In order so to do the lady used to be out of the house at or before 06.00 cleaning the local school for miniscule pay. As I recall, at home she hardly ever seemed to sit down - but what a brilliant cook she was!

And then there was the boat(s) and fishing the salty waters of The Solent. Of course the girls had no interest in those things but myself and the boys sometimes, weather obviously permitting, took Joan out with us, launching off the Lee on Solent slipway close by Raynes Road and lifting Joan and her wheelchair aboard. But even that form of recreation faded and died as my wife's condition deteriorated, as the boys took themselves off and as I was 'encouraged' by the dear old HSBC to reduce my accumulated borrowings. Looking back on them, those times remind me of a game of musical chairs. At some point the music had to stop and in 1985, so it did.

Dee, my friend and lover since the early 70's and her boys, Max and Rudi, now in their late teens, were more of a solution for me than a problem. A kind of haven of normality. And now, in 1985, they became *the* solution. Read on if you will ...

41. What are we; who am I?

When in 1970 I had been required to undergo a three day physical and mental selection procedure for sales director (manager at first) of Sweetheart International I visited one Dr Ralph Arnold, a diminutive, somewhat eccentric psychologist; a leading figure in his profession. For some three hours in the morning and two more in the afternoon he sat opposite me in his London office as I underwent test after test. Example: *write your signature on this paper fifty times.* He clicked his stopwatch. Having done so he passed me a fresh sheet of paper with the instruction; *you are right handed, now do another fifty with your left hand.* Stop watch on. And so on and on and on. No explanations, no apparent rhyme or reason. Sometimes the same 'test' repeated hours later. When I met my new boss, managing director Alan Watchman and co-directors Don for production and Richard for finance I learned that we had all gone through the same somewhat harrowing selection procedures.

Months later, after we had set up the factory in Gosport and our offices in Fareham Dr Arnold came down to see us all at work. Apart from the fact that the pocket dynamo did his level best to seduce my secretary I remember that visit very well. I learned that the main purpose of his assessment was to ascertain whether we, as a team, could act as a team or whether there would likely be destructive clashes of personality. He produced a square paper divided vertically and horizontally - *'my introversion / extroversion* register', he told me; *Your tests are collated and result in a dot on this grid; if your dot falls at the bottom left hand corner you are an extreme introvert, top right hand corner and you are an extreme extrovert. If you are beyond this square in one way or the other you are dangerously unstable, even psychopathic. Where,* he asked, *do you think you are, Bryan?* Now, I had always thought of myself as a thinker, an introvert, somewhat inclined to being reserved, but nevertheless I felt a salesperson should always lean towards extroversion so I put myself low down in the upper right hand quartile but near the centreof the page. He grinned. *Yes, almost everyone wants to be there - it's the fear of abnormality.* He put a dot near the top right. *You are an almost extreme extrovert. All top sales people are somewhere up there and all of you think you're introverts, wherever you put your own dot! No, I won't tell you where your colleagues are except to say that the group of you do have the potential to operate as a team.* A load of bollocks? I don't know but what I do know is that we worked extremely well together although within three years I was the only one of that carefully selected team of four still employed by the company!

Anyway it's now 1985 and for me the roof is threatening to fall in. To the outside world I am a successful director of a profitable company which has, since its green grass beginnings fifteen years ago, wrested market leadership from all its entrenched opposition and which is now a major employer in its locality. Almost everything about Sweetheart International Ltd bears my personal thumb print. I have gained the respect both of the trade and the town. But what of me, myself, a forty one years old chain smoking, pub-going, speechifying family man - albeit with some unusual qualities, methods and habits at work and at home? In precise order I love my wife and family, Delia and her family, our boats, our dogs, nights in new cities with my team, the Highlands of Scotland, the folk in my sales office and of course England and St George. There are a few things I don't like, principally my crazy new world-travelling boss Roberto Gasparini and Margaret Thatcher, still busily closing down the heavy industries that had made our nation rich and powerful in favour of her and her husband's money-shuffling pals in The City of London.

So that's my best shot at a 1985 self-appraisal. You may recall my much, much earlier blog about how at school all we fifth formers were required to write and then have delivered 'in public' an essay - its subject, *'Myself as others see me'*. I assure you this is not an easy thing to write and even less easy to hear being read out! I suppose it can never be the truth, the whole truth and nothing but the truth because we all look in the mirror darkly, do we not? Nevertheless I tried my damnedest then and have done so again right here. As I say I am, in 1985, probably heading for a terminal clash with new managing director Gasparini and whoever the hell might own Sweetheart International this week, and I have a wife with advanced, untreatable multiple schlerosis and a son beset by a rapidly escalating schizophrenia - plus of course plenty of bank borrowings. What happens, I ask myself, should I be fired or walk away from my job?

On the other hand I have a real and present saving grace - a secret or not so secret second family in Delia and sons. Looking back from the present I know Dee was the rock to which I clung throughout the wild waters of my life in the eighties. Had I been stronger or a more decent man, depending on your point of view, I would or should have let her go and been swept away to God knows where.

I devise a plan, a crzyplan some might say, a plan that needs merely that legendary 'one mighty bound'. First I would talk through my plan with Joan and, if she concurred, I would ask our children whether or not they can accept such a situation. What was it? I would attempt to persuade Dee to come live with us at Lee-on-Solent where she could look after my wife and our joint families. If everyone agrees and when things have settled down I will sell our house, releasing its capital and wiping out my bank borrowings before raising a mortgage with a minimum deposit on another home for us all. So very simple! But that is merely step one. Step two, I shall resign my position with Sweetheart before they fire me, for I detest and will not tolerate for long, (or they will not continue to tolerate me for much longer), the way they want to run the company. After that I'll use my trade contacts as a base from which to build my own packaging design and logistics consultancy. Step three is just a background shadow as yet, disclosed to nobody; but I shall create an opportunity to go back thirty years and begin again: I shall at long last get down to the writing of fiction. I think I can write stuff worth reading and secretly still yearn to do so - hopefully for money, by the way. Oh so simple; I told you I was an optimist!

Slightly revising my plan I met with our first born, Kairen, in London where she lived with husband Roger and, by that time, the first two of her children. I laid my cards on the table. I'm not sure if she said go for it with or without great enthusiasm but she said she understood and thought it might work. So after that I spoke with Joan in our living room when we were on our own. I need not have worried. My wife was always the pragmatist and of course she knew me, warts and all, better than anyone in the world, (even myself!). Her longstanding inability to be the wife and housewife was never her fault whereas my having taken a mistress was, if you like, my weakness. Whether she said yes or no to the plan I would abide by her decision, I told her, and I meant it. That would be that. We would continue as best we were able and in any case she, Joan, would always be my wife. There were tears but by then tears were not new to us, for as I have recorded here her life had been really and truly unkind to her and to me and so to all of our family. Eventually she agreed to give it a go but first she wanted to meet with Delia. After that, and before speaking with the other three of my grown up children I sat down with Dee in a Lee-on-Solent Cafe called the Bluebird, thoroughly expecting to have my plan rejected; killed at birth. After all, in spite of our longstanding relationship what attractive, sensible young woman would exchange her independence, her job as a legal secretary and the life she had made for herself and her boys for a man ten years older than her, a man carrying so much baggage and with with so much of doubt about his future? She heard me out in silence then looked me straight in the eyes; *When can I meet with Joan?* she asked quietly, adding, *on my own Bryan, please.*

42. Hayling Island

I'll not forget showing Delia into our home and introducing her to Joan. I left the two of them together with a cup of tea and took a walk down to the beach, my mind in a turmoil. I knew if this didn't work, for any reason or for no reason, for either or both of them, I would be looking for a nursing home for Joan. She was now permanently wheelchair bound, suffering considerable pain. There was no way I could keep on looking after her myself or expecting my sons to do so, neither could I carry on paying for professional outside support of the kind she really needed. I had asked my fellow director Peter Viggars M.P. about state finance for this but the answer had come back with a zero. My leaving work and becoming a state supported unemployed carer wasn't an option. I knew I could never be a good enough housekeeper / nurse and my job was the therapy I needed. Add to that the fact that we would definitely lose our home anyway without my income. If either Joan or Dee said 'no' I would be saying goodbye to Dee - my personal lifeline through these hardest of hard years. I would be very much on my own. I need not have worried. I next called a meeting with Julie, Bob and Stuart with myself and their mother. There were no objections and considerably more understanding than I had any right to expect. They all knew the seriousness of our family position.

Joan and Delia formed a fair to good relationship from the start, a relationship that varied from functional to great to hilarious over the following two years. Delia moved into her own bedroom at 45 Raynes Road. Our two daughters were married with distant homes and families of their own. Our sons had their own rooms when they were home and not away at the fishing. It was time to look at the next part of my plan - i.e. sell the house and buy another one.

Joan, Delia and I sat down together and looked at possible locations having first decided to move altogether away from Lee and the Gosport / Lee-on Solent peninsula. A fresh start for us all beckoned, yet we must contrive to live within commuting distance of my Gosport office. Somewhere nice and detached with four bedrooms - and close by the sea - that was the order of the day. Several times we took the car across to the Isle of Wight on house exploratory jaunts. Twice we came close to making an offer there, but on each occasion something negative emerged re the properties in question - negative enough to make the three miles long, expensive ferry boat ride from Portsmouth to Ryde on the Island tip the balance. So we eventually forgot about the Isle of Wight. Finally we found what we sought, a pleasant postwar detached, a stones throw from the sea front on Hayling Island, which is not an island but a peninsula by Langstone Harbour and a twenty to thirty minute commute from the office. Our offer was accepted.

By 1985 Joan and I had lived in 45 Raynes Road Lee-on-Solent for fifteen years. We and our family had grown up there, my career had, in all the circumstances, flourished from there. To us and our two* dogs it was home. I had not anticipated my reaction when that 'for sale' sign went up. I have never been one to fall in love with bricks and mortar but I did feel the odd lump in my throat. Fortunately the house didn't take too long to sell - for a price some six times that of our original purchase. But it was that good old property owning delusion, for my salary had advanced by about the same percentage and so had accumulated inflation and bank debt. On the other hand of course the Hayling Island house we were buying was about the same price as the one we were selling. After paying off mortgage and bank and funding the deposit on Hayling there was not that much left but at least I could relish my new, debt-free situation, even though having to live with monthly mortgage repayments much more than they had been.

All four of our boys - my Robert and Stuart and Delia's Max and Rudi got on well together. Hayling being a holiday town with much nightclub life, young folk pubs and plentiful teenage girls, it suited them all too well! My oldest, Bob and Dee's youngest, Rudi, became especially friendly in spite of - or perhaps because of Robert's incipient mental illness. And Max and Stuart, being closest together in age, were similarly friendly. Perhaps too much so. They were often accompanied by Stuart's friend Fraser on their Saturday (and all other) nights out. Picking fights seemed to be part of the fun. *Why do you have to do that?* I asked one of my well-bruised warriors; *because he looked at me and this girl*, came the incomprehensible response. A quite bewildering rota of girlfriends arrived at the house. I rarely knew quite whose was which if you see what I mean! The boys would sometimes go out sea fishing together - rod and line, not commercial, for by now Robert's late unlamented oyster dredger was long in the boat knacker's yard, R.I.P bloody *Kerry Jane*. Dear old *Culash* had been sold and little *Limanda* had been wrecked by Dee's two rapscallions. We were now boatless so they had to borrow their fishing boat from friends. One day they arrived home with the biggest lobster any of us had ever seen. It weighed in at some fifteen pounds, was older than all three of the boys combined and seemed not at all pleased to have become entangled in Stuart's fishing line. Of course we had no cooking vessel large enough to accommodate such a gigantic crustacean. One of them had a brainwave; *we can boil* (yes, that's how you cook lobsters) *her* (yes, all the big ones are female) *in the top loader washing machine!* Wonderful. The washing machine broke down and 'she' tasted like reinforced cardboard. The double whammy!

One thing I did share with all four of our male offpring to a greater or lesser extent was arachnaphobia. I had loathed and detested spiders since one had tickled my eleven year old bum whilst I was sitting on the toilet. One day Max announced that he had discovered a wasp nest in the attic. Quite what he was doing up there I don't know, but I have not seen my long unused golf clubs from that day to this! Anyway all five of us climbed the ladder to devise a plan for the good riddance of our unwanted boarders. Suddenly Stu shouted **oh, no!!** It was the biggest house spider I ever saw. We fought each other to tumble out and down the ladder, much to Joan's hilarity. She had been watching the pantomime from her wheelchair at the bottom of the stairs. She always had been partial to that kind of banana skin joke and she didn't mind spiders. Just as well. Here's a flash-back … On our first night as a married couple we had stayed in an hotel en route for London. Ready and waiting, nude on the bed and posing like some imagined Greek warrior whilst Joan divested herself of her going-away outfit, I glanced up. Directly above me was a spider on the ceiling. I moved off that bed like lightning, imploring my lady to catch the xxxxxxx thing and get rid of it. *If you lose it*, I said through clenched teeth, *we're getting out of here*. She looked at me in pity, said; *don't be daft; it lives here, Bryan. It won't do you any harm*. Nevertheless she did catch it and pop it out of the window. It took me several or a lot more minutes to rediscover my amorous intent.

Hayling Island could and would have worked for us all had it not been for twenty three years old Robert's mental condition. For weeks or months he would take off for goodness knows where, funded by us of course, then arrive home often dishevelled not to say evil-smelling and unwashed, once riding a stolen motorcycle. For years we had been turning a blind eye to his mental abberation. It was Julie's husband, Rob, with his background in military medicine, who forced me to acknowledge that my beloved eldest son was suffering advanced schizophrenia. On another occasion Bob was found by alarmed policemen sleeping in a one man tent on the green just outside Buckingham Palace in London! Bob had a close affinity to his disabled mother and she to him. To the end of her days Joan was convinced that his schizophrenia was linked to her multipleschlerosis. But his general behaviour and his convictions about other world voice messages were getting more and more alarming. He was physically very strong indeed, to the point where, one day I found myself in a hospital A&E department with several broken ribs, the result of a single one of his punches. He had never overtly threatened Dee but she was becoming more and more terrified, never sure of when he might appear and what he might do next.

The situation was impossible. Time for more change.

* I'm not sure if I mentioned it earlier but Stuart's show-ring success with his dog Seth had inspired Julie to want a vizsla for herself! Hence our dear old Chloe, a lovely young lady animal although never a match in the show ring for her older mate. Lightning may strike twice but how very, very rarely!. In spite of our best efforts to avoid it, Chloe became pregnant to Seth and so became the (sometimes reluctant) mother to five lovely, incontinent, sandy coloured bundles of hungry energy.

43. End games

It is well nigh impossible to put into words the true life and soul - the *spirit* - of the industrial sales unit which I had, over fifteen years built up at Sweetheart International plc. By 1986 I still had Ted Pool and Alex Mattewson, my original field salesmen recruited in 1972 and by then area sales managers, together with the fifteen others who had been selected, (indoctrinated!) and trained by the three of us. I cannot think of any member of that sales and marketing unit ever leaving us of their own accord, presumably because we were that phenomenon called a team where the sum is far greater than all of its parts. Certainly none of the succession of Wall Street and City of London owners of the company ever understood it / us! All they understood was our sales results and our sales results were almost always outstanding as a platform on which to grow the company's profits. I had a sign on my desk - that quotation from Henry Shapiro on first meeting me: *'The only thing that happens inside a company is cost. All profit comes from the outside by way of a customer's payment.'* Should sales have fallen down no doubt I would long since have been made to walk the plank like so many of my managing, technical and financial Boardroom colleagues. But as it was I was very proud of that sales team and always did my best to shield them from the harsh winds that from time to time inevitably blew around the company. As if in return, whether or not they knew it, my team and the company itself protected me from the harsh winds that had been blowing around my domestic life.

Yet I felt quite sure that the latest owners of the company, certainly Roberto Gasparini, the youngish, hawkish Italo-American they had put in charge, would seek and eventually find a way to, as it were, break up the happy business home. Reluctantly I had to prepare myself for the softest possible landing and of course for my subsequent take-off, for what on earth could possibly happen to me - or more realistically whatever could I make happen in the afterlife? I talked over the situation with my friend and leading customer Mike Jacobs of Raines Dairies. He introduced me to his friend, one of the brightest guys I have had the pleasure of meeting. Funny, I can see his face and hear his voice but cannot for the life of me recall his name. He was a young City lawyer, Jewish, well versed in employment and dis-employment law. This man listened impassively and in silence to my story and my suspicions. Then, *this is how this sort of thing goes, Bryan*, he told me; *the Gasparini fellow will call you into his office one Friday afternoon and tell you to clear your desk forthwith because you're fired. He may or may not call it redundancy but that makes no diffrenece; you're out. When this happens and you're invited in, whatever you do, DO NOT GO. Go home at once, call me, and do not re-enter those offices any more without me in attendance!* One of the biggest mistakes I have made I made when, one Friday afternoon almost a year later Gasparini sent for me. Forewarned being forearmed but cocksure of myself as always I went in without calling my lawyer friend! Game, set and match, Gasparini. But more later on that.

In the last episode I told of my involuntary visit to the QE Hospital in Portsmouth after my eldest son Robert had turned up in a lot more than his now customary disarray. Remember, this was a strong, good looking young man, six foot three inches tall and extremely strong. I don't know how much of his ravings that day were the result of the psychosis and how much of it was down to his cannabis addiction, but I do know he had his mother in huge distress and Delia in mortal terror and myself in great physical pain with several broken ribs! I called the doctor, both to me and to Robert. Visibly shaken after attempting to talk to my son, the doctor took me to one side and told me he would be sectioning my son. A vehicle would be arriving momentarily to take him to St James' mental hospital in nearby Southsea. Fiercely I told him the vehicle would not be necessary for I would take Robert myself. Doctor shook his head, said, *well Bryan, on your own head be it. But if you do get him to go with you, after St James you must go directly on to have your chest x-rayed at the QE hospital..*

Surprisingly Robert agreed to go with me without fuss and bade a relatively calm farewell to Joan and Dee. On the way to the mental hospital he entered into one of his quieter, more rational interludes. We were almost there when he said something so shattering that I have never forgotten it: *I will never be able to have a family of my own, Dad, will I?* I had to stop the car, filled with released emotion. I cannot write more about this moment, nor about Bob's commital, nor about the great pit of depression into which I fell whilst driving away, having left my beautiful young man in St James' mental hospital. But I will say this; having that day had the first of many subsequent opportunities to talk with psychiatrists about the condition called schizophrenia, and knowing how much cannabis Robert had been smoking, whenever I hear somebody telling me that cannabis is harmless and should be legalised the old red mist really does come down. I long to invite them into one of the secure mental wards where I have spent so much time with my son, stinking wards filled with drug induced zombies, repressed violence crackling in the air. And I will say this; my first wife had multipleschlerosis and my second wife lymphomatic cancer and my son schizophrenia, and if I myself had to choose between the three of them which one **not** to have it would definitely be schizophrenia.

That incident was the final nail in the coffin of any kind of 'normal' lifestyle for me at that juncture in my life. All change. Although, as I have said, Dee got on well with Joan, and all the boys mercifully got on well with each other, the tensions I have just described were too much for Delia. Frankly she wanted out; I hasten to add, not from me but from the general situation at home. I totally understood. Eventually I found her a rented place in the little village of Titchfield. But that meant I had the same old dilemma. On the one hand I could give up my job and become a nurse / housekeeper, presumably living off the State, on the other hand I would need to sell the Hayling Island house, having lived there for little more than a year, then find Joan the best possible nursing home. I could not afford the fees without selling the house. That became the inevitable chouce. I myself would go to live with Dee in Titchfield. Rudi was the youngest and the only one of our combined family of six 'children' still living at home and of course we still had the two dogs. Rudi and the dogs would all live with us in that rented house; a family much reduced in so many ways.

This, without doubt, was the darkest hour of my life since my parents split, when I had found my ten year old self motherless in a strange boarding school. But Hayling had not been without its lighter side. We all had enjoyed the good life there, notwithstanding Joan's and Robert's illnesses. There were always the laughs. I recall once driving home to Hayling and seeing Rudi roadside trying to hitch a lift. Of course I stopped to let him in, which he managed to do with some difficulty by laying back the passenger seat so that his shiny Mohican haircut would not be bent over on the Ford Granada's interior roof! I asked him, *why, oh why do you have your hair like that, Rudi?* His answer so astonished me as to preclude all further questions. *Because I can't dance*, he said. He might at that time have been telling the truth, 'though we hadn't been long living in our new Titchfield rental when the young fellow started earning part of his living dancing topless in a Portsmouth nightclub!

The next of what would become a series of increasingly attractive rentals took us all to Osborn View Road in Hillhead, not far along the Solent shore from Lee on Solent. This was a spacious, rather lovely house and garden. By then our lives - human and canine - had begun to take on a new and happier shape, for Joan was being very well cared for in her Hayling nursing home, Dee had found a lovely walk with the dogs down the river to the sea and I still had my job as sales director of Sweetheart International. My sales team were producing the usual good numbers. I went over to see Joan at least once a week at weekends. She seemed relaxed and quite happy apart from her inevitable enquiries after Bob. I would take her in her wheelchair down to the bottom of the nursing home garden, where we would park ourselves close by the sea, comparing notes about the rest of our family - and times recent as well as all those good times long past. Then, on the way back to my new home I would call on Robert in St James' hospital. He seemed slower, duller under the influence of allthe placatory drugs but was still pleased to see me whilst still talking oftentimes without total rationality. The psychiatrist in charge said he was taking his medication and soon could be released from hospital. But, the leading doctor warned, he would be best off living apart from the family and only then if he continued voluntarily to take his medication. If he didn't, said the psychiatrist, Robert would be in and out of institutions for the rest of his life. When he did come out I found him a flat in downtown Southsea. At first he seemed quite settled. That was just as well, for Delia continued to be very frightened whenever he hove into sight. Sometimes I would take him to see his mother in Hayling Island but these meetings were quite frankly disturbing for all of us, for Joan was and would always be convinced he just had a different form of her own illness.

As I have reported, one Friday in May 1986 I was called in to my boss and the axe fell. In all truth, although I have written harsh words about the company ownership and Roberto Gasparini, the eccentric New

Yorker they had put in charge - and I will stick by those words here - I cannot really blame the powers that were for getting rid of a long serving, successful sales director but now probably seen as a bit of a lame duck, domestically much dislocated.

I spent the ensuing weekend fielding well meaning phone calls from customers and almost, if not quite all of my colleagues. Virtually all of my team would be following me out of the door over the next months, some voluntarily and some not. End of an era. As I say I had many messages of support but the one I remember the most came from Dee, who never flinched by act or by sign; *You can do more with your life than sell plastic cups, Bryan*, she said.

Could I really?

When Monday arrived I woke up to find myself in a strange kind of limbo. For virtually the first time ever I didn't need to go off to work! I could barely get my head around being, for the second time in my life, out from under the comfortable safety of the employment umbrella. I took a long solo walk along the beach, stopped, looked over the water to the Isle of Wight, breathing in the salt air. The sea was calm and the early day sun was shining. All of a sudden I came to realise the true meaning of that word we all use, so often and so very recklessly; **freedom**. Wonderful, but freedom, I mean real personal freedom is also quite frightening when first it is encountered. I was fifty four years old, jobless - all but moneyless for most of what I had was needed by Joan's nursing home fees. On the other hand I had good health and most of all I had Delia and our dogs. I bent down to pick up an oyster shell, thinking ruefully of Bob's long gone dredger, the Motor Fishing Vessel Kerry Kane.

But hey, OK. The world was still my oyster, was it not?

44. On our own

1987 had begun for us with New Year's Eve in a Gosport jazz club. We were with our friends, all of us cigarette smokers. (Dee had been a non-smoker until we met, after which she said she got tired of me offering her a smoke, so opted for the quiet life!) As midnight counted down our ashtrays overflowed with a veritable Vesuvius of dirty cigarette stubs, the air was thick with smoke and the taste of old tobacco was on the lips of everyone you necessarily kissed. At this point, totally on a whim I announced that I would never smoke another cigarette, a pretty bold claim after thirty years of up to fifty of the buggers a day. Dee at once said she would give up, too, if I did. All the others laughed. For a week of intense virtual silence at home not to say murderous intent we began to relax. Neither of us wanted to be the one to break down. The urge to light up a cigarette and inhale its smoke took a long time to die but die it did, and has never come back to life.

Back to the May of that year ... In the immediate aftermath of my redundancy/sacking Dee and I embarked on a long planned holiday with our friends Ray and Audrey Gaskell. Fortunately I had the use of my company Granada until the month end. We sailed from Portsmouth to Le Havre and drove down past Limoges to the house we had rented in the Dordogne valley. Apart from the clash of interests and disinterests between us and out friends which became more obvious as the fortnight progressed it was heavenly. Long walks through lush woodlands for Dee and I, local sightseeing trips for the four of us, tiny restaurants in tiny villages, balmy weather ... wonderful. But Dee and I were early risers and Ray and Audrey much more stay abed. One of our early morning walks resulted in this poem ...

Just some cherries

Waking early we looked on that Dordogne day.
then dressed, quietly let ourselves out.
taking the narrow road that curved downhill
through bursting early summer woods.

dense green branches often meeting over our heads.
It is quiet; we talk quietly as we go.
When you talk to each other not at each other
there's no need for other than quietness.

This seems a bigger place than Hampshire.
As you walk, the hill lasts longer.
Distance across to the next hillside is greater.
Trees are crowded together more closely.
Light is lighter; shadows darker hiding more.
The rainstorm when it overtakes is bigger, too,
but we walk on, not bothered by the size
Nor by the drum-intensity of its warm drops.

I can feel the penetration of that place and time
Into senses obfuscated by thirty years of
fifty noxious cigarettes each passing day,
by loud noises in small rooms only some of it music,
by seldom being challenged naturally by things natural
(other than the slight panic of the passing of the years;)
by the senseless cycle of earning and paying.
By unnaturalness between all the caught-up people.

Finally at the bottom of this valley
on the outskirts of a village still sleeping
walking by an ivy covered wall of stone
overhung by the branches of a cherry tree.
Swollen fruit hangs tempting in front of our eyes.
Bunches of cherries droop, still rain-globulated,
butter into high-lit blue-red into magenta, cerise,
framed by shining leaves of that life-green,
tight-smooth the cherries are to my fingers.
I taste the free rain, bite to the stone
and the eye-closing sweetness of this valley
spurts Into every corner of my mouth,
floods over all of me and all my memory.

I remember looking and drinking in the beauty
and the comfort of her happy, rained-on face,
In her straight eyes a reflection of this shared awakening.
In her hand, too, were just some stolen cherries.

That holiday took the sting out of the forced dislocation from my employer and second home of seventeen turbulent years, the company I had been instrumental in conceiving and growing from nothing to a dominant and profitable something. But on our return of course I had to wake up to reality. One summer evening I drove 'my' large motor car back to the premises of Sweetheart International, left the keys with a less than interested security man, exited the place for the final time with suppressed tears behind my eyes and returned home in the little Honda we had bought ourselves. At age fifty three I was now, for the second time since the age of twenty four without the use of a high end company car.

I called the City lawyer to whom I'd been introduced a year since, apologised for ignoring the man's original advice, outlined my situation. Sighing over my stupidity he told me I had two choices; either sue the company in Civil Court for wrongful dismissal or take the company to an Industrial Tribunal. The former would take much longer, cost much more and would be a gamble - win and the sky's the limit, lose and all you have is the cost! The Tribunal would happen much more quickly. If I won, which I almost certainly would, he averred, I would get a maximum of ten thousand pounds, of which between a third and a half would belong to him, my lawyer, even if he stayed locally with us to avoid hotel costs. This would be a very much reduced fee, he added, and I believed him. He also said something of such importance I can remember it now, even if I've forgotten the man's name! *The biggest issue in front of you,* he told me, *is to forget about some kind of revenge or embitterment against your ex-employer, much as you might want to indulge it. You have to put behind you the past and get into your future without carrying negative baggage. Sweetheart International will shrug its shoulders and move on with narry a problem. It's now just a mark on your c.v.. This Gasparini guy for you ceases to exist.* Easier advice said than done of course, but it didn't take long for me to see the sense of it after the Tribunal was all done and dusted, having duly awarded me the maximum compensation.

Industrial Tribunals consist of a lawyer, a businessman and a union man. I still feel that surely even Gasparini would have been shamed by their written verdict after three full days. I very much doubt it! This success I owed to my lawyer and many of my colleagues who gave evidence on my behalf - the ones who had by then left the company of course! This scenario had been and still was being enacted in the

States. Maury Fiterman contacted the ex-owner, Henry Shapiro in his St Moritz super hotel. He was asking for help. Henry's answer? *Hey, sorry, you've caught me at a bad time.* End of phone conversation! Not much of loveliness grows in the big business garden.

After buying the little Honda the next thing I bought was an Amstrad personal computer. I just had a gut feel that, when I had learned how to type and worked hard to polish up my grasp of basic computer technology this machine would become the window to my next work world, and so it would prove. I had first learned the rudiments of typing thirty three years previously when I was preparing to leave the Royal Air Force. In addition I had quite recently learned some of the dark secrets of computing on a course 'Computing for Senior Managers' at IBM's Hursley HQ. So, now it was brush up time. Although, as I say, my real wish was to develop a personal business as packaging design consultant, without real conviction at the time I applied for several director level jobs as advertised in The Telegraph. I remember being short listed for two of them, one on the Isle of Wight and the other in Essex. Apparently I suited neither and neither suited me. I then embarked on the usual networking, offering my consultancy services far and wide. This was the point at which I discovered where my potential money earning value might really be. Managing directors and sales directors were ten a penny - and you had better be around your mid-thirties, whereas I was fifty three - but my interest in and talent for packaging design linked with production technology and foods marketing was something saleable in the appropriate industrial markets. Over the years I had developed many packaging product ideas and would go on to register several patents in my own name. Of course I had a load of top level food and drinks industry contacts. I secured my first independent consultancy brief from United Biscuits and enjoyed designing a pack for 'biscuit finger choc dips'. Quickly, another 'brief' hove into view, this time from Geest Industries for a special kind of salad pack. Both briefs required me to produce concept samples ... fortunately I knew a man in Bristol who was expert at creating them. I was on my way but when my progress was interrupted by a call from one Harry Evans, owner of Dolphin Packaging in Poole, I took a step back. I had previously neither met nor heard of Harry or Dolphin but over a very liquid dinner I was asked if I would like to join their key account sales team, headed up by his brother. The salary was fair, the expenses reasonable including a company car (!) and the work interesting. The lure of a renewed steady income proved to be too much and after discussion with Dee I said yes. Mistake! Truly it is much easier and much happier to move up the employed ladder than down it.

As I drove home to Hillhead late that night I could feel the car moving around under the force of one of the most violent storms imaginable. In the morning it was chaos. Fallen trees everywhere, the nearby yacht haven like a boat breaker's yard and serious damage to many houses though not to the one we rented. Dee and I took the dogs out on a long walk, discussing everything as we went. Dolphin Packaging was forty miles away. Why not move closer? At this point of course it became clear that one of the several advantages of renting as opposed to buying on mortgage is your relative freedom of movement. Oh yes! Chloe and Seth looked up at us, tails wagging as if in total agreement. With all six of our children off on their own we only had the dogs and ourselves to consider - plus of course the weekend trips for me to visit with Joan. Her Hayling Island nursing home had by then closed down and I had found her a really good place, nearer to us, between Portsmouth and Southampton. Within the month we found ourselves yet another beautiful rental - one that accepted dogs - in the little village of Sopley right in the heart of the New Forest. Yet another chapter beckons.

45. Looking for a home

If my life were to be divided into parts, I suppose the first would have been everything up to my marriage to Joan Wood in 1955, the second everything from then up to 1970 when I walked out as sales manager of Lily Cups in Liverpool. The third part would be with Sweetheart International from 1970 to 1987 when I found myself 'released' by the company. Parts four and five begin here. These memoirs are labelled 'Me, My Life', but of course my life was always and continues to be touched by others, many others of more or less importance *to* me, making more or less impact *on* me. Top of my 'importants' list are or were each of my two wives, my children and Dee's children, third our wider family, fourth my friends and after that all others. But yes, this is about me, not about all or any of them. After all neither I nor anyone else has a possibility to access a second party's innermost thoughts and deeds, nor to understand the how and why of events of importance, in turn, to them. It's no different when that second party is family. So I must leave them to speak (or more probably *not* speak) for themselves.

Having said that, it will not hurt at this stage to summarise ... That previous episode left Delia and myself in 1987 about to take up my new employment at Dolphin Plastics (of was it Dolphin *Packaging*? I can't remember) of Poole in Dorset, and about to move from Hillhead on the Solent into a new rental in Sopley, a hamlet lying within the heart of the adjacent New Forest. At that stage I had just moved Joan into her new and quite luxurious nursing home, *South Winds*, near Southampton. My eldest, Kairen, and husband Roger already had four children and were still living in north London - still are in fact. Roger was and is in construction management, Kairen was continuing with the studies which would lead to a degree and eventually her doctorate in psychology. Julie and husband Geoffrey had their three boys and lived in the Midlands, where they owned and ran a snooker club. Robert was travelling 'below the horizon out of sight' all over the country, (and Ireland), surfacing from time to time in hospitals, inevitably in need of funds. We met in such places and would continue to meet often over the next few years. Stuart had met and was living in Poole with the young and lovely Lorraine, his future wife. He was small boat inshore fishing for a living having given up his itinerant life on the big crabber, *Kingfisher*. Dee's eldest, Max, had met with Tracey and lived in Dorset, shortly to move on to Tracey's native turf in a Manchester suburb. Rudi, our youngest, who had been with us in Hillhead, decided not to migrate with us to the New Forest, preferring to stay in the Fareham / Gosport orbit where I think he had already met his future first partner, Nina.

Only two of these five original 'partnerships' were to survive intact, with Robert by now an inevitable, invisible question mark. And myself? Battered but unbowed I think you could say. My lower level new job at Dolphin Packaging was interesting enough as it combined selling (packaging) with packaging design and development. It represented a total change of business life for me, not having responsibility therefore worries about those I employed. That was probably just what I needed after the hiatus of the preceding years. I and my new colleagues were encouraged by the owner, Harry Evans, to return to our homes each day, no matter how far the distance to and from our last customer appointment. Four hundred mile daily return trips were not uncommon. Harry detested hotel expenses almost as much as those entitled 'customer entertaining'. In the general office at Dolphin there was a chart on the wall where salesmen's movements, forward and current day, were recorded for all to see. Harry was a self-made, now wealthy man; a genuine obsessive and a genuine eccentric given to working all hours. That may well have been the reason why he lived alone, his wife, I was led to believe, having deserted him. One day in his office he confided in me that his visiting housekeeper always left an unlit open coal fire in his living room for him. He would light it on arriving home at whatever hour. In front of it would be two armchairs, between them an occasional table complete with decanter of malt whisky and two glasses. He said he would come home, set a match to the fire, sit down in one of the chairs, take a swig of the hard stuff and ask himself a question out aloud. Any question; *perhaps*, he continued, *how was your day, Harry?* He would then move to the other chair, pour himself out another dram and answer himself at length, again out aloud whilst gazing into the flickering coals. And so on ... *A conversation with myself*, he said, *which is a good way to leave no unanswered questions or unmade decisions about the business and allows me to sleep well*; (that and presumably the whisky!)

I had a great deal of respect if not exactly a liking for Harry Evans. His finance chief had instructions to leave one piece of paper on his desk with just one number on it each and every morning. With this one number, set against previous, he knew instantly the financial health of his business. That number? *Exactly how many kilos of formed plastic had left the factory yesterday on route to customers?*

Harry Evans was for me the perfect example of rags to riches on the back of a simple good idea well and forcibly implemented. He had been some kind of ship's officer sailing out of Liverpool when he saw in a pub how a metal suit of armour, part of the decor, attracted so much attention. Knowing precisely zero about mould making and thermoforming, he spent a few hundreds of pounds on having made some silver plastic shells in the form of miniature, lightweight knights in armour, then selling them at vast profit around all the pubs within reach. To his astonishment his shining knights went viral! He then bought himself a simple thermoforming machine to make them for himself. Goodbye the wide oceans! Soon after that he was into plastic trays for such as sandwiches, convenience meals, multi-packaging of food product etc etc. If it could be thermoformed from pvc or, later on, from any other plastic, Harry was your man. Soon he couldn't keep up with just garage production so he obtained finance for a 'proper factory'. The rest, as they say, was history. Dolphin when I worked there had a value of more than ten millions of pounds sterling. Shortly after I left he sold out to a massive American packaging conglomerate, the Sealed Air Corporation. I believe he then took to his magnificent yacht, his intent being to sail the world. Good for you, Harry. Although I have to say he seemed to me never the happiest of men, and had become definitely one of the loneliest, I liked him a lot for his frontier spirit of adventure.

My employment by Harry Evans at Dolphin lasted little more than a year. As I saw and felt it, I had dropped from the premiership of packaging to the next division down or even the one below that. On the other hand I am sure Harry saw me as a catalyst for expansion and promotion but was unprepared for it when I began to instigate uninvited changes in procedures, technologies, policies etcetera. He called me into his offices one morning. We had a good chat starting with, *Bryan, I don't know where you're going - and I don't know where you think you're taking me.* I left on good terms with a generous settlement that included the company's (now my own) motor car. We shook hands, wishing each other well. To tell the truth we had a good deal in common even though that had proven of no real long term use to either of us.

Driving home to the New Forest and Dee I felt nothing but exhilaration; once again that sense of freedom renewed! I was fifty six. I did not know it then, but for the rest of my life I would work for nobody but myself. We walked our pair of hungarian vizslas that same afternoon hour after hour through the New Forest, I think my mixture of joy, adventure and, yes, probably a tinge of plain old fashioned fear transmitted itself to Dee. It was such a lovely day. Shafts of pure sunlight made a multicoloured patchwork of the forest floor. I recall us eating our sandwiches sitting on the bank of a little brook of crystal water, alternately talking quietly and listening to the birdsong, when out from under the bankside vegetation emerged a metre long snake, a quite wonderfully marked creature making his or her sinuous progress through the shallow, water. We didn't know if he or more likely she was an adder and therefore dangerous or a grass snake and therefore just a harmless thing of exquisite beauty. Either way we bade him or her farewell and went upon our way. This was his or her home. We needed to find our own.

46. Pensions, dreams and adventures new

The second in line of my five Sweetheart International managing directors, Lionel Klackan, had many qualities that appealed to me and from which I learned. On the lighter side I remember some amazing evenings out with him in various places home and abroad, notably Paris, Brussels and Amsterdam. A tremendously fun guy, he was good with my customers and my senior staff. And of great later importance he had been extremely able when it came to the laying down of feathers in the nests of his boardroom colleagues, including especially his own, through the company pension scheme. I am to this day a perfectly legal co-beneficiary of his expertise in that area.

It is usually the directorate of a company that is, severally and in total, responsible for its employees' pension scheme. Such was the case at Sweetheart International. The Directors were the pension fund Trustees. I was one from the company's beginning. I can say hand on heart that I was punctilious in the execution of my own duties but I was struck by the potential for the abuse of company pension money by those charged with its governance. I was also taken aback by the borderline machinations - call them sales efforts - of the pensions industry in their effort to grab from the Trustees the lucrative management of company pensions. The poor old rank and file employees, whose money we are talking about after all, don't get very much of a look in even now after the revisions laid down following the infamous 1990 Robert Maxwell affair. It came as no surprise to me when that truly bad person took for himself, (then duly lost), the millions of pounds sterling of pensions money rightfully belonging to thousands upon thousands of his workers, aided and abetted of course by the New York / City of London gang of 'bankers' calling themselves Goldman Sachs. Naturally nobody went to jail. Of course not. Not under a Thatcher government, even as wounded as by 1990 it / she had become.

Because of my grave suspicions as much as my desire to put everything Sweetheart International behind me, fairly soon after I left the company I withdrew my 'pot' of money from the company scheme - quite a substantial sum, and invested it in an annuity. A wise decision, for I knew how vulnerable was the scheme to the ravages of predatory owners and those invisible suits in the corridors of Wall Street.

For the first time in my life I now had to look after my own financial tax and future affairs so I appointed an accountant. Unfortunately for me he was a nice guy but the wrong one. Two years later when we were still living in Sopley, in the New Forest, I received a lovely little letter from Her Majesty's Revenue demanding c. £20,000 in back taxes, or else. I called my accountant only to find him 'out' - apparently forever, and no sign of the receipts that I had been religiously sending on to him and of which HM Revenue had seen neither hide nor hair! Frantic on the spot enquiries in my man's home town revealed that he had been spending more time in the local hostelries than in his office or home. *Where can I find him now?* I asked, to a miscellany of shrugs, downcast eyes, renewed mouthfuls of beer. I had to cash in half my annuity to pay the government. Self-employment is not always the bed of roses it might seem to the employed or even the unemployed! For the years up to age sixty five I made up in part for my loss by subscribing into my own private scheme.

Having left Dolphin, now on our own again I renewed my efforts to develop a business (or packaging) consultancy, making what can best be described as faltering progress. Fortunately we were always equally lucky with our rentals and our landlords - that is, what little we ever saw of any of the latter. In Sopley Dee and I and the dogs lived the good life in that wonderful converted barn of a residence. The village, twenty minutes form Christchurch and the coast, consisted mainly of a classic Hampshire country pub complete with tinkling mill stream surrounded by a dozen or so old houses then miles and miles of heath, heather and woodland. Lovely!

One day, like I don't know how many thousands of others in my kind of situation, I announced my intention to write a novel. Easy, thought I. With one mighty bound .... ! The house had a upper mezzanine floor. I carried my Amstrad computer up there, switched on and typed these words ...

Rose Feather

Chapter one

She stepped inside, wrinkling her nose. The Brown Ball Snooker Club's damp stair carpet smelled of the dirt carried in from the street on the soles of a great many shoes over a great many years. She unbuttoned her wet raincoat, took out her cue case. At the top of the stairs she opened the door, slipped into the dimly lit room, crowded, silent, made her way as unobtrusively as she could through the spectators. Billy wasn't working behind the bar. There was only this big blonde woman she'd never seen before. Rose tried a smile but the woman, unimpressed, made no attempt at a welcome, just examined her in that familiar white woman way.

"What's happening?" she whispered, not really wanting to know.

The woman sighed. "You want a drink, dear?" then shrugged. "It's a money match on. The Italian boy, Roberto .."

"Yes," Rose interrupted, not meaning any rudeness, taking off the coat, "I just wondered who was winning."

All my life I had been thinking - dreaming! - of writing fiction. I had recently bought Diane Doubtfire's remarkable little book called (something like); *How to Write a Novel*. Basically, you must create a strong central character, she advised, one through whose mind and life your story unfolds. This character will have a grand plan but he or she will in chapter one meet with a set-back. Each effort he or she makes to overcome that set-back only leads on to the next unexpected set-back. And so on, right down into the depths of despair. Eventually, with that one mighty bound he or she takes action to overcome all the odds and meets his or her well-earned triumph. Piece of cake!

Driving thousands and thousands of boring business miles over the years I had constructed whole passages of fiction in my mind, often stopping somewhere to write up the notes. So by now I had the storyline for my first effort fairly well mapped out. My main viewpoint character was to be the pretty young coloured girl, Rose Feather, daughter of Henry Feather, a fading snooker star, old rake and owner of a snooker club. My young lady would be bold enough to penetrate the heartland of the game of snooker, the sexist world of working men's and political clubs and she would be good enough to challenge the big professional players, all of them (then as now) male. And why the hell not? I remembered Barry Hearn's words back when my daughter Julie was one of Britain's first female snooker pro's. *The first lady player to consistently make hundred breaks will be a millionaire!* Well, my Julie couldn't make it but my Rose surely could be that girl! Being something of a club player myself and having attended the world championship in Sheffield many times - and knowing how great were the TV viewing figures amongst the ladies - I reckoned I knew enough about the inside and outside life of the game to make it the scenario for a novel that would sell and sell. Today the New Forest; tomorrow the world!

Filled with excitement I had consigned quite a few chapters of *Rose Feather* to my PC's memory when progress was stopped by a single phone call. The caller was Brian Mullally, a business friend when I'd been at Sweetheart and he had been production manager with Northern Dairies. As it transpired, Brian had been head hunted and now had a similar role in Saudi Arabia. He wondered whether I might be interested in a consulting assignment for his new employers, Almarai Dairies in Riyadh, Saudi Arabia. Would I be interested? Would a duck like to take to the water! I took to the road and we met in the

East Midlands Airport hotel. After that, for the immediate time being I forgot about being a novelist in favour of earning some real money in the Middle East.

I had visited that nation whose Arab natives call simply *The Kingdom* some years earlier when exploring the potential for Sweetheart's export sales. I had taken with me Howard Cheek, one of my sales team who would shortly be promoted to manage our Scandinavia sales office in Stockholm. How vividly I recalled Howard's first encounter with Saudi Customs. He had brought in with him a softback novel, its cover showing a pretty lady with a moderately low cut neckline. The Arabian customs officer picked up the book, ripped off its cover and handed the innards back to an astonished Mr Cheek without black-eyed expression and without a solitary word. I'll be writing about my first experiences as a consultant in Saudi Arabia in the next episode. And what an episode it turned out to be!

And my precious *Rose Feather*? I did continue with it in between times then, with ten chapters in the bag I approached a senior person in the world of publishing. I had no idea how stupid that move was. I should have known that no publisher would look at a part-written novel and only one in two thousand submitted novels by unknown authors would ever see the printed page. But amazingly the lady in question, the head of the newly created Orion Books, thought enough of my submission to comment kindly and request first sight of the completed typescript. I should have dropped everything and gone for it at that point. Of course I didn't, for things were moving fast for us in The Kingdom. Ten years later I had the opportunity to continue. Eleven years later I stopped again. I now have nineteen chapters of *Rose Feather* on my PC, plus two other complete, self-published novels and two books of short stories and two books about life in the Highlands of Scotland. I do hope to finish *Rose Feather* before I die. Also there's another three parts written novel in the offing. But I hope that one fine day my imaginary young lady will emerge to meet her triumph ....

47. Milk and sand

It was now 1990: I met Brian Mullally at Heathrow, bound for Riyadh in Saudi Arabia. I could not have imagined that for the next ten years I might as well have had a commuter's season ticket to Terminal four and BA flights to the Middle East!

I spent the following two weeks carrying out consultancy investigations at Almarai Dairy, which was and presumably still is such an impressive, market dominant set up, vertically integrated right through from growing the cattle feed to rearing and maintaining the cows under massive open structures way out in the desert. To keep them relatively comfortable the hundreds (or thousands) of Holstein beasts were constantly sprayed with water brought up from the 'aquafers' that cross deep under the Arabian peninsula from west to east. As a result of the most rigorous management milk yields are significantly higher and carry substantially less bacteria than those, for instance, in the UK. The milk is then emptied into huge silos at the processing plant, ready for bottling and labelling or for segregation and processing into consumer packed cream and various cultured products. One product of special appeal to me was the Arabic 'laban' drink. A bit like a European style drinking yogurt but sharper and absolutely gorgeous. I would buy it daily, were it available here.

The main one of several Almarai milk processing plants was situated about an hour south of Riyadh, near the town of Al Kharj. Driving through Al Kharj for the first time, Brian Mullally at the wheel, a well bearded gentleman stepped out in front, bringing us to a stop with a mighty thwack of his big stick. Brian said and did nothing, expressionless, until this stern faced fellow stepped aside. Driving on he told me the man was an untouchable - a religious policeman called a muttawa (unsure about the spelling), who was simply reminding us that this was a holy day, a Friday, and that therefore nobody should be working or driving about, especially an infidel. Relationships and responsibilities between the secular police and the religious policemen seemed to me often to be quite obscure although the latter were undoubtedly the senior. You did not, ever, argue any point with the muttawa! And, I was often reminded, you never, ever, made eye contact with a Saudi lady. Nine out of ten shoppers in the big supermarkets were men and what females did appear showed only their eyes through narrow slits in their head gear. What I recall most about them were my glimpses of their beautiful shoes, uniformly expensive no doubt. I was told to beware, for they were quite fond of surreptitiously goggling or oggling westerners like me! For some reason, I was further informed, those ladies were particularly fascinated by e males of silver hair! In my ten years operating my businesses in Saudi Arabia not once did I meet personally, never mind exchange any words with a female of our species - Ah, not quite true. I've just remembered. More later on that.

The Al Kharj dairy plant incorporated a large and very well organised storage and distribution system. Dozens of loaded refrigerated vehicles left there each night for destinations as far away as Jeddah on the Red Sea, Dubai, Abu Dhabi, Bahrain and Kuwait, all places hundreds, even thousands of kilometres distant. My role was to report on the efficacy of everything Almarai except the agriculture and farming sectors of the business, with a special brief for packaging logistics. That is, the pallets and crates and the individual bottles and containers complete with lidding, labelling and graphic design etc. Plus of course the machinery supporting them. Much of the requisite technology was outside my previous experience. Fortunately I proved to be a quick learner with a strong design imagination that appealed to the Almarai Executive.

Almarai had been suffering significant product damage to goods in transit. Early one morning I was shown by Brian into the back of one of their massive refrigerated vehicles, unbeknown to its Plilipino driver or anyone else, just before it set off filled with product bound for Dammam, some four hundred kilometres distant. My role was to try to see for myself at first hand the why and the how of damage in transit. (I tried to forget the fact that these Philipino drivers, driving unlimited mileages on straight and featureless cross desert roads constantly fell asleep at the wheel and ended up in or on the sand, sometimes still upright but more often not!) The main problem very soon became clear as we traversed a speed bump or a pothole. All the loaded crates - including the one on which I was sitting - lifted off the floor of the vehicle and came back down again with a resounding thump! That realisation led to the company re-equipping its fleet with vehicles incorporating a new kind of pneumatic shock absorber. I recall on another very early morning going out with an Arab van salesman on his rounds of shops, large, small and tiny in a suburban sector of Riyadh. This was my main introduction to the real way of life of modern Arabia. In spite of its strangeness and sometime harshness I found myself liking and respecting this country, and the Middle East in general, and its peoples; give or take the senior ones with whom I eventually crossed swords. As I will reveal, that was my mistake; a fairly senseless position to take against a people whose flag actually features crossed swords - and uses them most freely!

But it is fair to say I really liked this assignment and it certainly led on to many years of well remunerated and satisfying consultancy with Almairai Dairy and others all over the Middle East. Over that period of time I designed and commissioned from an Italian mould maker injection moulded crates, stackable when loaded or empty, and compression moulded pallets from a company in England, thermoformed cups and containers from a plant in Dammam and blow moulded bottles in various sizes from a company in Riyadh. I also worked with the mighty Tetrapack (paper cartons), and with a French glass bottle blower, various labelling and labelling machinery companies including the one in Northern France for which I became Middle East agent. I remain good friends with the owner, now retired. On the strength of the increasingly well known success of my efforts for Almarai, as time went by I gained consultancy work with and for many of these supplier companies and with many of Almarai's competitor dairies, as well as from packaging companies trying to sell their product into my operational area. However, treading the fine line between helping one dairy or European supplier without compromising my work and integrity with the others became a constant worry. The markets in the Middle East are small in scale by comparison with those in Europe and are thus quite incestuous.

Back home it was time to move on. I was commuting from England to various parts of the Kingdom of Saudi Arabia and other parts of the Middle East on a regular / irrregular basis. The New Forest seemed just too far from Heathrow and the locations of our combined families for it to make much sense. Therefore Dee and I left Sopley and rented yet another splendid old detached cottage in the village of Micheldever, close by the M3 motorway and only an hour from the airport.. It had plenty of space for my office and our visiting family and a wonderful village inn called the Half Moon. It was also close to some beautiful bluebell woodlands and the South Downs Way with which we, especially Dee, and our dogs were to become so familiar. The advantages of renting over buying were by now becoming clear to me, if less so to my partner, who would have preferred buying on a fresh mortgage. Certainly we could not have afforded to purchase the level of properties with which we had now become used, and the flexibility and certainty renting afforded us had become more and more obvious, given the sort of rental 'contract' we always looked for and invariably were lucky enough to find. Of course we still had the usual problems with some, but by no means all of our family, including especially the ill and perpetually itinerant Robert and the *South Winds* care home-bound Joan. Our time at Micheldever was not exactly paradisal, but we were getting closer to it as the nineties unrolled.

48. Some kind of peace

In 1990 Dee and I with our dogs and cats made our ultimate Hampshire house move. Laundry Cottage sits in the little village of Headbourne Worthy just to the north of Winchester - indeed has done so since early in the fifteenth century. It is today a protected building with thatched roof, daub and wattle walls, oaken cross beams, great big chimney nook and a lovely little minstrel's gallery. The cottage itself now serves only as this property's living room, connected through a modern kitchen area into a Victorian section of three bedrooms, two of them en suite. We were fortunate enough to agree a private rental deal with the owner, London solicitor John Duckworth. John and his partner Rosemary over the years became good friends. That rental arrangement lasted unchanged for the next twelve years as I commuted back and forth to my various business interests and part time residences in the Middle East.

Laundry Cottage was so named because one of its bedrooms used to be the laundry for a nearby 'Big House', long since gone the way of all things. In our garden, buried deep into a grassy bank, there was a world war two air raid shelter, emplaced there by John's father. I myself would not venture into its dark recesses - arachnophobia yet again! - but some of our many grandchildren visitors most surely did. Whether I was home or away Dee would invite all the grandchildren all together with parents, either just for tea and games or for longer stays. I well remember how on arrival all the little girls would gang up in one end of the property and all the boys in the other. Warfare invariably ensued but with zero fatalities or even any injuries other than to some over-excited child's pride! One teatime in particular I remember well. We had shoved several tables together in order to accomodate all, I think, eleven grandchildren. All except the one latecomer were seated when total silence fell as little Josh arrived with his father Rudi. The seven year old came in, stood there stock still surveying the assembly for a moment then burst out with, *who wants a fight then?* There were no takers. Not immediately anyway. But there was lots of laughing. I should add that Josh was one of the smaller ones.

Our pair of hungarian vizslas plus two very old cats had accompanied us all the way from Raynes Road to Headbourne Worthy. Laundry Cottage became their home as much as it became our own. There were familiar walks along the river Itchen and up on St Catherine's Hill with its clever maze created generations since, so it was said, by Winchester College schoolboys. There were many other favourite walks including Stockbridge Down , subject of the poem below, and the great field we called the racetrack because it had once been used for point to point horse racing. Dee walked the dogs twice daily in all and any weather. Me too when I was home. So we got to know and love so much of the Hampshire and New Forest countryside and its wildlife. Each day provided us with a fresh adventure, exploration, or what have you. So many incidents about which I could write. But this I wrote sometime in the early nineties ... I wrote it for Ella, our number one grandchild and now our first teenager ...

UP ON STOCKBRIDGE DOWN

Just walk with me on Stockbridge Down
I close my eyes and see us there
I hear our foot-fall's icy crunch,
Out-face the numbing breeze and know
The silence of the world below,
Asleep beneath grey-scurrying quilt;
Come sit with me on frosty stump
And fill the steaming cups, content
With January's snow-drift smother
And here and now with one another
'Till Spring can fight her way, contrive
To force the ground with her strong thrust
To make surviving feathered ones
Sing fair to life's continuum,
For to such songs their lovers come:
Soon there's this miracle once more
Bright petals blaze within the brush
Our hill is tinged then floods with green.

You stop to bend to touch a flower,
So easy, feeling nature's power
On Stockbridge Down: Such crowns
Of England bear the marks of Man -
Old earthworks, limey pathways cut -
But this we know, that when we go
They'll not take long to overgrow...
When summer comes let's climb the hill
And stop to gaze o'er quilted fields
Of crops, breeze-stroked like squally seas;
But why must yellow rape defile
- Man's greed so violent, so vile?
In far-off strips of trees, with silver
Glint does weedy river lazy flow
With musky scent of rising trout?
This landscape merges with the sky
In hazy distance. By and by
We'll sit together, stretch out on
The cush'ning burnt brown grass, hard earth
And listen to small living things
That drone and buzz and chirrup, and
Just be content to love this land
Whilst overhead a sun-crazed lark
Step-dances over washed out blue.
Oh yes, lay back and close your eyes
And smell this English summer's day
And dream of its extended stay

One day we noticed a kind of lesion on our lovely Seth's head. He was fourteen. On the advice of our vet we took him to the Queen Mother's Veterinary hospital in north London. For a few days he stayed there for tests. When we came back for him and to hear the verdict it was with indescribable sadness that we learned he had a kind of inoperable cancer. Well, actually we knew it already from the way he was and the way he looked and the way he looked at us. We took him home and made him as comfortable as possible. His fur was now falling out in tufts. It seemed that old Chloe, mother to his puppies and his lifetime mate knew all about it. Several days later we simply had to put an end to his suffering. Whilst waiting for the vet to arrive, Seth lay unmoving, uncomplaining in my arms, alternately in Dee's. We talked to our friend, talked and talked to him about all the good times and all his favourite wild places and the wild creatures he knew so well, so much better than us. I know he heard me but of course cannot tell if he understood. As our vet carried his beautiful body out of the house I felt such an intensity of sadness as I had never felt before. I am not ashamed of my unaccustomed tears that day. This magnificent animal had truly been with me and the ones I loved, for us all, always tail wagging, always loving throughout the trials and tribulations of our past fourteen years. And now he was gone ....

Only A Dog

Russetmantle Seth, Hungarian Vizsla, died 4th December 1992...
In the gathering of the darkness, the crying of the gulls.
'Only a dog', some might say but not those who knew,
those with the eye, the mind to understand, who,
meeting, seeing the life in him, filled to the brim
with all the magic of those things they saw him do
wondered at such grace even as his light grew dim.

You reached out to touch him when he looked to you
and watched as he ran, leapt, moved soft in undergrowth
and stopped to point a bird or greet a dog he knew:
when called by kindly death you knew he was not loathe
but did you feel, as I, the pull of some old goodness, too?

Our ancient progenitors along the sacred Nile
might better understand than we who have lost touch
with what's now covered by the petty works of Man
perhaps would know why he was loved and is so much
a part of all that lives and all that is not vile.

He is...

In the night-breeze sigh through moonlit trees
in the gold-red flicker of our Winter fire
in the green-burst rush each Spring o'er the leas
and those to be of which he is grand-sire:
in the light, in the land, in his world now at peace.

So no goodbyes, old boy: your memory does not dull:
you champion of our hearts, you knower of all sorts.

sleep you out the ages 'though life through time annuls
and thank you for the wonder that each day you brought
to the rising of the sun, to the crying of the gulls.
(8th December 1991)

On Boxing Day we drove the seven hundred miles with Seth's ashes up to his favourite beach in the far northwest of Scotland, returning New Year's Day. Here is what I wrote about that ...

A Place For Seth
New Years Eve 1991

This pact he made with nature for himself,
Not Dee nor me, the dog is ours no more.
Now here's his place, this heathered grey brown shelf,
Strong rocky arm flung round an ochre shore
On which with her he'd run in flying sand
And loved the cream-capped swell of ocean wave.
Seth knew each salty smell of this sea-land
And there is nowhere else he'd rather have;

He looks across to Skye, as from the croft,
And with the calling of the birds his norm
He'll sleep through rain and shine of summers soft,
In comfort feel each shaking winter storm.

Clean cuts sharp iron spade through root, black peat,
We bend to place named urn and champion's scroll.
Six rocks we, breathless, bring up from the beach,
This celtic place Seth's memory shall extol.
In failing light and our sad task achieved
We go in silence, stumbling down the path.
There was no bad in him for whom we grieve
But how we suffer in his aftermath.
We ford the burn then pause, about we turn
And just still see his cairn atop the mound:
Already snow-birds drift o'er him we mourn
'He's ours,' faint comes their melancholy sound.

As midnight nears the piper holds the stage,
In Gaelic swirl brings in another age.

Our glasses touch and then at last our eyes,
Minds now with he who's gone, we know our prize:
His final gift, last comfort, certain truth;
The good each does alone surviveth death.

Too soon we leave this hard and long-loved place
From rain-swept brae we turn to distant shore
And there a dancing light, such wondrous grace -
Oh Seth, our friend, we shall not miss you more
For you will be the upsprung green of spring,
Each dusty summer's calm fecundity,
In autumn mists you will be lingering
White winters too shall hold your memory.

Chloe, soon, again shall run fast by your side
And best of all for Dee and me it's true
You'll see us from another puppy's eyes
- But always there shall be this place for you.
Now: New Year's Day of nineteen ninety two

The first Gulf War was such a strange event in so many ways. Not least it was really not a war. I remember whilst on a stint of report writing at home in Hampshire receiving an e-mail from my friend and Almarai sponsor in Saudi Arabia, Brian Mullally; *It's started,* he wrote. I'm in Riyadh. *Saddam's just sent us over a nice present. Scud missile landed not far from the compound. Kuwaiti royals on the run they say.*

My workplace had become a boiling cauldron.

49. Money in and money out

January 1990: It's after midnight and I'm in Riyadh airport awaiting my flight home to England having just finished my second assignment for Almarai Dairy. Consulting work is now beginning to open up for me both in Saudi and in England; a veritable sunflower opening up to the new light of a new day. Sipping a coffee I begin a casual conversation with an Indian businessman, a total stranger. In the course of it I tell him of my hopes. *What will you be calling your business?* he asks. *Bryan Islip Business Industries,* I say. He shakes his head. *It is too much. The acronym*

Bibs is better. He makes a peculiar kind of humming drone deep in his throat, then says *yes, 'Bibs'; It is good karma.* Thus is born *Bibs-industry Ltd*, co-owners Bryan and Delia Islip of Winchester, UK and wherever else we wanted to base ourselves, especially in the Middle East; downtown Riyadh for a start.

All money is real but several times in my self-employed consultancy career in the late eighties and nineties I generated opportunities to make what is often called 'real money'. In 1990 'Bib-seal' was the first. A contact had let me know that Coca-Cola was on the lookout for promotional ideas. I looked again at the familiar paper Coke cup with its essential hollow base. Could I think of a cost effective way to enclose that space? If so something 'promotional' could be enclosed; perhaps a party balloon or Christmas cracker type gizmo, joke etc? The cup was made of PE coated paper. Perhaps I could heat seal PE coated aluminium foil to the PE coated bottom rim of the cup? Dee and I did a lot of ironing board kitchen experiments. It worked! Through a Coca-Cola marketing agency I presented my concept. They went for it straight away - an order for five million Bib-tabbed 12 ounce cups, foil underseal specially printed with a one-in-a-thousand prize number for the upcoming World football Cup to be held in Italy. I hot-footed it to London's Chancery Lane and the dusty old office of John Orchard, a wonderfully and highly intelligent man, one of the world's leading patent agents. Just for my interest John escorted me around the massive UK Patents Office, showing me some of the old documents appertaining to historically important inventions, James Watts' steam engine amongst them. The Bib-seal patent was duly applied for and the required world-wide searches for conflicting patents began to take place.

It was only a few months to the World Cup. Not having or wishing to spend half a lifetime ironing Bib-seals on to five million paper cups I drew up the outline of a small rotary machine. Perhaps it would do the job? Dee and I went up to Cheshire to a machine manufacturer I had known and persuaded them to rent us five specially modified machines with a promise to purchase them later, if and when the Bib-seal concept worked. Next I rented a factory in Devizes. I had got to know and to like a bright young man called Tony when I'd worked at at Dolphin. He agreed to come on board to manage our operation. We then hired twenty or so young students plus other unemployed males and females - enough to run our unit round the clock, seven days a week for two months.

Everything worked, if not exactly to plan; much nail-biting in fact, but we met our Coca-Cola deadlines. True, our costs exceeded our income of £93,000 by a few thousand. It had been a very steep learning curve but now at least we were in business. I had begun to negotiate new Bib-seal orders home and abroad when the ceiling fell in. A friend in the USA who had been in the cups business as long as me, pointed out some of what is called 'prior art'. Apparently a US patent twenty five years old. Although it had proven redundant for technical reasons it was close enough to obviate my UK application. Anybody could do what I had done without paying me a penny. In fact the patent holder could sue me (but luckily did not) for a lot of money. Goodbye Bib-seal. Is there really nothing new under the sun?

Altogether the early nineties were for me a relative calm after the furore of the eighties and the earlier pressures of the seventies. I was spending most of my time earning a good and satisfying living in the Middle East, based first in Riyadh, next in Al Khobar and latterly in Bahrain. But my consultancy business also took me to every part of The Kingdom of Saudi Arabia and to all other parts of the Arab world, as well as to packaging and packaging related machinery companies all over Europe. Quite early on I needed to bring in some of my old business friends to help me establish 'Bibs' both at home and abroad. For Saudi Arabia in particular Tim Henderson-Ross joined us, and in our newly implanted Winchester office, Jane Green, ex buyer for Marks & Spencer agreed to manage things mostly with Delia. Several others also came on board, most often on an irregular assignment basis.

Exciting times but I think, on reflection, the good old trap of one or even several bridges too soon and too far!

In the course of this consulting work I had several opportunities to become exclusive agent for European packaging material or packaging machinery companies. I had the contacts and these companies had the products. It could be very rewarding of course. An agent's ten percent of a machinery installation that could easily run into hundreds of thousands of pounds sterling is not to be easily ignored. But the problem for my consultancy in becoming an agent for a packaging or packaging machinery manufacturer was that in so doing I might all too easily compromise - or at least appear to compromise - my consultancy position. After all, as genuinely hard as I tried to be impartial in giving my advice, one can hardly be seen to be totally objective if one has potentially a large reward for favouring one potential supplier's product over another's when one is agent for the former! Especially so if said agency is 'undeclared'. I decided early on to restrict Bibs-industry to only four agencies but even so it is fair to say that although these agencies yielded me a lot of money, in the end they landed me with more problems than benefits. Oh well, we all make mistakes. Don't forget I was operating in a region where all kinds of commissions and what we (and Sepp Blatter) would call back-handers was the perfectly normal order of the day! Having said as much, I can add with hand on heart and not trying to appear holier than thou that I was myself neither giver nor receiver of any such unearned largesse.

Typical of this dangerous dichotomy, Almarai took my advice to re-equip their milk bottling plant with stretch-sleeving (i.e. labelling) machinery made by a French company called PDC. Dee and I had become good friends with the owners, Jean-Claude and Margaret. We were now the Middle East agent for PDC as well as for the actual stretch sleeve material as made by Bob Barratt's UK company, EPS. That proved to be a very good investment for my Saudi client and an equally good one for Bibs-industry. My mistake was that I did not declare my interests in PDC and EPS at the beginning, which led to a nasty situation with my Irish management friends in Almarai. By that time I had become virtually part of the Almarai family, often accompanying them to rugby matches in Paris, London and Dublin, playing poker and brag and partying with them in their residential compounds in Riyadh and so on. Although I continued for years to work with Almarai, especially on the packaging innovation and design front, the initial relationship and degree of trust could never again be quite the same. Not helping matters as regards my impartiality, my consulting services were soon in high demand by virtually all of Almarai's Middle Eastern dairy competitors and half the plastics packaging manufacturers who tried to get a foothold in the region.

Although I was now an expatriate in the tax office sense of spending no more than ninety days in the UK I was a commuter rather than a full-blown expatriate. Life for even a part-time expatriate in the Kingdom of Saudi Arabia could be extremely pleasant. The authorities make sure that each residential compound is home only to those of similar nationality or culture. Therefore you would find a compound for say Pakistanis next door to one for Europeans, although never the twain shall meet. I remember walking with Brian Mullally around his compound one evening. Noting that an adjacent compound for Asians I remarked on how surprised I was that the Pakistanis had such a love for dogs, several of which were chained up outside the huts. Brian looked at me strangely. *Bryan,* he said, *they certainly do like their dogs. They like to eat them!*

A European or American compound would be very well appointed with its own restaurant, swimming pool, post office, shop etc. The air-conditioned houses were generally of a high standard and many expatriates had their wives with them, some even their children for whom special schooling was provided. Weekend parties were the order of the day. Of course there are two things that are not permitted, even on the compounds. Alcohol is one and any religion other than Islam is the other. Discovery of being in possession of an alcoholic drink or a Holy Bible leads to prison and a quite terrifying entanglement with Shariah Law. A senior manager friend (not at Almarai!) fell foul of this and it was his experience in a Saudi jail that formed the start point of my first published novel, *More Deaths Than One.* Yet everyone knew that alcohol was commonly distilled in the compounds and mixed with Pepsi Cola to produce a noxious, very powerful drink the expats call 'Sid'.

I remember one hilarious occurance on a compound when dozens of fermentation glass bottles actually exploded. The roof of the bungalow literally lifted then settled down about five centimetres out of place leaving the window curtains trapped half inside the building and half outside! As for religion, of course the internet covers all and any religion in which one could possibly have an interest, try as hard as the locals might to censor it.

By 1993 Tim and I had our own villa in the Dwidag compound, he living there more or less full time and myself commuting to and from Winchester. Life was an adventure new each day. Our Winchester office was well up and running under Jane Green - Delia's O Level accounting skills to the fore! The consultancy was doing well, having branched out into packaging design and associated graphics and our agencies were lucrative and blossoming. All seemed set fair. Then I flew home to meet my friend and mentor Bob Barratt at EPS in Leicester. My proposal; why not set up stretch-sleeve manufacture in Saudi Arabia close by the dairy and soft drinks markets instead of importing the product into Saudi Arabia from the UK with all the attendant hassle that entailed? Bob agreed to make me a director of his company and I would manage the new venture in The Kingdom. All we needed was the right Saudi national as sponsor. Enter Sheik Faisal.

Not content with being agent, business consultant, packaging inventor, designer and super salesman I was now to become a manufacturer. A bridge too far? Delia thought so but I was able to talk her round to the idea of becoming rich instead of merely earning a good lifestyle. I should have listened to her but I'm glad I didn't, looking back. When things Middle East imploded the best part of both our lives was to ensue.

50. Storms and sunshine

In the early nineties my beautiful, sometimes bearded son Robert would turn up unexpectedly at our home near Winchester. First stop the bathroom - although Bob would never consent to the actual use of soap. (*Man-made chemicals secretly killing us all,* was the problem.) There was about him this all-pervading smell of stale perspiration and both kinds of tobacco. Most of his clothing would go into the washing machine and the rest in the dustbin. Luckily he was my size. Then after hours or days with us we would see him off on the road again. At other times I would hear from concerned, well-meaning officialdom asking for money to set him on his way home. When he was present with us there was always this sense of other-worldliness and sheer physical strength that so frightened Delia and so depressed myself. Whatever had happened, I wondered, to all that potential, so obvious to everyone when he was a child? A question without answer, for now he was where I / we could never be or ever want to be.

When Bob did turn up at home invariably he would accompany me on one of my visits to his mother in the *South Winds* Care Home. These were very often truly heart-breaking times, Joan in her wheelchair sitting with us out in the South Winds garden or in local pubs, Bob so mentally and Joan so cruelly, physically disabled. Those stuttering conversations were quite surreal, for both of them were sure that their own conditions (not that Bob would openly admit to having a 'condition'), was somehow related to or caused by the other's condition. At more private times my one on one conversations with Joan always focussed on our eldest son, notwithstanding my efforts to feature news of the rest of our family and the world at large. Not long before her death in fact Joan repeatedly asked me to promise that |I would 'always look after Bob'. I made her that promise even whilst knowing that I couldn't possibly honour it. My lovely son was out of my - or anybody's reach. But I believe it helped her and I suppose a mother will always seem to care most about the most vulnerable of her offspring. And me? By contrast I was typically just trying my best to normalise everything.

Sometimes I would travel with or without Dee to visit Robert or help retrieve him from custody or from mental hospitals in sundry places. I recall Dublin, Taunton, Stirling in Scotland, Portsmouth and central London. On one occasion I received an irate telephone call from a certain Mr Workman, farmer and owner of the Shell Island camp site in remote West Wales. Shell Island was where, some fifteen or more years previously, our family had spent such happy camping and fishing holidays. Workman told me that a dishevelled Bob had turned up out of the blue asking for money or work or accomodation, preferably the former. That was a bad conversation. On another occasion I learned he had got himself a job on a fishing boat based at Ullapool, close by the site of our latterday holidays. That employment did not, could not last long.

I loved my son Robert and still do. And I still loved my wife Joan, the mother of my children, and our other three children, all by then with their own families, therefore mine as well. But Delia was the one who lent to me a certain kind of sanity. Years before she had been through her own brush with the terror of a partner's mental illness. No need to go into it here except to say that it had left her with her own set of mind-scars. Looking back it seems incredible that this woman would stand by me and mine through those dark days. Besides the family my other saving grace was our new pair of dogs, both Hungarian Vizslas like old Seth and his mate, Chloe, who had outlived him by some year and a half. We were convinced that Chloe had gained an 'extra year' when we brought in Mati, a lovely, over-lively little bitch puppy, then six months later the puppy dog called Sorosh by his breeder. We only found out by chance much later that Sorosh means, in Hungarian, *beer drinker*! But how well I remember the time when fifteen years old Chloe, with the other two already in the back of the car for the first of their daily walks, just sat down by the kitchen door looking first at us and then at the car before getting up and walking slowly back into the house. She could not have made it more obvious that she had had enough. And so ... but don't they call this a vale of tears?

I may be giving the impression that all was doom and gloom in those early nineties at Laundry Cottage. Not so. Apart from family visits of which there were many, and all the joys of grandparenthood, there were the quiet fireside evenings in that lovely fifteenth century thatched cottage and those daily walks in all weathers through the Hampshire countryside. Even today up here in the far north of Scotland I can relive those walks - the wildflower covered rolling chalk hills or alongside the river Itchen with its weedy, trouty scents of summer or bluebell time in Micheldever wood or sometimes going back to revisit our favourite tracks through the New Forest. And we loved to walk the mile or so along Worthy Lane to visit the Saturday farmer's markets and fine shops of Winchester. Oh yes, and my favourite pub, *The Eclipse*, where we met and made some good friends and acquaintances. Dee was always a bit wary of my attraction to *The Eclipse*. When I like things and people too much I possibly was inclined to drink overmuch as well! I was never as good z drinker as many of my family and friends! Winchester's unique *Hat Fair* was the city's most ancient celebration and a particular memory for us. All kinds of street entertainment, much of it highly eccentric. A lot of good music and eating and drinking. A wonderful let your hair down Summer's day out, often with our families. Yes, good times; very good times.

51. A Few of my favourite and unfavourite things

A memoir should be about oneself; about the likes and dislikes and feelings that go to paint the self portrait. Glancing back from my early 1990's 'blogger chronology' I realise I've probably focussed more on events than on myself now that I have interrupted my narrative at that point - at least as was myself back in, say, 1993. I'm not sure if and where I might have reversed my feelings since then but to round out the picture here are or were my top likes and dislikes - apart of course from family and friends ...and in no particular order ...

Likes
1. The wilderness
2. Good company
3. The ocean
4. Watching most sport
5. Reading Hemingway
6. Listening to great music
7. Painting pictures
8. Writing fiction
9. Composing verse
10. Reading Shakespeare
11. Pubs and restaurants
12. Good wine and whisky
13. British royalty
14. The City of York
15. Dogs
16. Manufacturing industry
17. Porcini mushroom gathering
18. The scent of bluebell woodland
19. Sea fishing
20. Small boats

Dislikes

1. Westminster politics
2. Airports
3. The City of London
4. Older age / disability
5. 'Retirement' (no chance)
6. Loud noises / loud people
7. Aggressive religion
8. TV weather forecasters except Carol
9. Most but not all abstract 'art'
10. Standard motor cars
11. Multiculturalism
12. Divorce
13. Tesco
14. Travelling by other than train

15. Madonna
16. Hospitals and medicines
17. Hypocracy
18. Unearned privilege
19. Spiders
20. Mobile telephones (but not computers)

I'm quite certain the above will be inexplicable, even anathema to some folk. No apologies, we all have different backgrounds, different experiences from which to cull our own likes and dislikes. These are just mine (or those that I can immediately pin down). And if they should inspire any of you to fly away from me and this, no apologies. Sorry, perhaps for not being sorry!.

52. Arabian nights

1995. It's now forty years since the opening of Karen's baby eyes in Newmarket General Hospital. So much water under so many bridges since then. But we had by now found ourselves a good measure of that elusive thing called happiness. I was by now fully expatriated, earning our living almost entirely in the Middle East. As I think I must have said, expatriates were not liable to pay UK taxes provided they spent no more than ninety days a year in the UK. Perhaps I stretched that ninety days a little bit but nobody other than myself was counting. Some of us commute to work an hour or so daily down the road and others ten hours or so via Heathrow to Riyadh or Jeddah or Dharan or Bahrain or Dubai or Quatar. Wherever was the money. Easy dollars? No.

The routine on landing at my destination was always to find and join the shortest interminable queue at immigration then be very patient and ultra polite to the immigration officer. I would hire a car, exit the airport and find my way to my pre-booked hotel or, after I had set up a permanent residence, to my home from home. When in Saudi Arabia it was of course goodbye to the demon drink - unless I was invited to a friend's (native or expat) home for dinner. Having said that, at a certain social and financial level in The Kingdom some of the illegal hard stuff magically might become available.

One old friend now resident in Riyadh, I'll call him John, had worked alongside me through the early days of Sweetheart International. In fact he had been production director when I was marketing ditto. John was a thoroughly good, middle of the road Geordie business executive. But his was one of those stories that really are the stuff of a novel. His domestic life in the UK had it seemed not been of the happiest and, on leaving Sweetheart he had secured a high level job with a large, government owned company in Riyadh. After a while he became so content with life (and the money) out there that he was minded to make one last effort to save his marriage. Perhaps his family could be persuaded to come and join him? He flew his wife into Cairo and joined her for the legendarily romantic trip of several days and nights down the Suez canal to the ancient city of Luxor. Unfortunately on her first night off the plane in Cairo she fell foul of the stomach complaint common to those adventurous enough to dine out in that city. Afterwards, for several days and nights cruising down the canal the Englishwoman would be below in bed writhing around under medical care whilst he, John, would be out on the deck in the moonlight, leaning on the ship's rails watching the empty desert glide by, next to him a rather beautiful and as it transpired high born young Saudi lady. Inevitably they fell into conversation and then - or possibly later back in Riyadh where she lived, inevitably they fell in love. Now, everyone in The Kingdom knows the extreme penalty under Shariah law for both male and female if found in unwed company with each other, especially inside a motor car, never mind in any bedroom type liaison. But in spite of all their efforts at ultra secrecy their affair was leaked, so my friend was called in to see his big boss, a Prince of the realm, and presented with a first class ticket on the red-eye that very night back to London. *You are crazy,* he was told, *This woman was promised at birth to the son of Sheikh xxxx. If you are here in the morning you will be arrested.* Robin knew well that, even had he managed to get himself on board that flight, his young lady would be doomed - and I do mean doomed. If he stayed they were both doomed. *No sir, I will not leave her,* he responded. *I wish to marry her.* The Prince recoiled in shock; *Impossible,* he was told; *unless you convert to Sunni Islam straight away and wish to live here and behave in all ways in accord with the custom and the Law.*

Well, by the time I re-met John in the mid-nineties he was a thoroughly remarried man and a Saudi in all but birthright. He spoke Arabic, knelt to pray five times daily, wore the long tunic called a thawb and the traditional Saudi red-chequered headress called a keffiyah. He and his lady lived in a large and sumptuous apartment in central Riyadh. Several times I was invited to dine with them - the first and only times in my ten years working out there that I had the pleasure of a woman's company or even spoke to one. Saudi males on getting married are granted a piece of land by the king. John proudly indicated on a wall map his very own piece of the Saudi Arabian desert. The apartment looked down on to a beautiful private swimming pool. John chuckled. *When xxxx has a party she invites all her lady friends,* he said. *The view from here is great.* So far as I know my friend is still there with no desire at all to 'come home'. Oh yes, sometimes there really are happy endings.

My visits to The Kingdom were not all work. By the mid nineties I had many friends there, both expats and 'local'. The expats almost always lived on a compound reserved for people of like race. These berths offered residents and visitors alike absolutely no hardship. Sid-fuelled parties seemed no different than similar get togethers at home even if most of the partygoers were male. Invariably someone would suggest a game of cards. I had to be sure of having plenty of Saudi riyals before joining in for these were highly paid executives, natural risk-takers. Well I guess my gains and losses, large as they seemed, probably evened out over time.

I shall write about my experience of life with the locals on another occasion.

Back home we had closed our Winchester office in favour of setting up in a wing of Laundry Cottage as HQ for Bibs-industry. Jane Green had gone her own way and Delia was tending to the books and the bank and the VAT. One day I was with a client in Jeddah when Dee called me on my mobile* in a state of panic. *I've just had a call from the VAT Inspector,* she exclaimed. *What shall I do?* Knowing well how assiduous she was with her bookkeeping and how terrified she was if ever she thought she, I or we might have broken any law I said, *do nothing, darling. Just calm down.* Several hours later she called me back. *How did it go?* I asked. She laughed; *well, this man came in and spent ninety percent of the time trying to convert me to his Jehovah's Witness. He hardly looked at the books.* On another occasion I was sitting in front of an extremely important Saudi Prince - a potential client - when again my mobile rang. A month earlier our new bitch, Mati, had come into season. She was too young for puppies and not wanting the pleasure of a litter of puppies running around, much to our dog Sorosh's evident disappointment we had taken him away to board with a friend in the West Country. I knew Dee was that day set to to bring him home after the normal twenty three days of Mati's 'heat'. *What are we going to do, Dee* wailed. *As soon as I brought Sorosh home and into the kitchen I turned around and they were at it in a tie. They are still. Take her to the vet for the day after pill,* I advised, to the evident surprise of the immaculate His Excellency. Problem solved.

* Yes, I bought my first mobile - the size of half a housebrick - as early as 1990. It cost us a fortune but was worth it to me. Many's the night drive across the desert when the boredom and incipient depression would be assuaged by those so very expensive conversations with my lady, all those miles away in Headbourne Worthy.

53. The golfer and the sheikh

In 1995 after Tim Henderson-Ross left my employ and from my new operational base in Riyadh I employed a young Englishman of considerable personal presence, an expat already living in The Kingdom, up to then employed by DHS, the world-wide courier service. I'll call him Robin.

Now, every businessman (woman) knows there are four elements to the making or the losing of money in business...:

(!) Getting the work - that is, marketing one's goods or one's service,

(2) Making and delivering the goods or providing the services that have been ordered by a client - in best order and on time.

(3) Getting paid for the ordered and delivered goods or services

4) The organisation that knits together the whole operation.

I had hoped Robin could support me on all fronts. In a small operation versatility always has to be key. Everyone has to be capable of doing everything as well as a specialist in one area. Robin, my personable thirty something, proved reasonably good at (1), of little or no use at (2) - i.e. report writing and advising, creative work etc. He was largely an irrelevance for (3) but not at all bad at (4), i.e. linking with sponsor, getting all the necessary paperworks done, banking, travel etc, etc, which is why he lasted with me for some four years. But the laddie always had problems. His problems began with difficulty in getting out of bed in the morning and ended with his over enjoyment of an overcrowded night time social life amongst the younger elements - especially female - of the vibrant expatriated communities in Al-Khobar then Bahrain and Dubai. Perhaps the beginnings and endings of each of his days were linked in reverse, if you see what I mean!

Be that as it may, however exasperated I often became I always enjoyed Robin's company. I liked the guy, tell the truth, almost envied his devil-may-care attitude. His well-educated life as a teenager in England had focussed on the game of golf, his handicap having been down to scratch at age seventeen. I've often thought how awful is must be to have a great sporting talent but one that is not quite great enough to earn you all the multimillions and the enduring fame. Nobody would relish the life of a journeyman near-miss golf professional. Few can stand it for more than a few years.

Be that as it may, it was Robin who, in a roundabout kind of way, introduced me in 1994 to a quite high-ranking Saudi Sheikh in Al-Khobar - let's call him Faisal. In Saudi Arabia you have to 'sign up with' a local sponsor in order to enter The Kingdom if you want to live and/or visit for work and monetary gain. My sponsor at the time was a Riyadh based Prince, a fair man but one with limited interest in the business of those from abroad coming under his wing. Faisal on the other hand was a British-educated Sheikh, a bright guy interested in what you were doing although not at all interested in hard work when he could find folk like myself to do that kind of stuff. Deeply religious of course, in the Sunni / Wahabbi tradition. In fact Faisal's grandfather had camel-ridden with king-in-waiting Abdullah Al-Saud and the locally famous British officer called Captain Christian in 1916 when they combined to subdue the other desert tribes by force of arms. This allowed British diplomats to draw lines across the map of Arabia, thus to create what is now Saudi Arabia and the neighbouring Arab States.

Faisal became a man I thought of as a friend. He was not the eldest son, therefore not the leader of his clan, but was very well connected; wealthy of course, with his main home in the East of the country at Al

Khobar and another just over the Causeway in more westernised Bahrain. Such a sponsor as Faisal is absolutely essential if you want to do business in the Middle East. I would often join him at his beachside mansion of a residence on a Thursday or Friday - the Moslem holy day - to compare business notes and anecdotes, often with his high powered banking and business friends in attendance and always with the option of the 'forbidden' Johnny Walker Black Label uniquely available. Male Philipino servants would ply us with a marvellous array of food although never much before midnight. Before that out would come the karaoke mike. All in turn would be encouraged to deliver a song or a ditty. This was where I first tried and became quite famous for my awful version of Sinatra's *My Way* and those Irish folksongs, *Mother Macrae* and *Sweet Sixteen*. Songs I would never attempt in public without a good ration of the hard stuff! I have to confess nobody previously had bothered to applaud my on and off-key tenor efforts, alcohol-fuelled or not. Faisal also had a pokey little downtown hideaway with a pool table and etcetera. Good for workday extended lunchtimes!

I have to say that I came to like - even admire - Faisal and most of the ways of Islamic life. You were always safe from crime in The Kingdom though not always, as I shall relate, from the cruel arm of Shariah law. Although there was never a trace to be seen of the female of our species, in a strange sort of way you quickly grew accustomed to an entirely male and, as I say, mainly peaceful society. There are always opportunities to share in the incredible wealth of the place via creative business efforts provided you came to work and learn and live by local rules, both written and unwritten.

Rule number one: Arabians, as being the people favoured by the Prophet Mohammed are superior to the rest of the world. One overwarm evening, strolling barefoot along the beach on a Thursday night Faisal said, *Bryan, I suppose you wonder why we seldom perform work - as is normal to you in the West?* I said something like 'I wouldn't be so rude, Faisal'. *I'll tell you why,* he went on; *It is because we,* (he was taking 'we' to mean highborn Saudis such as himself) *come from three thousand years of a slave owning culture. When we need labourers we go for them to the Indian subcontinent or to Africa; for clerical duties we recruit from India. When we want management or more creative people such as your goodself we go to Europe or The States. In different ways you guys are all our slaves. For the payment of them these days Allah has given us the gift of oil.* That stopped me in my tracks. I had never been called a slave before, even though intimately familiar, as are most Westerners, with the term 'wage-slave'! I looked out over a calm, star-spangled sea and up to the heavens then back to Faisal's beautiful mansion, lit up in the night like Blackpool front. I took a mouthful of dear old Scotland. *But what about you guys when the oil runs out?* I ventured. He chuckled quietly. *You in the West must worry about that,* he said. *Your peoples were accustomed to live in one of two cultures - capitalism or communism - were they not? But now, overnight, you have only option one. Communism is dead in the water. Your capitalism is secular, almost entirely without a spiritual dimension. Yes, your capitalism will disappear soon, as will the oil. You then have little or nothing left. Chaos. We on the other hand have Allah. We shall prevail even if we should go back to the deserts of our Bedouin grandfathers.* Out of politeness I didn't argue the point. But I guess I would have found argument without intense rudeness difficult anyway.

Faisal told me how he had taken his teenaged son to a local 'place of punishment' where an adulteress was for buried up to the chest in the sand, surrounded by jeering villagers. As the local Sheikh the crowd had parted to make way for both father and son, he told me. His son was awarded the special privilege of throwing the first stone at the poor lady. Faisal informed me without any obvious emotion that it hit her head. I tried not to register my shock. I can only hope that stone killed her outright. If not the following hundreds most surely would.

By contrast I remember Faisal taking me one night to an extensive place of giant sand dunes in his four wheel drive Lexus. Similar vehicles and trucks were ascending in the moonlight a certain dune and descending / sliding down at great and dangerous speed on to the flatter desert land below, where were the small tents and where glowed the camp fires of many small groups of Saudis. We joined the merry throng up and down and again and again before Faisal slid his poor £60K motor car to a stop by a group of four well bearded men sitting around their own fire. Somehow they seemed to sense Faisal's rank. They stood up, salaamed gravely and invited us to join them - I have to say without overmuch enthusiasm for me and my plastic cup of that old Black Label. I watched their gaunt, fierce, black-eyed faces in the firelight. Of course all the talk was in Arabic. These were proud, strong, hard people, capable of great cruelties and equally great kindnesses, secure somehow in a world of their own between past and present, unquestioning in their spiritual beliefs.

I thought of my own religious forebears: Simon Islip, died 1366, Archbishop of Canterbury under King Edward the Third; John Islip, died 1532, Abbot and builder in chief under King Henry the Seventh of many sections of Westminster Abbey. It seemed to me that there were many similarities in custom, spiritual attitude and behaviour between them and these peoples of the desert with whom I was sitting, painfully cross-legged on the sand. Of course these folk didn't burn people at the stake, as did my own, but in all probability that is only because there is an obvious shortage of wood in the deserts of Arabia.

54. Ah, Bahrain!

All newly adopted action means taking some kind of a chance. Most of us know that the really big hitters historically in the world of industry and business have been close to or have actually been themselves bankrupted. When you come to a crossroad in business, as in personal life, it is often necessary to weigh up the odds as carefully as you can but eventually to take the path of greater rather than lesser risk. If you have the guts, the drive or the stupidity, that is. Only history will tell which of these belongs to you!

I was at that crossroad in 1995. Having come out from under the umbrella of corporate employment and the property owning thing some eight years previously we were sitting relatively pretty. Of course a long shadow was cast over life from Joan's incurable disability even though she was being well looked after in the South Winds Nursing Home. Robert's problems were if anything even more disturbing. But it is as the old Irish song tells us; *What cannot be cured, love, must be endured, love.* As I say, in spite of all that Dee and I and our new young pair of Hungarian Vizslas, Mati and Sorosh, were living a more than acceptable lifestyle in long-leased Laundry Cottage. Our consultancy / agency, operating now over the entire Middle East, was riding high. I had a prominent Saudi as sponsor and an office in said sponsor's building in downtown Al Khobar plus I was renting a villa within a very good expat compound. I could come and go as I pleased, subject UK tax laws of course. Freedom! I would probably still be there had I not seen an opportunity to climb a few more rungs up the business / affluence ladder ...

It is as well at this point to bring in the Emirate (now I believe the 'Kingdom') of Bahrain. Bahrain is approached via a twenty five kilometre causeway from Saudi Arabia's Al-Khobar. Its capital city of Manama was and I presume still is far more westernised than its larger Arabic neighbour and is therefore a weekend target both for Saudi-based western expats and the more - how should I put it - fleshpot-loving young Saudis. My own stays at the Intercontinental Hotel in Manama had for years been a highly acceptable staging post for UK/Middle East flights in and out of the area. I have especially fond memories of a certain Italian restaurant there. The excellent singer/guitarist would surrender the microphone to anyone with half a voice professing to know the words. *Ciou ciou bambino* was one of the favorites, as was *My Way*. You know ... *'And now the end is near and so I face the final curtain etc etc ...'* Anyway much to Dee's amusement I determined to learn the words so I could take my turn with the mike and perform for my very first time in public! Dee often flew out to join me for short stints in Bahrain. She and I returned to that restaurant, then when the guy started on *My Way* I stood up, held out my hand for the mike and for several minutes wandered around the crowded tables. *What is a man*, I sang, accompanied by the guitarist, *What has he got? If not himself* .... Looking at all the faces I knew I had them. *Hey, a star is born*, I thought, *long in the tooth or no!* Then - calamity! I looked down on a particularly lovely young lady - one in possession of one of life's more impressive cleavages - and lost not only the words but the whole bloody plot. Serve you right, Dee chuckled as I sat down red-faced to a mixture of stuttering applause and general hilarity.

Back to the track ... I've got ahead of myself ... Why not open an office over the causeway in Bahrain? I wondered. With my visa there wouldn't be any problem coming and going across the Causeway and a Bahrain based business with a high profile address was more than acceptable throughout the region. With the right new staff I felt we could take ourselves from where we were to a whole new level. I talked it through with Dee. She was against it. 'We're doing OK as we are' was the gist of her argument. Of course, she said, our overhead costs would absolutely sky-rocket. I sat down with Robin, my single employee, to talk it through again with him. By contrast Robin absolutely loved the idea (why wouldn't he when much of his nightlife was over on the island!) even though for sponsor reasons and to keep his mind on the job he himself would be required to carry on actually residing in The Kingdom's Al-Khobar.

I consulted Delia once again, finally convincing her to go with me on the move. Taking the proverbial deep breath I rented a suite of offices in one of Manama's most prestigious tower blocks and then a magnificent residential penthouse apartment for myself on the 19th floor of another tower. Right outside my front door was a rooftop swimming pool. I scoured the island for suitable furniture and office equipment and began looking for staff. My new offices were high up in the tower. My next door neighbours were The Bank of Bermuda on one side and Cable and Wireless on the other, each of them large corporations managed by highly experienced Englishmen. The Bermuda man, Thomas, who was to become a special friend, introduced himself and enquired as to whether I might consider his Anglo/Iraqi wife, Dina, as my Personal Assistant. Dee came out for the interview. They got on famously from the beginning although I gather the talk was probably more of shoes and clothes than business. Dina was (is) a very bright lady, fluent in several variations of the Arabic as well as English of course, seemingly able at all times able to navigate the complexities of visas, travel, banking and general business life in Bahrain and the Middle East. Next we hired an Indian lady accountant and a sharp Egyptian salesman called Saeed AEl-Jeddawy.

Bibs-industry (Bahrain) was up and running, and how!.

There was a lot of driving - especially the 400 klix across to Riyadh, and a need often for several flights per week to Dubai, Abu Dhabi, Qatar or the remoter parts of Saudi Arabia. My consultancy / agencies continued to prosper. Quickly I settled into the new life. At weekends there were bars, especially the Harp in the Holiday Inn just opposite my residence, even cinemas to go to besides many good restaurants, shopping malls and the famous native 'Sukh' (open air gold market). Even an impressive zoo, would you believe! Most of my breakfasts were taken in the Sunset Cafe over the road rather than up in my apartment. Looking out from my nineteenth floor window I could watch the shrimp boats going out into the Gulf in the evening and could see as far as the airport in one direction and the famous Pearl roundabout / monument. (now destroyed after the riots) in the other. Once I took a special trip down-island to see the Arabian Gulf's very first, tiny, long since disused nodding donkey oil well - and that amazingly ancient, very famous Tree of Life.

Yes, expatriate life and social life was not at all bad! Courtesy of Thomas, Dee and I were invited to attend Bahrain's famous Poppy Ball (11th day of the 11th month to celebrate the ending of WW1), also many times to private parties and several times to the British Ambassador's garden parties.

At this point I found myself renting a house near Winchester in the UK, a villa in Saudi Arabia, a prestigious office suite and equally prestigious penthouse in Bahrain. Oh, and I almost forgot, a very nice Lexus for myself and Ford Galaxies for Robin and Saeed. Our combined mobile telephone bills amounted to around two thousand pounds a month. But cost mean nothing by itself, I told myself; sales income means everything - and sales were doing just fine.

55. A tragedy non-Shakespearean

In the summer of '95 whilst home from Bahrain I wandered into an antiquarian bookshop in downtown Winchester. This was not unusual. Dee liked to tour the shops; I didn'texcept for this one. Dee was as captivated by books new and old as much as I, hence the massive library we have carried around from home to home like the heavy shell on the back of a long-suffering tortoise. On this particular occasion I picked up a slim and dusty volume that was to become one of three books that I can say have definitely affected my life. Written by Professor Logan Pearsall-Smith in the USA and published in 1928 it was entitled *On Reading Shakespeare*.

Now, although I had done very well at school with English Literature and had kept up a steady regime of reading both fiction and non-fiction since then, I had never really got to grips with The Bard, even on those rare occasions when I had seen the plays on stage. Something difficult about the archaic language and the odd mix of prose and verse perhaps. Now here was the good Professor telling me to see the plays in the theatre of my mind by reading them in the fully interpretive Arden paperback editions, rather than through the voice and actions of actors on stage.

What first affected me so dramatically was the purity and beauty of the Professor's actual prose. The combination of his words and his message struck home with considerable force. Between the summer of '95 and the autumn of '96 I read, one by one, all of William Shakespeare's plays plus each of his narrative poems and sonnets. Indeed, aided and abetted by the Arden translations, (on my bookselves to this day), throughout that period of time I read nothing else other than newspapers! This poem was written at the time…

Finding Shakespeare

After sixty years
Focussing on right now
I found the two fine walkers
Coleridge and his friend
Mr William Wordsworth,
Had a brief skirmish with
That other wondrous set,
The dreamer Keats, the
Poetic mister Shelley
And the bad Lord B,
Went backwards in time
Through Swift and Pope
And Dryden to blind Milton
In his metronomically
Agonistic anti-Paradise
To find my friend John Donne,
A love-struck island to himself,
The whiff of something
Of great meaning thus
Becoming ever obvious;
Like incense
As the swinging starts.

Breathless, reading much of
Elizabethan stuff and such
I circled Shakespeare,
But warily, for a long while
Keeping nervous distance
Unsure about this Everest
Or maybe of my ability
To climb it or find the light
That so many others find,

Went back a long stride
But Chaucer was too tough,
Loved Spencer's Faerie Queen
Then fell on Tamburlaine,
From reckless Marlow and,
Ah! Here it is, (I thought,)
The source! that river
Of sweet scented mists
Still coiled and flowed
And thrust and heaved
And his words lived
And in his halcyon shade
I lay and took my rest awhile
And read how Shakespeare
Was perhaps Marlowe
Come live with me and be my love
They or some one wrote.
Although to me it mattered
Only that their words were.

And then in Winchester
In the dust-silent attic
Of that antiquarian book shop
Logan Pearsall-Smith's
Jewel of a treatise,
On Reading Shakespeare,
Lay opened in my hand
As when something flashed
Brightly in a muddy field
And you stooped to pick it up
And you were looking
Into the bright sun-colours
Of a diamond.

And so the good professor
Opened up the door
Switched on the lights
And there for me that wondrous treasury
Of works to brighten up my days
To hold an explanation for my nights.:
Thus, in the beginning,

Were his Words.

And so it was that I was reading in bed at 11.30 p.m.on Monday the 6th of August, 1996 when I came to this passage in *The Merchant of Venice* ... Lorenzo is at last alone with his Jessica in a forest glade ...

> How sweet the moonlight sleeps upon this bank!
> Here will we sit and let the sounds of music
> Creep in our ears: soft stillness and the night
> Become the touches of sweet harmony.
> Sit, Jessica. Look how the floor of heaven
> Is thick inlaid with patines of bright gold:
> There's not the smallest orb which thou behold'st
> But in his motion like an angel sings,
> Still quiring to the young-eyed cherubins;
> Such harmony is in immortal souls;
> But whilst this muddy vesture of decay
> Doth grossly close it in, we cannot hear it.

Just at this very point the bedside telephone rang. It was matron at the South Winds nursing home. Gently she informed me that my wife Joan, the mother of my children, had breathed her last. *Don't come now,* she said. *The morning will be soon enough.* I explained the situation to Dee, got dressed and drove off, arriving at the nursing home just as the ambulance was leaving. Instead of going in through the gateway I drove down to the nearby marina, switched off the engine and sat looking out over the starry black mirror of yacht studded Southampton water ...*Here will we sit and let the sounds of music creep in our ears: soft stillness and the night* ... the passage above reverberated in my head alongside all the good memories of long before: you may remember as did I the dance in York where we had first met, our holiday up in Ayr when we had ended up sleeping on the beach, living in tiny little Moulton with my sister Shirley and her husband John, the birth of Karen, (no letter 'i' in her forename then), our flats in Bateman Street, Cambridge then houses in Kings Heath and Solihull and Southport and Lee-on-Solent; the inevitable onwards and upwards not always welcomed by my girl whilst along came the new babies. You may remember as did I all the countryside walks, the camping holidays, the family Christmases. I thought about our making of love at a time when love was all we had and so was very precious; (Love does not just happen; it has to be made, doesn't it? And protected). All the fun and the adventures and misadventures. I thought about my previous weekend visit with our visitors, Joan's family from York and afterwards, the two of us on our own, the things she had said on what would become this, the eve of her death. Things that will remain with me and only me. *Bi-ig boys, they don't cry-ey-ey*, goes the song. I cried all right and am unashamed for *such harmony* is indeed *in immortal souls*. But for the first time in years, there in that Marina car park at one o clock in the morning my belief in an afterlife re-awakened itself. There has to be a world beyond this; one with and of beauty and with neither pain nor tears.

There was much suffering in the aftermath, especially in the passing on of the news to my family and Joan's family. I recall waiting outside Kairen and Roger's north London home late into the evening that following Saturday as they and their family were due home from the airport after their overseas holiday. It was for them a devastating return.

All of our children - even Bob, who fortunately fitted the clothes I lent him - and all Joan's people and all our grandchildren attended the funeral service at Southampton Crematorium but the event was somewhat sullied by the appointed Reverend forgetting actually to turn up! Fortunately our funeral director had the necessary qualification to officiate. I had spent much time in writing Joan's eulogy and I'm afraid it caused the service to overrun, thus stacking up the following funeral services. In that eulogy I quoted a line from one of her favourite songs; *You flying high in the air, me on the ground / Bring On The Clowns*. Yes indeed, bring on the clowns and bring on more tears.

Delia had elected out of respect to stay away from the funeral. We had been living together for some ten years and it had been eight years since Joan had needed to enter professional care. Yes, there was an element of guilt on Delia's side but I can testify that there was also a great deal of mutual respect between the two women in my life. My Joan knew well that I might not have been able to make it through the night without my Dee.

Soon enough I would again be a married man. One love does not necessarily destroy another. On the contrary, if one is lucky and tries hard enough it can re-inforce it.

56. Of new beginnings

On the 10th of October 1996 Dee and I were married. We deemed it too soon after Joan's death to make a big production out of it, so invited no family, only our two friends Jonathan and Dorothy. They acted as the necessary witnesses in a Brighton Registry Office somewhat reminiscent of a public urinal Afterwards the four of us we went out to a very ordinary Italian restaurant for dinner during which I drank copious amounts of Bardelino Classico, thus pretty much wasting the Grand Hotel's finest four posted bedroom suite. One other trivia comes to mind; over the road outside that restaurant was a public telephone kiosk in which a young man was busily jemmying open the cash box. We reported this criminality to the restaurant owner who simply shrugged his Italian shoulders and muttered *they're always doing that*.

The following day we drove along the south coast to my father's apartment, there to impart the news. Dad did not seem unduly surprised or much impressed although he had always been fond of my new wife. That day he spent the time whilst I was out buying a fish & chip lunch in showing her compromising pictures of himself and his 'chiropodist' lady friend! I must explain that my father, long since retired on a cost of living indexed civil service pension, had about him a certain unworldly quality. Thus he was happily living on his own in his elevated sea-front apartment for those last ten years of his life. In good weather he would sit out on his balcony armed with binoculars watching the girls go by on the promenade or, bikini-clad, sunbathing on the beach.

On the occasion of which I now write, when I asked him where I could go get some fish and chips for our lunch he looked in the telephone book and dialled something called, I seem to remember *The Chippy Plaice*. When they answered the phone he made the following enquiry; "*Do you supply fish and chips please?*". They put the phone down on what was obviously a joke call.

After that lunch Dee and I went on to Dover and across to France on the ferryboat, for we had been invited to another - one might say a 'proper' wedding with all the bells and whistles in Montdidier - in fact Margaret and Jean-Claude Vandevoorde's lovely young daughter Celine to her fiancee Thierry Dedonnink. We had become good friends with the family and by then Bibs-industry had been appointed Middle East sales agent for the special kind of labelling machinery invented by Jean-Claude and engineered in their 'PDC' factory. That wedding really was a splendid affair with many people in attendance including Margaret's Scottish family, some of the males clad in kilts of the Rangers FC tartan, I recall. There was much live and good music before, during and after the ceremony and a magnificent wedding feast unfortunately marred by some kind of a falling out between in-laws, (long since repaired, thank goodness.)

We had enough time in the days after the wedding to pursue Dee's deeply held, long-time interest in World War one. Montdidier is a small town close to the Somme that had been utterly destroyed in the cataclysm and subsequently rebuilt stone on stone. In particular Delia wanted to locate the burial place of the WW1 poet Roland Leighton. We found him in one of those tiny war grave cemetaries called Louvencourt. Later, on my return to business in Saudi Arabia, sitting in the evening in my Riyadh hotel room I composed a collection of verses under the one title; *IN WOUNDED FIELDS*. Each of the six stanzas was addressed to a deceased poet of the so-called Great War ... the one following is to Lieutenant Leighton, who had been expected to marry his long term fiancee, the writer Vera Brittan ... There is some unresolved mystery about that poet's latterday life and the facts surrounding his death on the battlefield ...

To Roland Aubrey Leighton: March 1895 - December 1915

We searched the lanes, found you in Louvencourt's
Small cemetary amidst a company
Of stones standing straight-rowed to attention,
Smart white in a slow rain, near where you died;
'Lieutenant R A Leighton 7th Worcesters,'
Says your monument; said that telegram.
"I walk alone although the way is long,"
You said, in private lines in your black book,
"And with gaunt briars and nettles overgrown;"
What pain you meant by this we'll never know.
Just such a light so bright as yours aligns
The many-splendoured ones on which it shines.

She capitalised your 'Him' as godheads do

Whenever afterwards she wrote of you.

Yes, "Life is love and love is you, dear, you"
You wrote, prize scholar bursting sweating out
Of your illicit wet night dreams of she,
Who'd written to herself; 'Impressive, he,
Of powerful frame, pale face and stiff thick hair.'
Would you we know had she not loved you so?
Dee likes to know you in those violets,
Pressed brown and withered, desiccated now,
You sent to Vee from shattered 'Plug Street' Wood,
Picked from red sticky ground around the head,
The horrid face and splintered skull that she
Must never see... what, she, Vera of the V A D?

Who, from your sceptic pact with her enticed
Your secret taking of Rome's hand of Christ?

And I, not knowing of you very much,
Looked in that brass bound book at Louvencourt
Read this year's batch of private messages
To you, young friend, mostly from those unborn
When that one, shiv'ring in his field grey,
Unsurprised to see you that cold night, glad
Of the Christmas gift, squeezed the steel trigger,
Exploding pain into your youthful frame...
From far and wide they'd come to speak their grief,
So many words to you who wrote so few.
Why stood you there, why dare the guns, Roland?
'Hinc illae lacrimae;' your code...
I still don't understand....

* Hence those tears'.... (Terence)

Jean-Claude's PDC machinery requires a kind of polyethylene film with precisely inbuilt stretch qualities. The machine cuts and applies it at high speed to milk bottles and the like as a form of labelling. I had located a small company in Leicester called EPS, owned by Bob Barratt, which could convert printed quantities of this special material into sleeving ready to export into Saudi for use on Almarai's PDC's, so had become agent for both both the machinery and the material it neede. I am talking millions of pounds sterling here of which I, as agent, was happy to collect ten percent.

By now well set in our new Bahrain environment and enjoying the very expensive services of five employees instead of previously only Robin, I came up with my next Big Idea! Rather than carry on importing the printed sleeving material into Saudi Arabia why not set up a local factory to convert it from printed sheet? I spoke about 'Sleeves-Arabia' to my sponsor Faisal and to Bob Barratt, getting clear the green light for GO. To make maximum financial sense out of converting material into sleeving I really needed a local plastic extruding company with the right skills to supply my Sleeves-Arabia with extruded and printed polyethylene reelstock. With Faisal's help I located and rented an empty factory in Al-Khobar then made a partnership deal with Bob to supply the converting machinery along with a young Leicester employee of his as supervisor. Regrettably I cannot recall this man's name. Anyway this fellow agreed to come out as my employee. He began by recruiting two Philipino production workers, who proved to be excellent. By then I had found a suitable materials supplier in Dubai (Call the company 'Al-Shark'. That was not its actual name but events three years down the line would prove to make it sound quite appropriate!) Al-Shark was at the time managed by an English expat named Darryl. A thoroughly reliable and technically perfect source - or so I thought!

I had the ideal lead-off customer for our stretch-sleeving in Almarai dairy. My Middle East house of cards was now almost complete.

57. A good and dangerous life

Whenever I was home in Hampshire I tried to make time with Dee to take the dogs out for walks twice daily; once immediately after breakfast and once around lunchtime. How well we got to know the sweet-flowing, crystal clear river Itchen and the pretty little villages down the valley alongside it, and all the chalk hills, the bluebell woodlands and New Forest ways of south Hampshire. These were happy times. Neither of us had in the past been overmuch for friends outwith business and our family/ies but now our social life was very pleasing, both in Winchester and out amongst the expatriated luminati of that most anglophile Bahrain.

The tiny, ancient *Eclipse* pub close by Winchester cathedral was home from home to a truly eclectic group of folk who, I think, wouldn't mind me calling them, for the most part intellectuals. Especially as one of them was World Quiz Champion! Most of them could, as they say up here in Scotland, 'take a good drink!' as well as being able and willing to expound their views on any topic under the sun; or, quite likely there in Winchester, under the rain! I thought of the Eclipse as being somewhat akin to an Elizabethan Coffee House. In addition to that pub Dee's dinner parties at Laundry Cottage were quite famous and great fun if sometimes a little on the OTT side. I remember one more than usually alcoholic occasion when a certain guest was seen departing up Bedfield Lane in his kangaroo hopping Rolls-Royce. I have to confess I was myself very much the worse for wear on that occasion. Truth to tell I never was a top-rate drinker, much preferring nourishment to punishment.

The British Ambassador in Bahrain held regular garden parties. I imagine all British Ambassadors have done so worldwide since diplomatic time began. Anyway Bahrain's were splendidly formal affairs held in the evening outside the Embassy building on its highly securitised, well-kept lawns. Dusty old palm trees, scents of tropical flora and expensive ladies' perfume hanging in the hot and humid air, everyone 'who is anyone' both British and Arab dressed up, doing their best to move assiduously group to group with glass in hand, talking much, listening little. But our ambassador was a splendidly radical fellow living a strict protocol were it not for the fact that he had broken ranks to marry his native housemaid. Long live the British individualist! Our mentor into these affairs was always Thomas Kelly, a strikingly bold fellow, husband of Dina, my personal assistant, much akin both physically and in personal projection to Charles Dance. We often had lunch together in one or other of the Manama bistros or in the Yacht Club or, when Dee was in town, dinner at their home. Thomas was one of those lucky ones, the classic English who would have been born elite even were they in some East London ghetto instead of a quite stately home!

On the darker side there is one incident that I cannot possibly leave out of my memoirs. Since retiring from (or actually having been kicked out of!) my last long-term employment in 1987 I had kept in touch albeit sporadically with many of my colleagues at Sweetheart International. Perhaps foremost amongst these was my friend Ted Pool who I had recruited and who had worked with me ever since the company became a green-field start-up in 1971. Ted's first wife left him, apparently to go off with her boss, about a year after he joined, taking their two little daughters with her. Just before that I well recall that lady coming up to me at a company Christmas party; *all right, Bryan*, she said quietly, *he's yours; you can have him*. At the time I had no idea what that was all about. Anyway Ted remarried and had three more daughters with his lovely second wife, Jane, all of them now teenagers. He had left Sweetheart after me, as had the majority of my team, and had gone to work for a competitor where his new boss was Peter Bright, another leading extrovert of the ex-Sweetheart brigade. One morning Peter phoned me with the shocking news that Ted had passed away the previous night in a West Country hotel room after a no more than ordinary dinner with some customers. Heart attack, as it transpired. Somebody other than a policeman had to go to visit the family. Peter said he was on his way himself but could Dee and I come, please? The three of us knocked on Jane's Lee-on-Solent door, steeling ourselves for what was to come. They were out! We spent the next few hours in the local *Swordfish* pub, coffee and soft drinks only. before the girls returned to their home. But eventually on that terrible day three smiling young ladies and one smiling mum opened the door to us - before those awful clouds of fear transmuting into terror came over their faces. Somehow they knew, even before we spoke. Tragedy transmits itself just as easily as do smiles.

The church was filled literally to overflowing for the funeral. That man Ted had so many friends, many of them his business customers. People would say he was one of the very few for whom nobody had a bad word. His and Jane's youngest, his twelve years old daughter did the reading. She was as good and as brave as was her father. Neither Dee nor I knew at the time that his second trio of daughters knew nothing about the existence of their father's first two. Jane said they had just never got around to telling them. It came as another dreadful bewilderment, even though it did not damage their deep-held love for their now deceased daddy. Besides, in the event those first marriage daughters by then in their twenties did not turn up for the funeral. I was proud to be asked by Jane to deliver her late husband's eulogy. Amongst other things I told the people about how, in the very early days of Sweetheart International, Ted and I once set out from Gosport to visit Northern Dairies in Hull and then Bibby, the fats company in Liverpool, then back home. So, in a single seven hundred miles day we saw the English channel, the North Sea and the Irish Sea as well as doing some substantial business. But why would I tell them this in a eulogy? Because not twenty miles on the road in the cold light of dawn Ted asked me to stop the car. I braked to a halt. *What's wrong*, I asked him. *Nothing*, Ted said. *Sometimes you have to take time just to look at the world, boss.* I looked. Over the dawning fields and woodlands of Hampshire the sun was rising, the sky a kaleidoscope of colour. Yes, Ted, everything can be beautiful. Including you.

58. Growing old gracelessly

I really cannot remember whether in these episodes I've written much if anything about Winnie Boulter, nee Smalley, Delia's Mother. On the basis that I haven't, let me explain that I first met Winnie not long after I met her daughter. She would then have been in her late sixties. Not many years before she had lost her husband, Bill, Delia's father, to a heart attack on board the Gosport - Portsmouth ferryboat. Of course a bitter blow for the family but not totally inappropriate - for an ex Royal Navy officer who had spent the greater part of his life at sea or latterly shorebound as Chief Instructor at Whale Island, Portsmouth's famously tough Gunnery School. As an ex wartime WREN Winnie was a really larger than life character, idiosyncratic in so many ways. For me she was the epitome of that wonderful poem by Jenny Joseph ...

When I am an old woman I shall wear purple
With a red hat which doesn't go, and doesn't suit me.
And I shall spend my pension on brandy and summer gloves
And satin sandals, and say we've no money for butter.
I shall sit down on the pavement when I'm tired
And gobble up samples in shops and press alarm bells
And run my stick along the public railings
And make up for the sobriety of my youth.
I shall go out in my slippers in the rain
And pick flowers in other people's gardens
And learn to spit.

You can wear terrible shirts and grow more fat
And eat three pounds of sausages at a go
Or only bread and pickle for a week
And hoard pens and pencils and beermats and things in boxes.

But now we must have clothes that keep us dry
And pay our rent and not swear in the street
And set a good example for the children.
We must have friends to dinner and read the papers.

But maybe I ought to practice a little now?
So people who know me are not too shocked and surprised
When suddenly I am old, and start to wear purple.

Well, Winnie Smalley would have been terribly disappointed were people who knew her never 'shocked and surprised' by her! And she surely did wear her favourite colour purple. Although from an ordinary enough background, by heart and soul she definitely felt herself to be of the elite, if you see what I mean! She told me with all seriousness that she, Winnie, would never re-marry unless to at least an Admiral of the Royal Navy! Well, one day in the eighties whilst I was still at a loss for how to earn a longer term living after Sweetheart International I decided that life as a painter (pictures not houses!) held considerable attraction and at least a glimmer of potential. So to properly equip myself and Dee with the associated commercial skills we decided to enrol on an advertised country house weekend to learn the arts of picture framing. Winnie was also a painter of watercolour pictures so we invited her to join us. However when we went to pick her up, to our surprise she had with her a somewhat abashed, fine looking looking elderly gentleman carrying both cases; his and hers! His name was Len Boulter, a 'friend and fellow watercolourist', as we were told. It turned out that Len had been an officer of H.M.Customs charged with the specially onerous duty of touring the Highlands and Islands of Scotland to certify the bonded facilities of the whisky distillers.

That first evening in the big house Dee and I were much intrigued by the sounds of merriment from the room next to ours - Winnie's room! Consumed with curiosity we knocked on the door. It opened to reveal the two of them in fine party mood. We had no idea they were sharing. Winnie did not drink alcohol but there she was, doubled up with laughter, champagne glass in hand! *Just come and have a look at this*, she demanded. In Len's case, opened on the bed, was a neat pile of silken cord. No, not what you are thinking - or Dee of I or Winnie for that matter. Len offered his indignant explanation; it seemed that he had a phobia about hotel fires so always travelled with this *rope ladder*. The fact that we were on the ground floor and that most of his international travel provided him with rooms high up - much higher up than his 'ladder' could possibly be effective in hotel tower blocks - that had nothing to do with it!

When, a few years later and in her eighties Winnie's overactive conscience got the better of her she decided she could 'live in sin' with her Len no longer. Even though their subsequent marriage cost her and her two daughters two of her three wartime pensions, the splendidly-outfitted deed was done in a downtown Winchester registry office. Afterwards she took me on one side, explaining, in all seriousness - *I know he's not an Admiral, Bryan, but he does have an O.B.E.* ('Order of the British Empire'). But, at least according to their oppressed housemaid cleaner, Len in his eighties still possessed a healthy interest in the opposite sex. What with him and my father I was beginning to look forward to my own old age!

59. Sending for reinforcements

I believe it was in the Spring of '98, a weekend day, and I was working on my PC in the Bahrain penthouse when my youngest son Stuart called from England. He was very unhappy with the scant rewards of life as a south coast inshore fisherman, he told me. I could tell he was serious. Now with partner Lorraine and their two little girls, even living in that idyllic Carefree Cottage right in the heart of the Dorset woodlands had lost its lustre. *Anything you can suggest, dad?* I said I'd talk to Dee and call him back. It so happened that Dee was visiting me at the time and was right then sunbathing by our rooftop swimming pool. For an hour I sat with her in the scorching sun - her that is, me under a great beach umbrella . We discussed all the possibilities as we saw them for our thirty five years old son. Clearly if he was going to make a change of career, better now than later, but qualifications? Stuart had suffered more than his fair share of hardship, growing into and through his early teens in the dark shadow of his mother's multipleschlerosis and then his older brother's mental illness. Little wonder he'd rebelled at school and followed Robert's example, running off to Cornwall and a life on the fishing boats. But Stu was a bright, honest, personable young man, far more sensitive than his outwards persona might at times have suggested. His wild oats had been well and truly sown and by now he, like his father, had forgotten where he'd cast them!I was well aware that Dee had a very soft spot for Stu. I recall how, ten years back in Hayling Island, when sensing she was feeling down and knowing of her liking for toffee fudge he would quietly slip a few squares of the stuff into her apron pocket.

For some time I had felt myself much overstretched by the multiple pressures of my Bahrain based design and packaging consultancy and Sleeves-Arabia, by now well up and running and producing good volumes of high quality product. I was all over the place, often making five or six flights in a week and/or 'commuting' across the deserts to Riyadh. Although I had good back up in the office and out at the Sleeves Arabia factory as well as, through Robin and Saeed, in the field, I had begun to think about divesting myself of some of the top load.

It is not easy taking decisions that represent a gamble with the lives and prosperity of those near and dear to you - or anyone else for that matter. Our Middle East businesses were after all anything but secure. Promising, yes. On an upwards curve, yes. Secure, certainly not! A dynamic new business quite suddenly employing ten people can never be that, especially when situated deep in some foreign field. At the end of our talk Dee and I looked at each other, weighing up the risks. Then Dee nodded, *Let's do it* she said. So I called Stu back. Would he like to come out to take a look around? If we all gave it the thumbs up, (precisely what 'it' would be by way of a job we could firm up later), then Stuart could bring his family out to live in Bahrain. However, I explained, he and Lorraine would perforce need to get married. Middle Eastern countries had a habit of asking to see the wedding lines of incoming couples! No lines, no entry. I knew this would be a test of their commitment, for neither of them had much time for that kind of mere convention!

So Stuart came out, liked what he found and I liked the way he conducted himself. Within the month came the wedding, two pretty little girls as bridesmaids. Not long after that I was greeting the whole family at Bahrain airport. Soon they were happily and safely ensconced in a leased villa within a compound with swimming pool, etcetera, and the girls were enrolled in a good Manama school for expatriates. They had a rented company car and friends of their own age outwith the business. Their new life was up and running. How very adaptable are the young - and the young at heart. Of course Stu had the business executive's L plates up but he very quickly got used to the dreaded necktie and suit - and his daily commute across the Bahrain - Al-Khobar (Saudi) causeway with its double, and doubly infuriating customs posts. Most Saturdays (their Saturday equals our Sunday) I would meet with Stuart, Lorraine, Jadine and Sinead at our favourite breakfast cafe, taking the opportunity to catch up with all the family. Thomas Kelly was quick to befriend my family as well, which meant they would be invited to the parties and gatherings that are such a feature of expatriate life in Bahrain. As I have said before, if you keep out of any kind of trouble in the Middle East life there can indeed be very good.

The role of the sponsor in Saudi Arabia is a many splendoured thing. Anything and everything from the simple arms length signing off of visa applications to being an active supporter in the often convoluted world of Arab business. I am not, in case you're wondering, referring here to corrupt practices. Plain old stupidity yes, but in fact I seldom came across any definite corruption other than by oblique reference to those ultra high level Middle East arms deals. In any case the latter are not regarded as corruption by high ranking Arabs; more the entitlement of rank. Our British values and laws have absolutely no meaning or force, a fact that our domestic politicians have had to learn to live with, however reluctantly.

My own sponsor, Faisal, was of course responsible for the lawful correctness of all our activities in The Kingdom but as I have indicted herein he was, I truly and firmly believed, more friend than arms length sponsor. Certainly he had allowed me to be privy to some of his more unusual social activities. But rule number two for expats in The Kingdom - after 'do not infringe religious Law' is, 'never put your entire trust in an Arab or believe he is your friend, western style'. Thinking back, I should have read the coldwater signs even as early as then, in 1997/8. Perhaps it was unfortunate that the advent of my son on the scene coincided with the permanent disability of Faisal's son following his motor car accident and Faisal's incredibly expensive, if unavailing medical efforts in Europe and America.

Stuart's participation in my business life and his whole family's presence in my personal life proved to be a major help as well as a great comfort. He had all the energy that once I had myself and that was now perhaps slow ebbing; he had an innovative and enquiring cast of business mind and the adaptablity / resourcefulness so essential to any expatriate. On the other hand he had a long way to go with information technology and had had one of my own weaknesses - that of impatience!

60. Days of wine and poppies

If I should live long enough, one day I think I'll amass these episodes into a proper autobiography. I'll call it ... *Me - Myself - So What?* After all who could be interested in reading the life story of a non-celebrity, barring possibly some of his/her immediate family? Yet I have a suspicion that there are some important clues to a wider answer in the parson-poet John Donne's sixteenth century words ... and this is a quotation very familiar to any who listened to my après dinner 'speeches': *No man is an island, Entire of itself, Every man is a piece of the continent, A part of the main. If a clod be washed away by the sea, Europe is the less. As well as if a promontory were. As well as if a manor of thy friend's Or of thine own were: Any man's death diminishes me Because I am involved in mankind, And therefore never send to know for whom the bell tolls; It tolls for thee.*

Any man's death diminishes me!! Of course. And he might have added, *Any man's life enhances me.* Above and beyond that I write simply because I like the architecture of the written word. I love the English language. I want to use it to express my thoughts of what has been and what is to come, and why. I think we all should have some interest other than just *what am I doing today?* Don't you?

Everyone is dressed up to the nines, there are round tables each of about ten guests and there is of course much dancing . A group of red-coated Chelsea Pensioners is flown in from London for the occasion. The officers of any British military in the vicinity are also invited. On this occasion it seems that most of the upper deck of a destroyer were present, clad in their best whites and having little trouble attracting dance partners from amongst the local young ladies. In particularly recall Tom Jones' Delilah being played and a rather beautiful girl being thrown about like a hysterically laughing rag doll. I also recollect Dee being asked to dance by a minute Chelsea Pensioner - an octogenarian whose nose barely reached her bosom!

On another occasion my assistant, Dina, agreed to accompany Dee on a shopping trip. The plan was for Dina to pick Delia up outside my office in Bahrain Towers, thence to the shopping mall. I could look out of the window to observe her standing down there at the roadside, waiting. After some minutes past the agreed time and no Dina I suspected the worst when I saw a car - not Dina's - stopping alongside her. She began to talk to the driver through his window, then I saw my wife hurrying to the building's security cabin, quickly leaving that in turn, to hurry back up to the office. Before she arrived there Dina was on the phone in something of a panic. She had been waiting outside our apartment building, not the office. A red-faced Dee told us the man in the car had stopped to ask her how much she wanted! Then, when she went into the security kiosk for protection the policeman asked her if and if so where she was 'in business'. she pointed up to the tower block and told him, *Yes, up there!* When the man began to talk money the penny dropped for the second time in ten minutes! There always was a special kind of innocence about my wife.

It is extremely hard to obtain a visitor's visa for a woman trying to *visit* Saudi Arabia with husband as opposed to *reside* with husband on a compound That's not straightforward either, come to think of it. In fact on only one occasions did Delia cross over into The Kingdom. That was when Faisal's wife, Nair, invited Dee through Faisal and myself to one of her parties. We stayed with an American business couple, good friends, on their nearby residential compound. At the appointed time a large chauffeur driven limousine with blacked out windows made its appearance. I waved off my lady, beautifully dressed up as she was. Saudi Arabian parties are of course attended only by males or only by females. Never the twain shall meet.

For years afterwards my wife dined out on her account of that party. It seems she had barely introduced herself and had hardly cleared the compound gates before Nair was relating details of her own personal life including her childbirth experiences - and expecting Dee to retaliate! Once at Nair's mansion of a home she was seated on the left hand side of Nair in a great, starkly white salon with starkly white leather settees arranged around all four walls. The only decoration took the form of golden birds in full flight around the walls. When each guest came in she was introduced to Dee before taking up her station on the settees in strict order of seniority (social status!). Dee was the sole westerner. The Arabic ladies were of all ages, all dressed in the black of course, but most of the younger ones at once removed the black to reveal underneath the kind of female apparel you would find in Paris, London or Milan. The older ladies, pure Bedouin with intricately hennaed hands, would prod Delia's stomach with their forefinger and, laughing raucously, comment to each other that she could not possibly be attractive to her husband; she was far too thin! Interminable talk of the most frank nature, accompanied by much laughter followed whilst a young woman did continuous rounds with the coffee pot (called a 'dallah'). Dee asked Nair who this strikingly beautiful young lady was. Apparently she had been the wife of a wealthy man who had divorced her by simple declaration, leaving her penniless. Her only way left by which to support herself was to become a servant to the woman (Nair) who had for long enough been her friend and an equal in Saudi female society.

Dee had been starving herself all day in anticipation of the feast to come but the hours ticked by with the hunger pangs growing and still no sign of anything to eat. Then at midnight she was led outside into Nair's high-walled garden where was enough - and strange enough - food as to make her heart sink. She had read the book of *'Good Manners for British Visitors to Saudi Arabia'* so knew it would be very rude not to partake, however lightly, of each and every offered dish. Especially - yes, you've heard about it - the piece de resistance for the principal guest in the shape of a barely cooked sheep's eye!

Meanwhile I am sitting in Virgil's front room long after my hosts had taken themselves off to bed, waiting with gathering concern for the return of my Delia. It was two o clock when the black limousine made its reappearance. Dee tumbled out bidding Nair her farewells and multi thanks. She had the dazed look of somebody who had just been ten rounds with Mohamed Ali. .

61. Udrigle millennium

Remember the millenium? You know, midnight thirty first December nineteen ninety nine when the world as we know it was to descend into chaos whilst all our computers crashed and burned? Dee and I had rented Joanna Mackenzie's lovely old Udrigle House, having driven the seven hundred miles north after Christmas. We half-jokingly figured that if this was to be the end of life as we know it we might as well be where we had long wanted to be. Two Christmases ago we had stayed here with our dogs, recharging batteries, wondering, as ever, why we needed, *really* needed to go back to our work and homes in Winchester and the Middle East. At that time I composed this poem for Joanna, whose ancestor William originally built Udrigle House for his new bride, Lilias ... it is reputed to be the oldest intact dwelling house in this part of Scotland

    Christmas at House Udrigal

    I dreamed a dream most magical
    Of times before House Udrigal
    Of clansmen, living by the shore
    And on the hill, well used to war
    Yet speaking, singing poetry.
    I dreamed this fierce northern land,
    Made beautiful by Nature's hand
    From ice and loch and living rock
    Was gifted to its Highland stock
    Whose origins are mystery.

    Those people lived in hardiness
    In turv-ed structures windowless,
    Until that chieftain did decide
    In honour of his fair haired bride
    To build a house for history,
    Named 'Outer gully' ('Udrigal');
    Here's where he dug away the soil,
    Well found on rock his place would be
    Safe from the storms, the raging sea
    Withstand all that adversity.

    Great boulders came up from the beach;

He chipped and shaped and fitted each
To those beneath, row upon row
And joined the timbers one by one
Built solid strong in symmetry.
And then upon a lintel stone, to mark
Above the fire, in letters stark
For all who here sometime might pass
That this was "Williams', Lilias's"
And shall be through eternity.

Then in my dream I gladly talked
With friendly ghosts of those who'd looked
Across this moody, salty-plane
To distant hills in sun and rain -
A view of such great majesty.
I spoke with lairds and tacksmen and
The crofters who had worked this land
Had built this Highlands House sublime
Sired of the wind, the sea and time
That always shall stay close to me.

Awake! It's Christmas ninety eight!
We walk the dogs and get back late
Then eat and drink and so at last
We toast our future and our past
For each is vital, equally.
And when we pull the curtains back -
A star-less night of stygian black,
But lights ride bright up in the sky-
And yes, we hear a baby's cry.
For this is Christmas, magically.

Bryan Islip
December 1998

Anyway it's now the dreaded Millenium Eve. We had been in good company over in Gairloch's Badachro Inn having enjoyed a long walk along from Red Point beach with the dogs. On the way from Badachro back to Udrigle House, (herself in the driving seat, for I have never left that Badachro Inn in fit condition), I thought we might drop into The Sand Hotel for a livener. Now, this hotel was always 'let out' to parties of friends / relatives rather than to individual chance callers although but there was a bar open to the public. It transpired that the resident group in place was a party of genuine, English, dyed in the wool, both sex Yuppies - dealers usually to be found in the money towers and champagne bars of the City of London. Why don't you join us for dinner, they insisted. *No, we didn't come up with that sort of clothing,* Dee whispered to me - actually quite fiercely. *Thank you very much,* said I, full of goodwill to all men. *We'll see you later.*

What a Hogmanay that was. First the banquet, us in little more than our dog walking clothes, the other twenty of so, half our age, in full evening dress! Anyway Dee and I duly applauded their semi-incomprehensible speeches and made sounds of appreciation re the quality of that splendid meal with its good and plentiful red wines, bubbly and vintage port. All free of charge to us! Then the real fun as the Scottish Highlands dancing began. I have not seen energy and activity like it since we were chased, tumbling over a hedge, by an enraged Hampshire bull. I have a vision of shrieking young ladies being hurled by the men without let or mercy from pillar to post - and even vice versa! No place there for shrinking violets although we old folk did manage to stay hors d'combat. I could by then in any case have barely stood, never mind danced any strip the bloody willow. As midnight came and went and everybody had duly kissed everybody and the company had ascertained by mobile that their cyber world was still rotating we all trooped out into the cold cold night. A bonfire was lit which was the cue for a continuation of mad gyrations only this time on frosted and tufted grass instead of parquet flooring. The celebrations were less than dampened when one lady fell down a ditch and did considerable damage to her ankle. At that we stole away into the night. I don't suppose by then we would have been missed.

As you may have picked up in previous episodes I am not a particular fan of the City of London with its sharpster banks and bankers. However, being kind at heart I forgave them for that one night.

62. The Icarus problem

The one thing about me that used to drive Dee nuts, (no doubt amongst others), was my propensity to develop a new idea and immediately shift focus from the previous good idea. This is a major failing. I have to admit my latest creative interest was always the one that got my primary attention. Still is! By way of illustration, today I should be travelling down south in Wester-Ross selling my greetings cards etc or ordering new stocks of them - important to the money-in department. Or I might be working on my new blockbuster(!) novel; 81,000 words in the can and about 20,000 to go but in which direction?. Or I could be taking up my paint brushes again. I know what I have wanted to paint since Dee departed but my easel still stands forlorn. Or I could be working on a Cinderella pantomine script as requested by Ullapool Rotary. Or creating the long narrative poem about life in Wester-Ross that will hopefully form the basis, with my friend the photographer and my friend the musician, of an audio visual production this coming Autumn. I always seem to want to be master of all trades! But instead of those things, here I am writing another episode of my personal memoirs. Why? Because this is my latest venture, therefore the one that captivates me the most here and now on this lovely morning!

This was very much my position in macrocosm in year 2000. Things were going well for my consultancy, Bibs-industry, now re-based in Bahrain. In fact I had a twenty four carat clientele covering most of the Middle East. In addition our labelling factory Sleeves Arabia was up and running, supplying good product to several major dairies and soft drinks bottlers. At that point in comes an enquiry from a British friend of a friend of a friend: a huge tobacco company would like me to find out why Saudi Arabia has no cigarette factory. More importantly, could they (said giant, multi-national tobacco company) create one?

Everybody knows the majority of Arab males are smokers of cigarettes imported by the multi-billion from the USA, Britain, France and Japan. Why no local production? My sponsor, Faisal, told me he could provide my client with the necessary contacts. I hurried back to Imperial Tobacco in Bristol, England. To say they are interested is an understatement. Together we proceeded to the City of London and a major merchant bank. What prospects for raising the two hundred million dollar finance for such a cigarette plant? Every prospect. What kind of a deal for Bryan Islip's Bibs-industry? Twenty thousand sterling for the initial introduction plus five percent of the investment for masterminding the project. (Not actually doing too much I hasten to add!) I am very quickly on a fully paid up first class flight with my new Imperial Tobacco friends to Bahrain, there to meet a couple of Arabs high in wealth and politics. The whole entourage of us moves on to Dubai, which is one of the United Arab Emirates. Another of the Emirates, the remote Fujairah is our final destination. This is where, agrees the local Emir, we can build the cigarette factory that is going to make me rich! It is a free of charge gateway into Saudi Arabia and the whole Middle East. Also for export because Fujairah in under mega development as the end point of a new oil and gas pipeline that will enable the tankers (and freighters) to load up without having to sail round into the Gulf itself.

We all fly back to Britain together; in-flight champagne all round and I receive my twenty grand. The very next day I also receive a message from my new pal at Imperial. I'm told that, from the company's highest level has descended an edict. *'Forget all about manufacturing cigarettes in the Middle East'*. No explanation given or would be given. My bubble is pricked! But the explosion is nothing to that of my Arab friends. Feverishly I canvas all other of the world's main cigarette brands. Blank. Nada. Nobody wanted to know. It was the beginning of the end for my consulting business relationship with my sponsor, Faisal, although I did not know it at the time. He wanted to take Imperial to the British High Court even though nothing had been signed on paper. Very reluctantly but at his insistence I obtained expensive legal advice. The advice? Forget all about it.

Months later I hear through confidential channels the reason for the tobacco industry's top level negativity. It seems that The Kingdom of Saudi Arabia's importation of cigarettes has for decades attracted duty - and that duty is of particular interest to the Monarch himself! Local production obviously equals no omport duty. The message has gone forth!

It was not long before Sleeves-Arabia also came under deliberate attack. More on that next time. My castle and that of the people who worked for me, not least my son and his family, was beginning to crumble. And I would soon need to begin to think about a new life.

63. All dreams must end

At boarding school in Abingdon my reports sometimes mentioned my inclination towards dreaming rather than learning. And yes, I suppose I have to confess to having always been a bit of a dreamer. More imagination than intelligence, you could fairly say. No apologies for that because that's why I can paint things that are not there, why I can write stories that ae not real (it's called fiction and by the way this blog is non-fiction), and why I can create a business from nothing. Such a business was Sweetheart International in Gosport UK and such was Bibs-industry in Riyadh, then Al-Khobar, then Bahrain. And such, latterly, was the manufacturing company Sleeves Arabia in Al Khobar on the East coast of The Kingdom of Saudi Arabia.

As mentioned in at least one previous episode I set up 'Sleeves Arabia' to make stretch sleeve labelling from reel-stock that I imported into the Kingdom of Saudi Arabia from Dubai. The Middle East market for stretch-sleeves didn't exist until I introduced the concept - and the PDC machinery - to Almarai Dairy of Riyadh back in the early 90's. I had gone to extraordinary lengths to find a sound supplier of the precisely formatted and printed polyethylene reel-stock. Without that I would never have attempted to persuade my friend Bob Barratt of EPS in Leicester, (makers of stretch-sleeving) to join me in the Saudi joint venture. *(At this point I have to confess to having completely forgotten the name of my nemesis - that is, the UAE company I had contracted to supply my new venture, Sleeves Arabia. Probably a case of not wanting to confront one's personal demons?)* Be that as it may, the main reason for my decision in their favour was the general manager of that UAE company, a British expatriate originally from Tyneside. His name was Darren. In due course Darren got things going nicely for us. Sleeves Arabia had good material coming in on time, material that my guys in the factory were able to convert into quality stretch-sleeving. This product worked well on Almarai Dairy's high speed EPS machinery. No problems for my customers equalled no problems but good money for Sleeves Arabia. Plan A looking great. Then I made (another) mistake. I persuaded Darren to leave my UAR supplier and join Bibs-industry in the Emirates. Suddenly not only did I have no technical / ethical link into my one essential supplier, but that supplier did not exactly take kindly to my taking away the technical brains of his business! The Arab owner clearly had no love for me (or, I have to assume, of my sponsor Faisal), and was obviously beginning to ask himself why he should not make his material into stretch sleeves of this own and supply my customer, thus taking all the profit rather than half of it. Did he really need Bryan Islip's Sleeves-Arabia? Well, no.

But instead of going ahead with investing in appropriate machinery and developing his own sales relations with my friends at Almarai the owner elected, Arab style, to put me out of business! How? Simply by supplying me with large quantities of technically imperfect sleeving reel-stock; material that would not possibly be stretchable therefore would be inoperable on my customers' PDC machines. Pandemonium. In vain I protested that I would no more pay for material not up to specification than I would pay for petrol that not only left my car kangaroo hopping down the road but would quickly burn out its bloody motor altogether!

Stuart and Darren and I attended the crunch meeting in Dubai with the supplier's owner and his acolytes. Absolutely no sign of any understanding or any sweetness, much less any light! In vain I produced from a world respected UK University laboratory a technical analysis of the Dubai company's defective material. The Arab owner glanced at the report for all of five seconds then tossed it aside, indicating that anyone could bribe a scientist to write anything one wanted! Having paid a lot of money for this completely independent report and with my whole position teetering on the edge, at that point I saw many colours including a brilliant shade of red! Tht made matters worse; all in vain, naturally.

Soon after this my Saudi sponsor, call him Faisal, asked to see me. Stuart and I sat in his office. He indicated that 'the powers that be' locally had woken up to the fact that a manufacturing business in The Kingdom was not owned by a Saudi national. Surprise, surprise! The solution? He, my 'friend' Faisal, would become the owner of Sleeves-Arabia with myself as managing director and Stuart as something else. By this time I calculated that I and my co-EPS director Bob Barrqatt had four hundred thousand pounds in Sleeves-Arabia, now being grabbed by Faisal! I think you could say my response was not entirely positive. *'Come, let us take a walk around the block, Bryan,'* he said. And so we did, during which I noticed (a) Faisal had little to say and (b) he was sweating profusely. When we returned to the office it was to find

Stuart sitting there in stony silence with Faisal's equally silent wheelchair-bound teenager son and a rather scruffy, equally silent uniformed policeman standing by. Alarm bells began to clang all around! Loudly!

The uncomfortable impasse continued, for some reason unfathomable in the local police station in front of a quite sympathetic senior police official. I have never been more relieved to get out of anywhere and cross over the Causeway border posts into Bahrain. I'm quite sure Stuart ditto. He must have wondered just what he had got himself intoi. We had been well and truly stitched up. I myself was clearly well kippered! It would be thus for me in The Kingdom of Saudi Arabia as far ahead as mind and eye could see. I had two options at that point; either take the dispute into a Saudi Court or retreat as gracefully as possible to lick my wounds in good old Blighty. That was on Thursday 8th September 2001. My natural instinct was to fight the bastards but on Tuesday 12th September the phone rang in my Bahrain penthouse. It was Dee, speaking from our home in Headbourne Worthy, Winchester: *Quick, switch on your TV*, she urged, *America's under attack*. I said something akin to *What the hell?* (As if I hadn't had enough bloody excitement!) I rushed down to street level, crossed over the road to the Irish Harp Bar. That pub had a giant screen in front of which the usual expat beer drinkers now sat or stood in shocked silence whilst young Arabs, the majority Saudi, whooped and hollered and blew kisses whilst the twin towers of New York spewed forth smoke and bodies in equal measure. And then that awful collapsing in clouds of smoke and dust.

My world also had collapsed and would never be the same again.

On Saturday 16th September 2001 I landed at a near deserted Heathrow. Nobody wanted to fly. The whole world seemed to think then that Armageddon was at hand. Anyway Dee and the dogs were waiting, the Jeep fully loaded for our long planned fortnight's holiday in a Braeside, Gairloch house rental. Travelling north and before reaching Manchester I related the sorry tale to my wife, who was doing all the driving. By then I had made up my mind. I turned to her, told her that I would never return to the Middle East. I had no idea what we could do for a living but that was it. Stuart would be staying on out there for so long as it took to clear things up.

Dee said, *That's great, darling. Don't worry, we'll be all right.* What a hell of a woman! I could have cried but didn't. Instead I slept most of the way to a Scotland so Bonny that it seemed to me that day more like the Valhalla of our Viking ancestors.

64. Seeing about Gairloch

From the turmoil of my business adventures and misadventures in the Middle East and the associated madness of the twin towers in New York City, our Gairloch holiday presented, in September 2001, a true haven of tranquillity. I think this is reflected in my painting at the time; *A Gairloch Morning* . I painted it in pastels. 'Painting' is probably an incorrect word for the use of sticks of pure pigment stroked across, then fing

r rubbed into a sheet of special 'paper'.

Never mind. It was a perfect morning as I sat on a smooth rock up on An Ard overlooking the whole length and breadth of the Gairloch to which I had first ventured with Joan and our young family way back in 1971. Later on I had returned in 1980 with Delia for her first visit amidst a November storm of rain and wind that I had been sure at the time would put her off the place for life. It had not; quite the opposite in fact. Who knows what it is that stirs into reawakened life one's individual genetic history?

Years later I made this picture into a greetings card. The back of the card bears a version of this poem ...

>*Seeing Gairloch*
>
>*You have to come here, I told them.*
>*But it's so cold and wet, they said, isn't it?*
>*I said, I want you to see what I've been looking at.*
>*They said, Well, why don't you tell us about it?*
>*Right, I said, I'll send you a card.*
>
>*Sitting in a café with a cup of tea,*
>*a Highland scone,*
>*I wrote...*
>*'Dear people*
>*You think you know about colours*

until you've seen an early day
over a cloudless Gairloch.
you think you know about distance
until your eyes have roamed around
the curves and contours of the world
through air so clear, this clean;
noiseless save the shushing of the sea,
the calling of the gulls as if to you and me

…perspective…

You know, just what are me and you,
within all things?
I swear you taste these lands
of time lost Highland clans,
so wild, so free - this everlasting majesty:'

And so they came, our friends,
and it rained and blew a gale of wind all week.
(A different kind of beauty.)
This place smiles not, shows not herself
so often, nor to everyone.
And they will come again.

I have told how Dee had already suggested it was time for us to think about migrating north. I am sure many people have such thoughts following their holidays Wester-Ross, especially if the sun have shone for them! But of course you need to consider life where the nearest supermarket and hospital is seventy winding, up and down miles away, where the winters can bring hundred mile an hour gales, where the summers will definitely bring hordes of biting insects in still conditions together commonly with much rain, where local society revolves largely around the church(es) and where we 'white settlers' can all too easily divide up into sects or cliques. Above all one needs to know that looking out of your window at the stunning scenery will soon lose its lustre unless you have need, and the talent or ability to make a living, thus creating a properly useful way of life for yourself. 'Retirement' is the soft and pointless option. But of course the PC machine on which I'm writing makes things all that much more possible.

Above and beyond everything there is this indefinable sense of calm by way of contrast to the generally overpopulated and hugely materialist turmoil of the world outside. Here the people generally have a smile and a wave for you - even have the inclination to remember your face and perhaps even your name.

In 2001 we discussed all the possibilities on the long drive home to Winchester and we continued to discuss them during the subsequent weeks whilst Stuart and Lorraine tidied things up for us in Bahrain before themselves returning to England, ending up in the appropriately named Carefree Cottage in the heart of a pretty Dorset woodland.

Almost exactly one year later we were to make our move north. But there are one or two episodes of this before that!

65. Ashes and new fires

In September 2001, for the second time in my life I had crashed down to earth. My businesses in the Middle East were in ruins. Gone the way of all things. I would claim this was through no fault of my own but it doesn't hurt to face reality. Inevitably it's all down to oneself. The decisions that led up to my reversals in the Middle East were my own. They say that to be a really top entrepreneurial businessman you have to bankrupt yourself at least once. I had not actually achieved such a painful distinction but had now come uncomfortably close to it!

I had learned at an early age that crying over spilt milk really is for babies and have often been heard to say that none of us deal all our own cards; it's just about how we go about playing them. Besides, we had enjoyed thirteen good or very good and profitable years and had lived exceptionally well in consequence.

After a month back in Laundry Cottage from the Middle East I had a phone call from one of my most important Saudi clients; another Arab gentleman who I would certainly have called my friend. Would I care to join him for breakfast in Dusseldorf at the Packaging Exhibition ? Of course. However I well understood that Abdullah Obeikan didn't want me to join him simply for some kind of boy to boy chat. He knew I work for money like everyone else and nobody wants to drag me out to Germany unless he's after something monetary so I suggested a fee of £4,000. No problem. Mr Obeikan spent most of the time trying to persuade me to go back to Saudi - even Bahrain - for a meet and make up with my ex-sponsor, Faisal. Well, no bloody way! Firstly because I wouldn't enjoy the risk of becoming the second bite of anybody's cherry, second because I would rather have hired a hit man for the cost of the air fare (joking, Faisal!) and third, most important of all, because our new and better life was just beginning to dawn on us. Unless something fairly juicy happened for Bibs-industry here in the UK we would be migrating to the northern Highlands of bonny Scotland. Whatever happened I would never again set foot in Arabia, a region where I had close-up knowledge of the majority of hotels, airports, cities and towns and relevant companies. Although I had much for which to be grateful in the Middle East I had no wish to renew my acquaintance with the place.

In the event nothing overly good did happen for me in the UK over that post- Middle East twelvemonths. I had a few little touches and some promising nibbles but nothing to divert us from our vision of life in the Highlands. Tell the truth I wasn't really trying. In July 2002 we placed an advertisement in the Gairloch and District Times ... *'Wanted to rent. Cottage close to the sea for writer, his wife and two well-behaved dogs ...* We had three replies, so we entrained for Inverness, hired ourselves a little car and drove across the hills in search of a new home. One place proved to be ridiculously small although had the saving grace of being close to a hotel and bar, one was OK but we didn't much like the sound of the owner (anyone who ever mentioned Mrs Thatcher's iniquitous short term rental contract was at once kicked into touch,) and the third was Peace Cottage in Mellon Charles, just along the coast from Aultbea. It was considerably dilapidated, especially when compared with our Headbourne Worthy home of thirteen years but seemed capable of much low cost upgrading besides being beautifully situated in the middle of a sheep croft close to the sealoch called Ewe.

Having done the deal with the cottage's owner, Brenda Peace, we returned by overnight bus (a salutary experience all by itself) to Portsmouth via Glasgow and London. Back at home it was clear that we had accumulated far, far too much in the way of furniture and accoutrements over our years in Laundry Cottage. We therefore had a couple of successful garage sales plus our very first excursions into the exotic world of the car boot sale.

I'll not forget in a hurry being directed to our 'pitch' at Winchester's very large weekly car boot sale by an equally large lady who might have done extremely well as an Auschwitz prison guard. The minute that woman moved away from us a host of rapacious looking gents turned up to inspect our stock with eagle eye. One of them offered us twenty quid for a box of books. Delighted with such an early success Dee took the cash, whereupon Mrs Auschwitz came running or waddling back, loudly accusing Dee of 'trading before opening time' - a crime of which we were ignorant, even if guilty, as evidenced by my lady having the offending twenty pound note clutched in her hand! Dee was very frightened. How come? Well, she was being physically pinned up against a brick wall at the time and she hadn't even said a word! Me, I was too astonished to raise a finger, a fact that later got me into some trouble of my own!

Poor Delia! Her precious household goods and chattels being whittled away for cash in hand. She didn't actually wave them a tearful goodbye but I know she would have felt like it.

Removal day came: September 1, 2002. Stuart and his friend Fraser had rented a seventeen metre furniture pantechnicon for us, which just about made it through Laundry Cottage's gateway if only after some necessary tree surgery. The stuff we had calculated would fit into Peace Cottage was quite literally squeezed into this massive vehicle and our two young men (only one of whom actually had an HGV licence!) set off on the seven hundred mile northbound trek. I gave them a three hour start, figuring we would overtake them somewhere near Glasgow.

At last Dee had finished cleaning the house to her satisfaction, the dogs were safely bedded down in the back of the Grand Cherokee and we said goodbye, not without some emotion to our home of thirteen turbulent, wonderful years. I pressed the starter button. Nothing! Dead battery. Eventually I summoned our neighbours and friends, a pair of retired doctors blessed with a set of jump leads. Finally we were off up Bedfield Lane for the last time, Dee and I not knowing whether to laugh or cry, scared that the engine would stall on the first roundabout. It didn't. That engine was to remain alive and active until next mid-morning when we pulled up outside our new home. Needless to say, the boys with truck had been there for hours and had by then piled almost all of our stuff willy-nilly into the cottage. They set off back to Hampshire as soon as we arrived. The got there, I was later told, at crack of dawn to return a presumably exhausted vehicle to its owners. I shudder to think of what superspeed trucking record they must have set up.

The boys off and away, in silence we looked around at the mess. My heart sank. *I'm just going to walk the dogs on the beach,* Dee said, quietly then, almot as an afterthought, *Oh, my lovely Laundry Cottage.* The Jeep actually started for her and away they went. I set about clearing enough space at least to sleep, convinced that my wife would before the day was closed be demanding an immediate return south. It was raining a light rain and the midges were up. When Dee and the dogs returned she looked at me, grinning. (Funny how the Highlands' insect life never really troubled her) She'd been chatting to a New Zealand lady on the beach. *Come on, Bryan,* she now suggested; *Let's go into Gairloch for some fish and chips.* In that cafe we made friends with another couple who, that very same day, had 'migrated' to Aultbea from, I think, Manchester. From the cafe window we looked out over a classic multicoloured Wester-Ross sunset. One that, for we two weary travellers might really have been a sunrise. Without saying so there and then, we both knew within ourselves that nevermore were we to live anywhere other than in this 'remore' place.

We had five thousand two hundred and ten pounds in our bank account and a couple of quite small pensions for income. But we had zero debt, our dogs Sorosh and Mati, a whole new and beautiful world full of wild provender for those who would seek it out, a whole new and beautiful life, the release of some kind of long-frustrated talent to write and to paint - and best of all of course we had each other.

And that, my friends, is one hell of a lot.

66. Rich and poor

I've been relatively rich and relatively poor. Which is best? Well, I guess I've treated those two imposters just the same. (Sorry about that, Rudyard!) But for the first time in many years our first months in

Mellon Charles, Aultbea, Wester-Ross needed to be - to say the least, frugal. I recall checking the outside electricity meter of Peace Cottage most days in all weathers, hypnotised by the steady tick tick ticking away of our slender resources. We rationed telephone calls to our distant family and collected as much wild fare as we could to supplement our food shopping. Succulent mussels from the rocks and cockles from the beaches and rocks that fringe the sea lochs, juicy fat blackberries from the wild tangle (within two months of arrival Dee had twenty or so jars of bramble jelly in the store cupboard) and four kinds of mushrooms from the local woodlands. What kind of mushrooms? Hedgehog, chanterelle, oyster, and most precious of all - those fat penny buns, or porcini, or ceps, depending upon what part of Europe you're in. I would have liked to add fish from the sea and the lochs but, as you will understand later, other things had to take priority over fishing, Like, racking up something in the pennies-in department. Besides, we had no longer any boat.

Two things we never economised on: the right food for our beloved pair of hungarian vizslas, Mati and Sorosh, and our daily one to two hour walks in all weathers, every single day without fail. Because Sorosh was not overly other dog friendly and because Dee had a horror of upsetting their owners we never walked the pathways, preferring to set off across the unknown, trackless terrain. Fortunately there is a great deal of that around here. When we set off without map or compass we had no idea how far we would go (or be able to go) or what we might find along the way. Over the coming years we were to 'discover' many places without sign of human presence, places where we would sit on a favorite river or burnside bank or bloody great boulder or fallen tree to eat the sandwiches and drink the soup or coffee we had invariably brought with us. Often we would sit there in a contented silence, much affected by the sheer beauty of what most would call wilderness. After my lady died I commemorated these walks - for myself if nobody else - in this poem …

I see her still

I see her still, and will
so long as I have seeing eyes alive
to the hills we walked,
with those beloved dogs.
So many, many lovely days;

so many, many trackless ways.
The hills are winter muted now,
their lovely colours sombre
as if in respect or tribute
to she who, leaving me alone,
embarked on that adventure
that all that lives must know,
this harder, emptier year ago.

I see her still, and will
so long as I have seeing eyes alive
to the stony, bouldery shores
or riverside woods
where we would each day
in all weathers find a seat
to eat our picnic lunch
often in silence, content
to watch the play of light,
oft-times the drift of rain or snow
on hill or moving water, smile at
the play of otters, divers, others,
listening to the crying of the gulls.

I see her still, and will
so long as I have seeing eyes alive
to the crystal seas of Wester-Ross
cold, clear, summertime blue,
'remote', where she would
take off her clothes and, breathless,
slip nymph-like in to swim,
framed by deep, dark-waving weeds,
laughing at me, at the cold;
or for the simple joy of it,
lithe mermaid in a perfect zone,
the one, forever gone
that we had made our own.

It was inevitably a slow process learning to adjust our lifestyle. We learned about a different dimension of time that's imperceptible to a holiday visitor. No point in dashing out for a loaf of bread or a newspaper. Once you're in the village store or the post office conversation is near bound to ensue. But hey, such dalliance may seem inconsequential but it is never a waste of time for it is how you live. And we already knew that if one is not to offend the local folk there's to be neither sight nor sound of any kind of working on The Sabbath.

After three months came our first Christmas and the much more important New Year's Eve (Hogmanay to we incomers). We sent out to the family a lot of home made Christmas presents - boxes of the local delicacy known as 'tablet' - a kind of fudge that Dee became a past master at making. Max and his Spanish girlfriend had come across to stay with us over the holidays. That first proper Highlands Hogmanay was a memorable experience. The routine here in Aultbea is quite time honoured. About nine pm you go to the hotel for a pint or several then wander across the road to the village hall - a relic of WW2 when this area became home to thousands of servicemen in need of rest and relaxation. The hall was jam packed with people from age about ten to about ninety, all rocking and rolling and highland flinging in wild abandon fuelled by wine and whisky and beer in plastic cups. Good home-baked cakes as well as traditional neeps and tatties was on offer (mashed up turnips and boiled potatoes - delicious!).

At about one a.m. Dee realised there had been no Auld Lang Syne, therefore no linking of handsor stomping in and out, etc. Most puzzling. But the following night we took Max and his Ava to our favourite Badachro Inn. The party seemed to be still going strong in there. We got into conversation with a young soldier on leave, a lad from a local family. Dee asked him about this lack of a midnight Auld Lang Syne. *Where were you?* he asked us. *Aultbea* we said. He shook his head; *On no, that's a Jacobite song. You won't hear it over there.* Of course none of us realised that Robert Burns, who wrote the famous song, was legendarily a secret Roman Catholic - or for that matter that Aultbea was a strongly Protestant village. I still don't entirely believe that young soldier, mind; but neither would I disbelieve him. History lives on up here.

I had set to with much vim and vigor to make Peace Cottage our home, making many small upgrtadings to the property as well as over filling it with our own furniture. Anyway by that first Christmastide we were well and very comfortably settled. Time then to find a way to bring in the pennies and the pounds if we were ever to lift ourselves above subsistence. So I developed a plan of sorts; one that would take us from major to minor in the demanding world of business. But the rules of the game remain the same.

67. Getting to know you

As incoming 'Sassenachs' desiring assimilation into the Aultbea community the best things we could have done were done by force of accident. To earn a few pennies, therefore have butter and even a little jam on our daily bread Dee got a job as a cleaner at Aultbea's Isle View Care Home. As all the other lady employees were 'locals' and Dee was a natural maker of friends we were soon in the swing of things. Her work wasn't easy of course. One of the Care Home's residents was a Gaelic speaking old lady who didn't like the English - even to the extent of locking my wife in the broom cupboard - but who ended up by being tolerant, even friendly, even to me! That lady was the one who as a nineteen year old student had travelled down to London one cold December day in the '50's in an unheated Morris Minor along with three male undergraduates, their objective being ONLY to 'steal' the Stone of Scone from under the throne in Westminster Abbey and transport it back to its rightful home in Perth, Scotland. Scottish kings from time immemorial had been crowned on the Stone of Scone, as had UK kings and queens since the Union in seventeen something) Amazingly their plan actually worked. Was / is it customary to leave Westminster Abbey's massive front doors unlocked? I wonder. In due course the forces of Law caught up with the miscreants and the 'Stone' was returned to London. Nonetheless Dee's new friend confided in her that the stone taken back by the authorities was not the real one. The real Stone of Scone was / is still, she said, hidden away somewhere in its rightful home - Scotland!

Dee didn't have to be a cleaner for all that long - maybe our first couple of years in the Highlands, after which I was able to earn a bit from my paintings - but we had many memorable - even enjoyable experiences in and around The Isle View. For instance whenever a resident achieved the ripe old age of one hundred years - not all that uncommon these day - there would be a gathering of staff and residents and friends in the main hall. The Lord Lieutenant of the County or his / her deputy would come across the hills bearing Her Majesty the Queen's legendary letter of congratulation for formal presentation to the new centenarian. Well, on this occasion Her Worship the Lord Lieutenant made her speech on behalf of H.M., stepped forward to the recipient's wheelchair and held out the letter, upon which the old lady refused it with the immortal comment; "I never did like that woman". Embarrassed silence all around followed by some rather forced light laughter.

The second best thing we did (again by accident) was to move into Peace Cottage, situated between two working crofts that were and are owned and run by the Beaton brothers. Peace Cottage was our rented home for the first four years of our Highlands life. Harold and Ian and Ian's wife Fiona proved to be the best of friends to us - i.e. the kind of friends who are there when you need them and leave you to your own devices at other times. For instance we had discovered, on moving in, that our expensive three piece Tetra suite would not fit through the narrow passageway from front door into living room, therefore we had to stow it in a leaky old open fronted cowshed out back. A few days later I explained the situation to Harold Beaton who at once went off to fetch his tools then returned with his customary economy of words in order to remove the entire dining room window, frame and all! The next thing I knew, our suite was safely in the living room and the window was back in place, good as new. Ian and Fiona (who worked and still does work at the Isle View Care Home) have a daughter called Rebecca - Bex for short. Bex took a real shine to Dee, and vice versa, especially after the twelve years old fell off her bike outside in our shared driveway. Dee rushed out to administer first aid and soothing words. The next day a large bar of chocolate appeared through our letter box.

In, I think, 2004 Dee's / our son Rudi and partner Nina decided to get married. To our delight they chose to have the ceremony carried out up here in the Aultbea Hotel. A great many lads and lassies from seven hundred miles south came up with them and occupied most of the available B&B accomodation. All our new friends, both local and incomer, were invited to the wedding. This mixture of near and far worked amazingly well and an extremely good time was had by all. Only a very few minor hitches such as Dee forgetting to bring the actual documentation to the hotel, in which waited the congregation plus a reverend who had clearly been at the celebrations a little early. I was despatched home for the papers. In something of a world record hurry, on my return I backed into the hotel wall much to the surprise of the congregation assembled inside.

That very first February I took out my pastels and 'painted' a winter snowscene. I called it *Across Isle Ewe*, for it is the view from Peace Cottage. The croft house in the middle distance is now the very successful Aultbea Smokehouse. I sold the original pastel to Mamie and Duncan, a couple with a second home in Gairloch. They became good friends over the years. But before that I had created a series of twelve Highlands Wildlife pictures using a method that involved me creating literally hundreds, even thousands of digitally coloured, custom, Word Draw 'shapes'. I exhibited them at a crafts market printed as greetings cards. That was in Ullapool. I managed to take eight pounds and fifty pence! Not long afterwards I did a sales tour of the local shops, not easy because, although I had spent a lifetime as a professional marketeer/salesman, I really did and do find it difficult selling my own creative works. Extoling the merits of my own work comes close to bragging, which does not come easily, perhaps because it was always high on the list of 'things not to do' at Abingdon School. Notwithstanding all that, with what quiet pride did I get home and drop more than four hundred pounds in paper money on the dining room table in front of an astonished, not to say delighted Delia! Our income tap was once again turned on, albeit with but a trickle, but I had big ideas - of course I did - and what a place in which to have them!

68. Oh, mine papa!

Throughout the first decade of this century Dee and I would quite often travel south from our new home/s in Wester-Ross to visit our families, sometimes separately and sometimes together. Although neither of us wished to live in our childrens' pockets we certainly wanted to keep well in touch with their lives and to ensure they had a good understanding of ours in return. But that was never easy for our lives had not been in any way 'normal' and it was certainly not normal to upsticks and migrate the best part of a thousand miles away to a new life and a new lifestyle at our kind of age, (sixty eight in my case, fifty eight in Dee's). But distance didn't matter. Also, as an early nest-vacater myself, I knew all about flying out from under the wing of mummy and daddy, but this time voluntarily and hopefully without loss of parental love.

My step-mother, Julia, had died in her eighties whilst resident in a Hastings Care Home. At her funeral Liz, one of Julia's nurse / carers approached me. *Don't worry about your father, Bryan,* she told me, *I'll make sure he won't be on his own.* She wasn't kidding! Before long the two of them were taking sea cruises together and then when he could no longer travel in comfort, no problem, Liz went on taking the cruises solo or with her daughter, naturally at father's expense. Taking more than cruises, actually. Be that as it may, by around 2005 it became clear that my ninety four years old dad was heading in the same direction as had his second wife. He couldn't possibly sustain himself by himself for much longer in his seaside apartment. Several times he fell over, suffering hip and other bone damage as a result and having great difficulty in obtaining any help. Several times he was consigned to spells in hospital. Therefore with his agreement I spent some time looking for the best place in or around Hastings in which he might in comfort end his days.

At this point I have to say that there had never been overmuch of the aforementioned parental love between father and I, although I must also add that we were probably closer together in the few years leading up to his death that at any time previously. Why should such disharmony have been? I think it went back to my boyhood perception of him as something of an ill-tempered tyrant. The days he returned to my mother, my three sisters and myself at home in Lancashire from his work in London - they were seldom if ever happy and all too often involved much angry shouting. Also, I probably blamed father for the loss of the mother to whom I had been very close throughout the war years.

I think my placement at age eleven in a public (boarding) school paid for by my wealthy Auntie Kay was at first not a happy time for me and a source of some scarcely concealed humiliation for father. All his life his brainy and equally good looking elder sister had outperformed him. But perhaps one reason above all was my failure to properly accept my step mother, his new partner, now wife, Julia nee Wicksteed. Then again, at Abingdon School I did OK but I let the family down (father's words) by my failure to shine either as Olympic class sportsman or academician summa cum laude. Having said that I astonished him and perhaps even myself by the high grades I achieved in obtaining my School Leaving Certificate.

As I have related the final estrangement came a couple of years after leaving Abingdon when I was coming up seventeen and father shot off with Julia to a new civil service position in Singapore, leaving me to enlist in the R.A.F for an early-entry National Service - actually for want of anywhere else to go. And, by the way, leaving my sister Shirley to rush into an exceedingly bad, much premature marriage in Newmarket. Both of us had emphatically been labelled *not wanted on voyage*.

Whilst stationed in R.A.F. Full Sutton, not far outside York, I met and fell passionately in love with beautiful Joan Wood. In those days one needed to seek parental permission to marry if one was under the age of twenty one. Father of course was consumed from afar with rage or disappointment, probably both. I don't know whether he was expecting his son to marry into the aristocracy or something. At any rate he showed no sign of fatherly congratulations, much less interest in my hoped for bride to be. He wrote me a long letter in reply to mine enclosing not a penny piece of the possibly expected although unasked for support, plus not a little condemnation and much advice - for advice read instruction - to the effect that, when I had finished a-serving of Her Majesty the new Queen I should at once apply to join the police force. Advice which I chose to ignore, as those of you who may have been reading these episodes will already know.

Don't get me wrong, my father was a fine figure of a man who some had earlier compared to the film star Ronald Colman. He had, as they say, 'a way with him'. His main interests were, in descending order, sitting on his apartment balcony in the shortest of short shorts watching young ladies parading along the promenade or cavorting on the beach, betting on horse races and the incredibly, unbelievably boring ex-nurse, Liz. Oh, I almost forgot; and the three local housewives with part time jobs as 'chiropodists' who visited him in turn, once fortnightly, at a cost according to his post-death bank statements of fifty smackers a throw. I had no problem with the latter; probably indeed a little admiration! His life, his money.

Anyway I found father the perfect Care Home, fixed everything up and went back north. When came the day for his occupation I entrained again for Hastings and proceeded directly to the Home from the railway station, expecting to find him comfortably ensconced and holding court. It was not to be. The ninety five years old had arrived earlier that day, sure, but had excused himself and promptly 'disappeared' according to an offended and much panicky matron! I went straight back to his supposedly vacated apartment. He was there of course, acting as if nothing had happened. He told me he hadn't liked the place after all, so had walked out through the kitchen door, flagged down a passing motorist and had been given a lift 'back home'. I once again did the rounds of Hastings and St Leonards Care Homes. This time he stayed in the one I found for him - and I stayed close by for three days to make sure he did. Some weeks later, during one of my regular phone calls he assured me that; *this place is good, son. I get washed down naked every day by two Chinese ladies.*

I organised father's funeral. It was sparsely attended by myself and my two surviving sisters plus Auntie Peggy and her daughter, my cousin, plus lucky Liz and her daughter, each of whom enjoyed a share equal to ours in dad's tiny estate. Oh, and touchingly the two Chinese nurses were there at the crematorium. I wrote and delivered his eulogy. It was not easy but, strangely, I loved the man more as he lay in his coffin alongside me and then went on his way into the furnace, and the unknown, than at any other time. Was he or was I the more responsible for our lifetime lack of mutual affection and also that towards my siblings. I shall never know. You didn't talk about such matters, did you? More is the pity. *To be or not to be may be the question,* father, but every man surely must merit the memory.

69. And the livin' is easy

As I have reported we made the fairly dilapidated Peace Cottage into a very much loved home between 2002 and 2006. What furnishings we had not brought up with us I mostly made, starting with my work bench and our extensive bookcases. Downstairs was our living room / dining room, a front room (that became Dee's mother Wynne's bed sitter, see later), a minute kitchen even if for several months with no cooker we needed to rely on our microwave and a shower room / toilet.

The Beaton brothers, crofters both, living one to either side filled us in on the history of the cottage. How fascinating it was. Peace Cottage had until recently been the Beaton family home since way back. Remember that in the days before and after the Great War this whole area was to a large extent gaelic speaking and needed to be largely self supporting. Everything you wanted or that needed repair you either did for yourself or got a more skilled neighbour to do for you. Bartering was the way to live. Labour saving domestic appliances were mostly in the future even 'down south' never mind up here, where electricity was yet to come. These were, and I think still are people of considerable strength, resilience, resourcefulness and bravery. It is to me no coincidence that the male Highlander had supplied half the warrior armies of Europe with kilted merceneries throughout earlier times.

A stream - or 'burn' as they say up here - ran in its deep, timeworn channel to the sea within five metres of our front door. Ian Beaton, a man I would guess twenty five years younger than me, pointed out the flat rock in the bed of that stream on which their mother had beaten / washed the family laundry. And Harold Beaton told us how, when the boys were little there had been no extension to the rear of the cottage, as today, therefore no bathroom or kitchen as such. He and his brother had assisted their father in adding such niceties to the building by bringing rocks up from the beach for the construction of walls. The trouble was that for some years afterwards the family needed to go outside and round in the open to access the new facilities because at that early stage they had provided no doorway access from inside! Of course nobody needed or wanted planning permissions, therefore nobody had drawn up plans either for their self-built houses or their property at large. The Crofting Laws in the mid eighteen hundreds went some way to establishing an English style land registration but to this day land boundaries are sometimes a source of irritable and most often unnecessary dispute.

Within a couple of years I had generated enough of an income from my painting, greetings cards, etc, to necessitate a return acquaintance with Her Majesty's Customs and Excise! What is it they say about that pair of unpleasant unavoidables - death and taxes? By then I had finished my digital wildlife series, painted a couple of dozen pastel landscapes and also a miscellany of oils on canvas.

At that point arose a problem in the shape of Dee's mum. Wynne Boulter, nee Smalley had always been very close to her daughter, Delia, and vice versa. Although Dee often flew south to visit her aging mum s it became very clear that the old lady missed her daughter very much. Also that she was suffering those scourges of modern old age - leg ulcers and incipient dementia. Like my father it became clear that she could no longer live in safety by herself in her Alverstoke home of some fifty years. Dee and her elder sister, Gloria, eventually found her a Care Home in place of the hospital bed to which she had in the end been consigned. She hated it and said how desperately she wanted to come live with us in Peace Cottage in spite of the fact that she had never been any further north than her Birmingham birthplace; unless to Belfast as a wartime WREN.

So we rented a motorhome from a company with the unlikely name of *Robin's Reliable Wrecks*, mistakenly thinking the name a bit of a clever irony - until the rear door fell off our ancient vehicle halfway up the hill coming south out of Inverness with another seven hundred miles to go! Never mind, that vehicle eventually served to bring Wynne north in relative comfort.

On the way south we stopped overnight in Chesterfield where I was presented at a major ceremony with a national an award; my very first, for my short story, *Speaking of Champions*.

Wynne settled down remarkably quickly at first, especially as a trio of district nurses did more for her leg ulcers in a couple of months that the entire Hampshire NHS had achieved in a couple of years. My abiding memories of 'Winnie' are legion, for she was what used to be called 'a real character'. I so well recall her propelling her wheelchair down the driveway to park alongside our little lochside road, where she (an ex wartime WREN as she never forgot to tell people) would sit gazing over the sea in the forlorn hope of seeing 'at least a small warship', its crew lined up on deck as per the tradition on entering Portsmouth Harbour. A couple of times a week I would take her to the Isle View Care Home where she could consort with her peers in the main hall. But she was a very strong willed old lady, was Wynne. She requisitioned a special chair. Woebetide any other old person who parked themselves in it before we arrived. One day I sensed there would be trouble ahead when a lady of one hundred and four summers was found to be in 'her' chair. Wynne was only ninety two but I could hardly believe my eyes on seeing her lifting the protesting centenarian by the armpits from 'her' chair on to another one!

After six months, out of the blue Wynne came out with the immortal pronouncement *I want to go home. If I never see another bloody mountain or another sheep I shall be happy.* Not everyone, you see, is easily transplanted! We found her a lovely place in Fareham. It was expensively called the *Merry Hall* Nursing Home and it was to cost her daughters all of their mother's three hundred thousand pounds of savings. That was another irony although I suppose it was as Merry as any such resting place could possibly be. I recall the dozens of fluffy toy animals crowding her daytime bed and, long before Merry Hall, the motor car in which she invested almost human qualities. I can still see the electric buggy in which she travelled, purple cape a'flying down Gosport High Street with such an imperious lack of concern for the following traffic. She point blank refused to use the pavement. I can see that immaculate, flower-filled garden at 26 Madden Close and I can see her beach hut on Stokes Bay outside of which she would sit in the summer sunshine talking with any and every passer-by, often blue of hair and dressed - well … let's just say 'strikingly'.

When we visited Merry Hall, often with Gloria and her husband Peter, we used to light some spark, where there really was no fire left, by breaking into some of the old wartime songs - *White Cliffs of Dover, We'll Meet Again* etc. At such times she would talk about Dee's father, Bill, and her Lancaster bomber pilot brother, shot down and eventually killed over Munich in the latter days of the war. And on one occasion she told us all about the great ocean liner she had been watching as it traversed the urban landscape outside her window - five miles from the nearest sea!

'When I am an old woman I shall wear purple,' wrote the poetess Jennie Joseph … . *'And I'll gobble up samples in shops and press alarm bells and run my stick along the public railings'.* Maybe not quite in those ways but with similar intent, that was very much my mother-in law, the unforgettable Mrs Wynne Boulter.

70. On the move again

I told you how, six months after settling her in with us at Peace Cottage Dee's mother, Wynne, having already become something of a local character, pronounced - quite out of the blue ... *Oh, if I never see another bloody mountain or another sheep again - I want to go home* and how, in collusion with Dee's sister Gloria we found her a fine en suite room in Fareham's *Merry Hall Care Home*. The transmigration was accomplished by me packing all the old lady's goods and chattels with the two dogs into the Jeep and setting off at six a.m on the 700 mile trek south. A couple of hours later Dee and Wynne took a taxi to Inverness and then a first class train to Southampton. I actually had time to unload at the Care Home before going with Gloria and Peter to meet mother and daughter on arrival at Southampton rail station. It was then ten p.m. Wynne came bouncing off that train, a woman re-kindled. Personally I was exhausted! Our pair of hungarian vizslas were good as gold, perhaps sensing in the mysterious ways of dogs that they were at least temporarily back on home turf.

Back inWester-Ross on our real home turf I set about marketing my artworks as cards etc with renewed energy, much aided and abetted by Dee, now resigned from her Isle View Care Home duties and doing the accounts, manning our marketplace stalls etc. Our tide had once more turned. We and our two dogs, although now visibly ageing, were indeed very happy. Good food, much of it local provender, a regime of different daily 'walks', an abundance of love, the simple life and lots of genuine friends - why would we not be happy?

At this point the contentment was inadvertently shattered by our widowed ladlady and good friend, Brenda, who understandably decided to sell her big old 'Kirkhill' manse house. As a result she needed to occupy her / 'our' Peace Cottage. We were therefore out, albeit at six months notice. This was the first and to date the only time any landlord/lady had asked us to move. Whilst we were still in the process of cogitating over our situation the phone rang. It was Kitty Wiseman asking us if we would consider her Loch Ewe Cottage for a long term rental? Dee knew Kitty well as they had been working together at the Isle View Care Home. I said, *yes of course we will look at it, and thank you. By the way where are you?* Kitty said, *If you look out of your dining room window, you'll see the cottage just a way up the hill.* We walked up to have a look around, hardly able to believe our luck. Loch Ewe

Cottage was even more perfect than had been Peace Cottage. It was part hidden in a little wooded dell, surrounded by Kitty's and her daughter Ann's sheep, chickens, geese and ducks. It was even nearer the sea shore than Peace Cottage, had plenty of room for work and comfortable living and was a lot better appointed. Perfect. Oh, and no difference in the rental - even more important as the years went on for even though our income was happily increasing, Dee's share of her mothers Will was being steadily eroded down to zero by those Merry Hall Care Home fees. This, genuinely, was never begrudged for we were both more than happy that the lady's final years were of well deserved care and reasonable contentment.

I have no doubt but that our five years in Loch Ewe Cottage were as happy as any years that Dee and I had shared, right up until the day of our dogs' passing. For some time Sorosh had developed pain in his hips as well as bad teeth and severe incontinence. Mati was almost but not quite in as bad a condition. Fifteen is very old for a vizsla. Then one awful morning our poor old lad could not get himself up. Of course, like all animals knowing their end is nigh neither he nor his eqally disabled mate Mati complained. But Sorosh looked at me through filmy eyes and I looked at him and at Mati and both of us looked again at both of them and we all knew ... I called the vet. He examined old Sorosh and shook his head and said that in his opinion Mati was close behind, would it not be kinder for them to go as they had lived - i.e. together? I held our boy and Dee held our girl as they each in turn received the fatal injection. The vet took what was of their earthly remains away with him in black plastic sacks. Even as I type this I cannot deny the tears. Look, I do not ever want to compare sadnesses but we had truly loved those dogs, those wondrous fellow creatures who had been with us through thick and thin from birth to death, the fellow creatures who so many, many times had lightened our darkness.

We buried the caskets containing their ashes in the beach-side hillock where the ashes of old Seth and Chloe had fifteen long years before been placed. May the four of them always run the sands together. One can always hope... even can believe.

71. Telling tales - finding words

I wrote many short stories between 2003 and 2006. Dee said they were for practice ahead of my first completed novel but I took each and every one of those stories very seriously in their own right. Two of them won prestigious national awards. *Speaking of Champions* and *Willie's Place* are included in my anthology, *Twenty Bites*, ISBN 978-0-9555193-3-8

Actually I had started and had completed 80,000 words or three quarters of an unfinished novel I called Rose Feather all the way back in 1993. (That typescript still resides within my PC. The other day I pulled it up on screen and had a look at it. Hey, I think it's really good! One day I hope to dust it off and carry on.

But in 2004 I finally got around to writing my first fully finished novel. It is called *More Deaths Than One*. When we came north Dee knew I was planning a novel with a certain deepky probing theme, however she had urged me to write a thriller first; hopefully to make some money! The back cover 'blurb' of MDTO reads ... *Thomas Thornton has settled down to expatriated family life in Saudi Arabia. He is wrongfully caught up in shariah law on drugs dealing charges but finds himself implicated in a far more universal situation. Injustice is a bitter pill - potentially a fatal one where your landing card is headlined in red italics: 'Death For Drugs Dealers'. Even with a past life as explosive as that of Thomas Thornton's, what odds against a future for himself, his family; what of his love for the ways of Arabia?*

When you finish the writing and then the interminable editing, re-editing and re-re-editing (etc) of a serious full length novel there is almost as much pride and satisfaction with your new baby as with the real thing - particularly if that first copy for retail has been produced by a 'proper' publisher.

Alas, I was to find out the hard way that getting one of the mainstream publishers to accept (perhaps even actually to read) a typescript authored by an ageing, first time novelist is something with a degree of difficulty akin to swimming up a waterfall! After the best part of a year of trying I gave in and decided to go the self publishing route. This of course entails its own unique and thorough understanding of digital technology, and of book layout, and (in my case) of cover design; and not least of being accepted as a serious writer / publisher by the international digital printer *Lightning Source plc*. And all this is but a prelude to that little thing called marketing! Anyway after failing to interest a mainstream publisher for me it was back to school time! Anyone can learn the technology who wants to try hard enough. More *Deaths Than One*, ISBN 978-0-9555193-2-1 is the first result, and one of which I am very proud.

I sent out a copy for review to a few national newspapers without hearing anything back, even whether they had been received, but the editor of the the Ross-shire Journal was more encouraging. His published review got my sales off to a flying start. Copies still to this day dribble out in ones and twos whilst never reaching the hoped for hundreds and thousands. And still to this day I receive the odd e-mailed comment from somebody who might have found a second hand copy somewhere and enjoyed the reading of it. It is still in print and available, as they say, from Amazon or all good bookstores (quote the ISBN) or as an e-book. Ditto the two non-fiction booklets *On Wester-Ross in 24 Paintings, Poems and Narratives* and *A Life in the Highlands in 24 Paintings, Poems and Narratives*. And ditto my second anthology of short fiction, *Twelve of Diamonds* and my second full length novel, *Going with Gabriel* - the one I had planned to write first until Dee effectively demoted it! GwG received much encouraging comment from people whose opinion I respect, including that in a very nice hand written letter from Sir David Attenborough.

As I write this episode of my autobiography I am close to finishing a third novel, one that I began to write in 2009. So what? So why? I have no idea. It cannot be for money - the chances of fame and fortune, even if that is what I seek are slim indeed. But I just looked up one of my old poems. Perhaps in this lies the answer ....

> **Finding Words**
> *After sixty years*
> *Focussing on right now*
> *I found the two fine walkers*
> *Coleridge and his friend*
> *Mr William Wordsworth,*
> *Had a brief skirmish with*
> *That other wondrous set,*
> *The dreamer Keats, the*
> *Poetic mister Shelley*

And the bad Lord B,
Went backwards in time
Through Swift and Pope
And Dryden to blind Milton
In his metronomically
Agonistic anti-Paradise
To find my friend John Donne,
A love-struck island to himself,
The whiff of something
Of great meaning thus
Becoming ever obvious;
Like incense
As the swinging starts.

Breathless, reading much of
Elizabethan stuff and such
I circled Shakespeare,
But warily, for a long while
Keeping nervous distance
Unsure about this Everest
Or maybe of my ability
To climb it or find the light
That so many others find,
Went back a long stride
But Chaucer was too tough,
Loved Spencer's Faerie Queen
Then fell on Tamburlaine,
From reckless Marlow and,
Ah! Here it is, (I thought,)
The source! that river
Of sweet scented mists
Still coiled and flowed
And thrust and heaved
And his words lived
And in his halcyon shade
I lay and took my rest awhile
And read how Shakespeare
Was perhaps Marlowe
Come live with me and be my love
They or some one wrote.
Although to me it mattered

Only that their words were.

And then in Winchester
In the dust-silent attic
Of that antiquarian book shop
Logan Pearsall-Smith's
Jewel of a treatise,
On Reading Shakespeare,
Lay opened in my hand
As when something flashed
Brightly in a muddy field
And you stooped to pick it up
And you were looking
Into the bright sun-colours
Of a diamond.

And so the good professor
Opened up the door
Switched on the lights
And there for me that wondrous treasury
Of works to brighten up my days
To hold an explanation for my nights.:
Thus, in the beginning,
Were his Words.

I have a feeling I might have registered this poem previously. If so, no apologies. It is relevant here.

72. Animal magic

I think I've said previously that from 2005 Kitty and Ann Wiseman's Loch Ewe Cottage represented, for us - especially Dee, some sort of heaven on earth. The old cottage was coal-fire cosy, situated close by the lochside and in a secluded spot within the same remote, tiny village of Mellon Charles as was Peace Cottage. It had a very reasonable rental and even, as it later transpired, an option to buy. We had all our own furniture, books, pictures etc - in other words all the stuff we had brought up from Winchester in 2002. Ranking as a benefit equal to all those for my lady, we were surrounded by the Wiseman's croft animals.

Bearing in mind that hungarian vizslas are by breeding and nature hunting dogs and that they had been brought up in an urban Hampshire setting, there had been in Peace Cottage a fair amount of necessary 're-training'. Most especially when first the two of them set eyes on sheep, chickens, geese and ducks - not to mention the odd (wild) red deer - just by our back door! But in a surprisingly short time all threatening behaviour had ceased and everybody settled down to a life of harmony, or so we thought!

One day we were out visiting, leaving the dogs lazing in the garden sunshine, the back door open into the dining room. We rarely if ever remembered or found it necessary to lock up either our home or our parked car for crime was and is virtually unknown here. However we returned to find Mati, the picture of innocence, as far away on the lawn as she could possibly be and Sorosh, the picture of guilt, trembling under the dining room table surrounded by feathers and one very dead cockerel. We were horrified. Kitty had two cockerels who were always at it tooth and nail and, to my exasperation constantly competing with each other to all-hail the crack of dawn - about 03.30 in the summer! Confronted by the scene of the crime, in somegthing of a panic myself, I determined in true murder mystery fashion to hide the body. As fast as I could drove it miles away and consigned the late lamented to a watery grave. However when I returned home, Dee, conscience stricken as always, insisted I go and confess Sorosh's crime to Kitty. Kitty's main comment was, *where is he? He'll make a goodly soup, so he will*. Upon which I was forced to confess to the greater crime of criminal waste.

On another occasion Kitty told Dee that *something's getting into the barn and taking or eating the eggs*. It so happened that Dee had spotted the miscreant. One of the locally much detested hooded crows had found a hole under the eaves of the building. That same day Kitty went into the barn to collect eggs, hand in hand with her seven year old granddaughter, only to surprise the thief at his criminality. Caught red handed the crow tried to exit the barn at high speed through the opened doorway, upon which a hen jumped high in the air, talons uppermost, and brought the crow to ground. To the horror of the little girl and the delight of Kitty all the chickens then fell upon the thing and literally tore it to pieces in front of their eyes!

Down on the farm truth is often, at least to me, stranger than fiction. As an instance, at one time Ann and Kitty were losing their precious ducks one by one nightly. Very distressing, especially as they had spotted the culprit, the female otter who had given birth to a litter of cubs (kits? otterlets? Not sure of the correct terminology) in her holt) under a broken down old shore-side building. This furry friend had been feeding her family right royally at Kitty and Ann's expense. Anyway, to put a stop to the slaughter the crofter ladies brought the ducks up to a place nearer their house but that same night the bold otteress actually came into their back yard, grabbed a duck and made off with it. Ann was just in time to rush out and take hold of the duck's legs when the poor thing became jammed, being pulled by the retreating otter through a hole in the fence. Ann won that tug of war. That was very much a phyrric victory, for the duck did not survive its ordeal. The next night Ann was lying in wait. When the otter made its appearance she dashed outside, grabbed the nearest throwable object and let fly with a tin of paint. Mrs Otter last seen heading rapidly back to the beach and her holt covered in white!

At lambing time in March Dee would help out Ann, patrolling the fields in the middle of the night to find and help any ewe that was in birthing trouble. I'm afraid I myself would turn over in bed and go back to sleep. Even in broad daylight the birth process is not of interest to me. I never attended the birth of any of my own, by the way. For a supposedly hard-nosed crofter Kitty was incredibly kind to animals, which is why she always has so many cats and dogs. When a sheep gets injured or knocked over in the road the crofter will usually despatch it without a second thought. Not our Kitty! She would take the creature into her kitchen, which instantly became an operating theatre, and do everything possible and some things impossible to mend it. Some of her sheep she kept for years after their commercial value was well out of date. There was one ewe I remember that she called *Shirley Bassey*. The poor animal had eaten the dreaded poisonous ragwort and therefore had a permanent wool-less sore on its back and only half an ear. But it had lived at least six years in such a condition. Apart from those defects it was an ordinary white woolly ewe. *Why do you call her Shirley Bassey?* Dee asked. *Because she's got curly hair of course,* Kitty responded. Of course; how very obvious! But a couple of years on we noticed Shirley Bassey one winter's day lying comatose in the field, one poor eye a bloody mess. The hoodies had been at it. You can hate those birds. For a time we did but nature will not tolerate infirmity and cares not if we tolerate it ourselves. By the way, with Kitty's help Shirley Bassey made a recovery even from that and lived on for a couple more years.

73. Sunday best

Early on in our Highlands life there were of course some things we missed. These were not necessarily important things; the Sunday newspaper for instance. There were no local shops open on the Sabbath in Aultbea. It was some while before we discovered that the Sundays did in fact reach the area and that you could order yours for collection in the public bar of the Aultbea Hotel. However to pick up your order you needed to run something of a gauntlet. I remember very well my first Sunday morning collection. As per every day we loaded the dogs and our backpacks into the Jeep, ready for our walk up on the hill. On the way I popped into the hotel for the paper leaving Dee waiting in the car - only to find four Wiseman brothers aligned along the bar and their one sister, Pat, serving behind it. All of them turned to examine this sassenach incomer. Obviously finding him fairly harmless the eldest brother, Johnny, offered me a pint of '80 shillings' - the local bitter beer. To be fair it was more than an offer. To decline would not have been a good idea in a village for which the Wisemans sometimes seemed to have a proprietorial inclination. That's when the problem began, for I was clearly expected to reciprocate the hospitailty. Now, I have never been more than what you might call an enthusiastic beer drinker of modest capacity. To buy pints for the brothers without one more (x four!) for myself would have been discourteous! Besides, I found the company increasingly interesting, almost forgetting one wife and two dogs waiting outside for their daily walk. After more than an hour said wife reminded *me*. She came into the bar as I was in the middle of a risky joke, surveyed the scene in a new and frosty silence then demanded the car keys and turned on her heels. Delia walked the dogs over the hill by herself that Sunday whilst I later walked or staggered the three miles home. When I reached there, to prove my (entirely false) sobriety I set to work cutting out my greetings cards, not intending to cut off the tip of my finger in the process. Much blood but little sympathy..

I think it fair to say that most of the locals attend one church or the other whereas only a minority of we incomers do so. One problem was that, even for the religious, the range of local denominations, therefore of actual churches was and remains quite baffling. It seems that whenever in the past there has been a division of theological opinion a new Church has been formed by breakaway and a new church building created to accomodate it. But it has not been unknown for the departing schism to conduct their own services actually in the open air for years before the building took place. There was one well recorded church gathering in a natural rock cave under the cliffs by the village of First Coast and yet another took place in a grassy hollow by the sea in Gairloch - these days a nine-hole golf course; by the way these days overlooked by a monumental stone church large enough for a small town but, as I say only one of severalo local houses of God.

There is a little autobiographical booklet written by Hector Grant, the first part of which is all about the Grant family's growing up in the settlement of Mellon Udrigle prior to world war two. This includes an account of the Grant family walk of some six or seven miles each way to Lords Day church in Aultbea and back, in all weathers, clad in their Sunday best. Recently I was invited by a retired sea captain to accompany him on his boat for a fishing trip.Whilst chugging slowly past Isle Ewe the captain pointed out a certain rock face that sloped down into the sea. This, he told me, was where the stones for one of Aultbea's churches came from. Great slabs had been hand cut from that native rock and slid down directly into a small wooden boat then rowed over one by one to the mainland. Goodness knows how long this process lasted but the large kirk (church) was Hector Grant's family's destination in the 1930's and still of course stands firm and proud. Another reminder that you don't actually need power tools or computers to create a work of lasting magnificence.

That kirk, and the other one opposite the Isle View Care Home, has been the site of many a funeral since our arrival in 2002. Funerals are important events of great solemnity in Aultbea. They have included the funerals of three of the four Wisemans who had been sitting at the bar that first Sunday newspaper day. Such funerals - and the wakes that most often succeed them - command the attendance of large numbers of men and women in black. Virtually the entire community of 'locals' as well as many of we 'incomers' are in attendance out of respect for the departed.

I have commented earlier about my perception of the value of Sunday observance. I can say now, without being a fervent believer in any particular church, that I have have since adolescence always seen the value of a biblical, physical day of rest. By the way, having reached thus far in these autobiographical episodes whilst skirting around the the matter of religion I am happy now to declare my belief in such a phenomenon as a human soul - a soul that could transcend death and attain an afterlife. I feel that such a belief makes for a considerably higher value to one's life on earth. After all, nothing should be worth nothing as may be implied by the title of this book. For me there is absolutely no value in trying to prove one God better than another or one God better than no God - or the reverse - as a kind of game of spiritual one upmanship. We all know what is good and life enhancing about a personal observance of the ten commandments, even if these days it is more than ever difficult to live by those commandments.

By the way I believe the Hebrew scholars mistranslated the crucial word commandments; I think it should be COMMENDMENTS. i.e. 'Recommendations' rather than 'instructions'. JC was not, according to the gospels, given the power to command. Perhaps it would have been best and easier by far if he had. By now we would all be perfect!

74. A touch of the Irish

I wrote about how Brenda Peace had rented her Peace Cottage to us on our arrival in the Scottish Highlands but how in, in I think 2005 she decided to sell her Aultbea manse house (vicarage) called Kirkhill House, thus needing her Peace Cottage to live in. As I have said it didn't take us long to move, literally over the road into Kitty Wiseman's beautiful Loch Ewe Cottage. Had Dee had her way and were she still alive we would be there yet - and probably for evermore. She absolutely loved the place. And so did I until something better came up!

Our good friend Brenda had sold Kirkhill House to the Hickey Brothers, two Irishmen in a substantial way of business living, each with wives and their own families down in the south of England. The brothers had no intention of living in Kirkhill or of even spending much time there but, having carried out some extensive improvements they wanted somebody local to become a sort of visiting janitor. Brenda recommended Delia (and me for what use I would be!) And of course we were glad of the money. Mike and Gerry Hickey are extremely kind and courteous people, as we have realised on many occasions since then. When they turned up in their high powered car at Loch Ewe Cottage to 'interview' Dee the two of them and the two of us and our two doggies didn't leave a lot of space in the living room for the old tea and biscuits, nevertheless we got along famously right from the start. Dee and Gerry in particular shared a deep interest in all things world war one. We had the job!. We would look in on a more or less daily basis to check Kirkhill's security and generally take care of things, for the place was hardly ever to be occupied by its owners.

My Pictures & Poems micro business was by then doing OK. Along with our Kirkhill income and our State pensions and two relatively small private pensions from my seventeen years at Sweetheart International plc - plus now with the Kirkhill supplement - life was financially well balanced enough. In adddition we were kept pleasantly busy, and in addition even to that we were very happy. Or content; I've never been too sure about the difference. Then in 2007 we were offered the sale of Loch Ewe Cottage - and came very close to accepting it. I should explain that Dee and I had often discussed and debated whether it was best for us to rent or to buy. Dee was always in favour of owning house and mortgage whereas for years past I had convinced myself of the advantages in terms of freedom of movement and home economics of renting or leasing - but *only* if one kept well clear of Mrs Thatcher's iniquitously one-sided short term rental contract. We had always, since I had sold our house in Hayling Island to fund Joan's Nursing Home costs, managed to find super properties to lease; properties with owners who respected the difference between what was *their* house butg *our* home, owners who realised that we were not about to degrade their property and who had no aversion to dogs or cats and who were willing to negotiate a private form of lease - a contract between two. You know, just like real grown ups!

Just as I was about to cave in to Dee's purchasing wishes re Loch Ewe Cottaqge two things happened. First, the general economy and accompanying house prices collapsed like a pricked balloon. So very obvious if one believes at all in the Law of Physice; w*hat goes up must come down!* Second, I took a telephone call one morning from Serena, Mike Hickey's personal assistant down in Kent; would I mind, she enquired, if she asked me what rent I was paying for Loch Ewe Cottage? In a nutshell Mike and Gerry would, if we wished, rent us the more than twice as large Kirkhill House at that same price level. Five years lease renewable; yes we could have whatever pets we liked and yes, we could operate whatever businesses we liked, obviously Pictures and Poems and potentially the B&B for which Kirkhill was pretty much ideal. On the owners' side they would want to build on a new and very upmarket sunhouse whilst we were there in residence. And we would make sure there was accomodation for the two of them on the rare occasions of their visits. My only regret about the deal, if a deal was to be agreed, was any inadvertent upset I caused to Kitty Wiseman, owner of Loch Ewe Cottage. She and daughter Ann and Dee had become good and close friends and did not want us (mainly Dee) to leave them. But my lady knew how I wanted to make the move. Thus it was agreed.

We were due to move house in the January. In the previous month the area had suffered the worst and most prolonged snows and ice in many years. One freezing morning I emerged from the car at the top of Loch Ewe Cottage's driveway only to perform a backwards somersault and land with a mighty thwack on head and back. Dee said the solidity of my head had saved me but honestly, all joking aside, I thought my back and/or hip was broken. I have never had to suffer overmuch in the way of physical pain I'm pleased to report, but that fall sure made up for it. Anyway late in January 2009, with considerable help from our local friends, we moved in to Kirkhill House. As it transpired this was to be journey's end for Dee. It could - indeed it may still be for me as well. But that all lies ahead ....

75. Sharing with strangers

Delia was a brilliant domestic manager. She could turn a cold and empty new house into a warm, attractive home at high speed, very short notice and ultra low cost. 'Minimalism' as a house style to her (and me) was anathema, nihilism, cheerlessness, characterlessness. No way! As large as Kirkhill House is, in no time she had positioned all of our hundreds of books and pictures because, again like me, she could not tolerate bare walls. We installed enough shelving to accommodate her collections of chinaware, and had interspersed our own pieces of furniture with those belonging to the Hickeys. What of ours would not fit comfortably within the house went into the detached garage, where it resides to this day.

Kirkhill's dining room became my office - where I am now writing this - and the front porch with its super daylight became my painting studio. There were four bedrooms, three of which would become available for bed and breakfast guests; there was a cosy kitchen with oil fired AGA and a sort of figure of eight living room, the neck of which took the form of an archway and which we immediately curtained off so as to contain the heat of the open coal fire within the half where we would sit, watch TV, read our books and do whatever private things we might want to do in front of the fire in the evenings. The other half of the figure of eight became our guests' dining room.

According to plan we started up our B&B that first spring/summer in Kirkhill House and continued it throughout the rest of that year and most of the next. Neither of us were at first quite sure about letting strangers into the house but we very quickly got into the swing of it with varying degrees of enthusiasm. Over those fifteen months of bed and breakfast operations we met with some really nice people, a few of whom remain to this day in touch with me. Our visitors were mainly Germans, Italians, Scottish and French but many other nationalities including all the Scandinavians plus Japanese and Chinese. Even a few English. I recall one Chinese family group who booked in by e-mail were a bit of a mystery. I couldn't understand why folk with such a prestigious home address as theirs, smack bang in central London, would be B&B' ing up here in the north of Scotland. Much bowing and smiling on arrival but little conversation as I cannot speak their language and they could barely speak mine. But eventually I learned that the young man was a junior member of the Chinese embassy. His parents were over here on holiday. Good people with excellent cameras constantly in action!

When B&B enquirers knocked the door or came in to their pre-booking we developed a routine. Dee would always greet them. Having established to her satisfaction that they approved of their accommodation and its price, we would sit them down in the living room with tea and biscuits for a jolly good chat - or, if I warmed sufficiently to them, a glass of the wine of the country; aka whisky, aka uiscea beatha, aka a 'wee swallee' as the Glaswegian locals have been known to remark. Wonderful how much of interest in a person's life you will discover or uncover in an hour! We discovered the truism that everybody is interesting for everyone. But everyone has more than one tale to tell of special interest to a writer! After that they would be escorted up to their room, instructed how to operate the telly and how to close the window blinds but never the ornamental curtains, then left to their own devices - and we to ours - until scheduled breakfast time. At breakfast, which had been ordered the evening prior, the Aga was a great boon. I myself was early on in our B&B life deputed and trained in the minutest detail to the gentle art of scrambling eggs on the gas hob. Dee herself saw to everything else on the Aga - watching over me from the corner of her eye and bossing me about without mercy when deserved. I would unashamedly fish for compliments from the guests - and often would receive them - about the deep colour/butteriness/texture/unique quality of my eggy offerings. Indeed I often claimed a Master's Degree in egg scrambling. But one day a most surreal scene developed when I tried to get away with a few black specks in my platefuls - a sure sign of my having burnt some of the butter. Dee went absolutely and unreasonably crazy, threatening me - in fact coming close to striking me with a heavy saucepan. We had a good laugh about it later that morning, talking of how we could have made a dramatic entry into the dining room, kicking and scratching and punching each other, rolling around on the floor Basil Fawlty-like, our waiting guests at the breakfast table in a state of shock horror. I fancy there might have been a touch of hysteria in our laughter!

We decided from the beginning that our evenings had to remain our own so no dinner was on offer along with the bed and breakfast, thank you, never mind the money. On only one occasion was Dee talked by a guest into providing dinner for him. Never again. This guest was a single man - a rather one-off character, a bit of an intellectual, I thought. As usual Dee went completely overboard with that evening meal, serving up three dinner courses that would have graced The Dorchester's dining room. When he was through eating that and drinking our good wine we were preparing to wash up, draw the curtain on our living room and say goodnight when he announced he would rather like to do some work on his PC. Would we mind terribly if he used our cleared dining table for the purpose? He worked better, he said, in a warm domestic atmosphere. I was so taken by surprise that I could not say no. So here he is in the dining area, curtains undrawn therefore able to observe Dee and I watching TV from our usual easy chairs in the living room. As was my habit I poured myself a stiff glass of Lagavulin. My heart sank when after a while I could no longer stand his sneaking glances. Would he like a glass of whisky, I asked? Would a duck like to swim? With hardly a thank you he demolished that first offering in very short order. I watched him hold the empty glass to the light, twitching it from side to side as some kind of heavy hint. You know the rest. One empty bottle of expensive malt whisky. Not a penny piece added to the bill, either demanded or volunteered. Dee said it was entirely my fault for being so bloody greedy. As ever she was right.

As a rule, when breakfast was done and all our chatting over coffee or tea had been played out and our guests had at last vacated (a) the dining area and (b) the building for the day it was laundry and housekeeping time for the rest of the morning. In general I looked after the vacuuming. Whether or not there was the merest speck of dirt I was required by my taskmaster to vacuum all carpets upstairs and down and - hateful job - all stair carpets - whilst she of course saw to the laundry. All sheets, duvet covers and towels were laundered either every third day of a guest's stay or every day if it was the dreaded one night stand. One good thing; Dee loved ironing stuff. She went into a sort of automated whirl, textiles flying in all directions. When the freshly laundered sheets were done and folded she would take them upstairs, put them on the beds and iron them again in situ!

This B&B thing may have proved interesting but by Jiminy it was damned hard work. Dee had a long history of occasional 'back trouble'. By the end of that second year the strain and pain had become altogether too much. Mysteriously there seemed nothing the doctors could do about it. After several successive mis-diagnoses and no diminution of the back pains there was no possibility of entertaining any more strangers in the house. But it was the best part of another year before a big, a very big cancer revealed itself in the form of complete lower body paralysis. Many times we had speculated about a cancer. Many times we had been assured that was not the case. Please forgive any medical skepticism. I know how elusive can be these cancers and I appreciate fully that no one of us can be mistake-proof.

But all in all 2012 / 2013 was the beginning of the end for my lovely lady.

76. What've you heard?

2009: We had over the years gained many friends in Aultbea and surrounds. My paintings and writings were attracting a bit of notoriety (I cannot possibly say 'fame', can I!) and of course Dee's early employment in the Isle View Care Home working alongside many of the local ladies helped. We could seldom visit shop or post office or take the two hour bus ride into Inverness and back without engaging in chit-chat. Chit-chat - or 'the craic' as most folks know it - is an all-pervasive hobby in these parts. A classic instance I well bring to mind concerns Delia's special friend, our ex landlady, Kitty. This lady had the reputation, supported by her own declaration at every opportunity, of 'not visiting,' which was itself pretty rare in an area where doors always seemed open to the passer-by. However Kitty made up for this by spending much of each evening on the telephone to her many lady friends, Dee amongst them. After we relocated the three miles to Kirkhill House, even before that when we lived in Loch Ewe Cottage, fifty metres away from Kitty and Ann, the phone would ring at exactly a minute after six. Dee would smile at me, mouth *Kitty* as she picked up, then would answer with her usual *'Delia speaking'*. The caller (Kitty) would not identify herself but would open straight up with *'What've you heard?'*. Dee herself had a strong aversion to the retelling of scuttlebutt. She often reminded me (warned me) of the dangers of gossip in a small community. Nevertheless, and in spite of answering 'not much' to Kitty's leading question, the two of them would hold extensive evening conversations about little or nothing.

At the risk of over-eulogising my late wife I have to say two things at this stage. First, I seldom if ever heard her utter a bad word about anyone - or any kind of indiscretion about anyone for that matter. She had the knack of being an involved listener but a non-reciprocatory one! And secondly, Delia Islip, nee Smalley was the original people magnet. Although she never went out of her way to engage with groups and was, indeed, always happy to be on her own, I think folk sensed that there was no evil in the woman, only genuine interest; perhaps were drawn to her on that account. It is true that without seeming to make any effort to do so, within a very short time after our arrival here she knew everybody in our orbit by face and by name.

I have myself always avoided joining extra mural clubs and associations and have indeed never been one to make many friends outside of a business life that took up all other than my family time. Therefore when I (and Dee) were invited to join the Wester-Ross Burns Club in, I think, 2007, 'honour' was the right word. I suppose it was well known in the area that I had a love for poetry. After all I was making something of a living out of publishing / selling cards and books incorporating my landscape paintings and associated poems. It may also be relevant that, as related in a long previous episode, my 19 years old fiancee and self had visited Burns' Cottage in Alloway back in 1954. Nevertheless for an unreformed Englishman and his wife to be invited to worship at the altar of Scotland's world-famous National Bard ... an honour indeed.

The Burns Club has been a significant part of our lives - and still is of mine. There are not that many of us 'members'; just enough to overfill one or other of our living rooms for our occasional meetings under the learned chairmanship of Ian Macmillan. Our meetings tend to have a pre-announced theme. Could be 'Burns the farmer' or 'Burns's fellow Scottish poets' or something that would at any rate inspire some study. I recall the theme back at our first gathering; 'A favourite Burns poem', or similar. I forget which one of my many favorites I read out but I do remember being surprised by my wife's choice. I didn't even know the ploughman poet had penned such a one as that he called simply '*Delia*'. It is quite amazing how many of his poems are entitled with the Christian name of a female. I wonder why? Anyway 'my' Delia had a horror of performing in public so at her request Ian read out her namesake choice, and he did so right nobly. Our meetings would proceed with good food, continue with all the drink and descend with much hilarity into Scottish Country Dancing, courtesy of that well applauded local expert, the lovely Elna. The congregation often continued on with the singing of largely sentimental Scottish or Irish pub songs, the words of which some of us sometimes actually remembered - some of the times. Some of the tunes ditto!

On one occasion I wrote a little playlet for our Club gathering. In my scenario Burns and Shakespeare were meeting in the afterlife. I selected fellow member Tony Davis as Mr Shakespeare. He read the part extremely well even though his accent was more rural Dorset than Warwickshire. Unknown to me at the time he is actually something of an aspiring thespian anyway. I cannot bring to mind who assumed the part of Burns. When I published this as a blog called *Two Gentlemen in a Far Away Land* it received well over a thousand internet 'hits'.

But the highlight of our Burns year is of course the January Burns Supper. It is usually attended by fifty or more. The program is strictly formal and so to a lesser extent is the dress code. Proceedings commence with the piping in of the haggis, then follows the President's fiercesome address to that haggis and the supper itself of cock a' leekie soup, haggis neaps and tatties; then cranikin, a Scottish kind of trifle for dessert. After that comes the all important toasts - an invited male does the toast 'to the lassies', a female responds 'to the laddies' and somebody specially priveleged presents the keynote speech; 'to the Immortal Memory' of our Bard. Over the years I've toasted the lassies on two occasions and presented the toast to The Immortal Memory on a further occasion. I thought long and hard about the wearing of the kilt. Number one, should an Englishman aspire to the kilt at all? Number two, what, if anything, does one wear beneath it? And number three, how do you manage to be seated whilst safely preserving your modesty? In the end I decided to go for it, so these days I hire a complete Highland regalia in the Ben Wyvis tartan from a lovely shop in Inverness. What's underneath? Well, I can only quote the traditional response to that question; *That's for me to know and you, lady, to find out!*

So have I now forgotten my eleven centuries of family history as a southern Englishman? By no means. We are what we are and I don't think it's in any way 'racist' to be proud of who we are, or from whence we have come.

77. Going somewhere else

For somebody who has had to do a lot of travelling as a part of his business life but who has seldom found it a joy, much less something in any way exciting, our position in the far Highlands of Scotland has entailed much road, rail and air mileage if I ever wanted to sell my products or if we ever wanted to see our family face to face. Of course we would receive visits from the family now and then, particularly in the early days, but the vast majority of our familial meetings of latter years would be away from home. I find this completely natural. The young always will find less of compelling interest in the lives of the old than vice versa. That applies just as much of course when we were actually ourselves the younger, meeting with our aged parents - Dee's mother, Wynne, and my father, Eddie, whether out of a sense of love or of duty - but most likely some of each.

'*Honour your father and your mother.*' is the Fifth Commandment. We still love our fathers and our mothers. Delia much more than I, it has to be said. But these days we do not necessarily honour old age. On the contrary, latter day generations are taught to honour youth, not age.

For me, the modern compulsion to be somewhere away from wherever one is, whether for so-called holidays or for business is one of modern life's great mysteries. How can that be when one is often so pleased to arrive back home again! Airports in particular I have long likened, if not to Hell then at least to Hades! Who really, really appreciates being encapsulated with a polyglot melange of people you would usually go out of your way to avoid, beset on all sides by noise and commercialism, being treated by robotic people ('handled' is a more appropriate word) like some computer fired piece of human jetsam? Actually I suspect the answer to that question is that, however surprisingly, most of us actually do like it. So very sad! You may be relieved to learn that I'm not going to be getting right here into the meaning of life. (Perhaps you'll need to await the publication of my novel in progress). But how many times in my life have I been propping up the bar at some ungodly hour in some airport - any airport, anywhere - nursing a drink and pondering what it's all about? What indeed is the answer to the question a sombre American semi-drunk sitting alongside me once gratuitously asked: *Hey, pal, what do* **you** *want chiselled into* **your** *headstone?* In casual prior conversation I had told him I was marketing director of an international plastic cup and container factory. In response to my silence*; Five little fuckin' words on that headstone of yours*? he suggested; *I - SOLD - FUCKIN' - PLASTIC - CUPS. Great!* Whatever, he'd made me think! Yes, I remember him still, or rather that which he told me.

As mentioned, by the mid-late noughties when I was in my mid-late seventies I was regularly travelling most of Wester-Ross and Easter-Ross on a mission to sell my cards, prints and books. My self-appointed sales territory extended from Achiltibuie / Elphin in the north to Kyle of Lochalsh / Castle Eilean Donan in the south to

Inverness in the east. The west is just water until you come to the Hebrides; I've not yet ventured over there thus far. Basically I'm talking a couple of fast road hours of driving in each direction, which is why my poor eight years old Renault Megane Sports Estate has suffered the ravages of fifteen thousand potholed, stony, snaky Highlands road miles each year. I have about thirty regular retail customers now - down from a peak of fifty two because I can't afford by time or health to visit the less productive shops any more. Most of these regulars have become my friends, which is why my 'trips' seem to take longer and longer. Not because I am driving slower and slower - not yet anyway - but because I'm taking more and more cups of coffee and indulging myself in more and more minutes of chit-chat! The fact is that, although my days of creating and managing 'proper' business have long gone I am still fascinated by those retailers I visit and those who supply me with materials - the why's and wherefore's of their ups and their downs, changes of strategy and tactics, etcetera; the kind of business issues that used to occupy me so absolutely.

You might well have gathered that I am not a fan of the two words, *holiday* and *retirement*. I hope that doesn't offend. Should it do so, then my apologies, I can only quote the usual; we are all different, aren't we? Even when I used to take family holidays it was always to *do* something with an objective, usually fishing or walking the hills or visiting relatives rather than simply to *be* somewhere, much less just to travel. I genuinely never felt the need to get away from work, as such. As hard as sometimes work was, both physically and especially mentally, and as welcome an opportunity to spend more hours with my nearest and dearest , work was my life - alongside my family it was my raison d'etre so why would I want to get away from it? And retirement? What's that all about? I would far prefer to die in the saddle! I may not be able to ride as fast or as far as of yore but it's better than walking, never mind standing still. You may or may not believe it but this has little or nothing to do with money but it has everything to do with why I was pleased to wake up and get up this morning and why I shall be equally pleased to do so tomorrow, God willing.

Back to travelling. By far my preferred means of getting from here to there would be by train, should rail be an option. There's something about the clicketty clack, the feeling of having all the options to pass the time that one would enjoy at home: i.e. the opportunity to view the passing landscape, the possibility of conversation with fellow travellers if that is what you (and they) want, the benefit of arriving smack in the centre of the city and not least the comfort and security aspect compared with car, coach or air. My most memorable rail journeys in these latter years have been London Kings Cross to Inverness on the overnight sleeper. The bar-room carriage was as good as a pub or a club as a place to pass the time, often late into the small hours if you got talking to someone with something interesting to discuss. Mind you, the two tier beds themselves were not specially comfortable when you found yourself staggering into your bedroom cubicle already occupied (always on bottom bunk, leaving you to the difficult climb!) by some total stranger (male of course) not especially impressed or good humored by your noisy arrival. As morning came and that great Scottish breakfast beckoned I became quite practiced in the art of appearing fast asleep whilst said stranger got himself dressed and out!

But there really is no place like home. No matter how many times you've moved it - home is still home!

78. Light into dark

By January 2011 we should have been sitting pretty. We had a lovely home in Kirkhill House and a strong running Bed & Breakfast ranking highest in the area on Trip Advisor. My Pictures and Poems micro business was doing steady business. Most of our six grown up children were well settled and equally well adjusted with families of their own. We had many close friends in the area and just a few good friends outside of it - the residue from our previous life down south in Hampshire. Ranking for us as highly as anything, we were in a most beautiful part of the world alongside other, like-minded people. (Not too many of them). Perhaps these feelings were reflected in my 2010 poem ...

A Land Unspoiled

Our day slows down as last light paints the sky
and you can feel the movement of the globe,
hear gentle surf, the wheeling seagull's cry,
watch land and sea in pastel colours robe
this Wester-Ross, where calming nature seems

a place of magic that itself redeems -
inspires an artist and a poet's dreams.

You think perhaps Blake's feet in ancient times
would want to tread a land unspoiled as this.
There's little discord here where most things rhyme,
and all is sensate to an evening's kiss,
when no-one's going far and peace is sought
and found; for what this is cannot be bought,
and things material count for little, less or nought.

And when you meet these folk, this land, this sea
You'll know to live here's more than just to be

But there was also the dark side of the moon, for nothing in heaven or on earth for we mere mortals seems destined to be perfect. Well, I cannot yet be sure about heaven but I most certainly can about earth. After all, the Garden of Eden is but a biblical memory and the Nordic Valhalla but a faded legend. Oh yes, and Milton's famous Paradise has been well and truly Lost. Amongst our problems we still mourned our lost dogs and still debated new puppies - always however without resolution. And we still had to worry about our one lost sheep. (I wrote above that most of our children were well settled, well adjusted. But not all of them.) And then again I naturally had some regrets over my business rise, the opportunities lost and in the end my business fall in the Middle East; whether through bad luck or my bad judgement or my Saudi sponsor's deliberate depredations I shall never know. But hey, frankly my dear, by now I no longer cared. The past was the past, the present better by far. I so wish I could say or sing with Ms Piaf, *Regrette, rien do rien*, (or something akin) but I cannot.

But the greatest blow came now, in the late summer of 2012 when we had to cancel our upcoming B&B bookings and put up the shutters on that business. My poor girl could by then hardly walk. The pain in her lower spine was all consuming. As much as I had tried to take over the more physical demands of the B&B job because I was reluctant to abandon our top ranking reputation and consequent financial benefit - it had become an absolute impossibility. Then, in the September, for the first time the pains overcame everything from her hips down. With lightning speed a total numbness set in. After a panicky last visit to the local doctor I was asked to drive Dee the eighty miles to Raigmore hospital for more 'tests'. When we arrived in the appointed ward, in spite of the gravity of the situation I recall a somewhat comedic episode when Dee found herself inadequately prepared for the requested stay over. I was despatched to the nearby Tesco with a shopping list that included nighties and panties (what sort, what size, what colour? *Oh please! Just use your judgement Bryan!*) Faced with such a massive range of choice as was on display I had no option but to enlist the initially somewhat suspicious help of two young lady shop assistants (having established to their satisfaction that this grey haired old guy was unlikely to have any nefarious intent.) They questioned me about my wife's figure, looks and personality. Dee's flame red paraphanalia I then bought and imported into Raigmore Hospital apparently caused quite a stir on the ward! Anyway I stayed overnight in the Holiday Inn, prepared to take Dee home the following day. But when I arrived back at the hospital at the appointed hour her bed was empty. She had been allocated a small room on her own. It too was empty. I was informed she was at that point away being prepared for some kind of x-ray. I sensed from the attitudes of the nurses that something ultimately dreadful was afoot. After a short while a lady doctor knocked and entered. She introduced herself, weighed me up carefully, I presume to see how emotionally fragile I might be, then gently, or as gently as possible let me into the bad news. My lovely had some form of bone cancer, later specified as non-Hodgkinson's lymphoma. She would be given radiography and probably after that the dreaded chemotherapy. And no, I could not take her home. She would have to stay here in Raigmore for several days at least.

Dee was ten years younger than me, a youthful sixty nine. If I was not mistaken I had just heard her sentenced to a very painful death; and myself, to a lonely old age..

I sought and found my wife waiting in the relevant x-ray department. She seemed to be on an amazingly even keel. No tears, just pleased to see me and glad at last to know the trouble, however big a trouble it might be. In fact she was more concerned about me than herself. How could I possibly cope with the minutae of feeding myself, keeping house etc? So very typical. I drove back home over the hills by myself, fighting all the negatives. It was a clear, full moon night. There is a viewpoint car park area close by Braemore Junction. I pass it almost every week and can never do so without remembering how I stopped the car there, thinking over our life together, hearing over and over again the good oncologist's careful words. The beautiful vale below reached down to Ullapool and the sea, bathed now in pitiless silvery moonlight. As readers of these episodes will know I had been knocked down a few times in my life. I guess most of us are but now, for the very first time I could not figure out quite how I would ever get back on to my feet. There should be no shame but still, at that time in that lonely plazce high on the hill I felt shamed by my useless tears.

As I shall relate, regain my feet of course I did, with more than a little help from my family and friends. One simply has to. Day by day by day and hour by hour was the key to unlock at least some kind of a temporary peace, some kind of a hope for the future even though my most fervent, most immediate desire was to go where my Delia was going; wherever that may be.

79. Living in darkness

After a week of hospital-bound radiotherapy Dee was allowed home. The numbness had gone but the pain had not. She was feeling but a shadow of her normal, former self. A fortnight went by mostly upstairs in bed. Without being asked, one by one all four of the doctors in our local practice came to visit her. I would show them upstairs, sit quietly in the background listening to what these very good people had to say to my wife, they who had so signally failed to diagnose the cancer at an earlier, possibly a more treatable stage. None of the doctors said sorry. Why should they? I have no idea whether or not a correct diagnosis would have been possible. Then a letter arrived setting an appointment back in Raigmore Hospital with a consultant oncologist. All too familiar with the often blank canvas outcome of such meetings, Dee and I sat down at home together to compile a list of fifteen questions to which we would request answers - even if the answer had to be 'don't know'. Even after Delia's diagnosis and radiotherapy neither of us felt sufficiently information equipped.

The consultant turned out to be a marginally interested lady aged perhaps thirty something who, for all her evident concern may have been running a touch late for something else. We already knew Dee was to be offered an extreme type of chemo-therapy. By the way that was an offer that could have been made in the letter or even verbally a fortnight before, thus saving ourselves and the environment one hundred and sixty miles of fossil fuelled car miles plus an entire day of our time and a half hour of the NHS's much more expensive time. The last (double) question on our list was ....

Dee: *If I do <u>not</u> accept chemotherapy what may be my chances of survival?*

Consultant oncologist: (when all obfuscation is removed) *Zero.*

Dee: *If I <u>do</u> accept chemotherapy what then may be my chances?*

Consultant oncologist: *Impossible to say; thirty to fifty percent*

Of course we decided to opt into the chemo, although had we known the true odds against and the extreme physical difficulty I do not think we would have elected to go through it.

I drove us back home over the hills, stopping only at a friend's house in Achnasheen then diverting to the Badachro Inn for some supper and the opportunity to consider things more fully and in as relaxed a manner as possible. This was the place where we had enjoyed so many happy occasions over the years, often with various members of our family on holidays long before we relocated north. How were we to best let our children know now about this awful turn of events? Conclusion: there is no best way; just the only way. But there were no more tears. We looked out over the bay with its moored yachts, its birdlife, the wild wilderness of Dry Island and the broad reaches of Gairloch itself. We were all right. Can an inanimate place really give you strength, I wonder? Why, yes - it can!

Over the next six months as Dee attended Raigmore for her chemo plus R-chop (whatever that may be) sometimes needing to stay in hospital and sometimes there and back home in a day, I was backing and forthing like the proverbial yo-yo. I would joke that my car didn't need a driver - it knew the way all by itself. On one occasion after the doctors had apparently changed their mind I had only just arrived back home after leaving Dee there, as instructed, when the phone rang. Raigmore: '*Oh, your wife can go home now, Mr Islip*'. Wearily I got back into the car. A second 160 mile trip that day! Cheers!

After the first chemo session Dee asked me to take a photo of her *'before all my hair comes out'*. Bear in mind that my wife had always taken great care of and not to say considerable pride in this hair of her's. The idea of losing it therefore would have been agony upon agony for her, now that it was coming adrift in her hairbrush. With the picture safely in my PC she quietly asked me to call Fiona; she wanted all her hair removed rather than have it fall out bit by patchy bit. Fiona was and still is my local lady hairdresser andour good friend. I watched and we both joked as Dee's lovely, long blonde pride and joy fell in clumps to the kitchen floor. By an odd co-incidence a friend of Rudi's had purchased a hairpiece of an almost exact colour match to his mothers's. That friend no longer needed it. Without our foreknowledge it arrived in the post the following day. It was the first of three wigs, and my own favourite.

Dee wasn't eager for the children and their families to come all the way up here to see her when, after all, she might be free of non-Hodgkinson's lymphoma by Springtime after the course of six hard chemo sessions had concluded. She knew her deteriorating physical condition would add worries upon worries for them all. That winter was a very tough one for the family and both of us. Having said so, it was not without its lighter side and its humour. Dee was pretty well daily receiving visits from our friends as well as family. We would constantly talk together about 'when I am / you are better' although always at the back of both our minds was that young lady oncologists' *'thirty to fifty percent'*. Of course I was doing all the cooking and cleaning and Dee spent most of all day every day in bed, in between chemo sessions. But a month or so after the end of chemo we determined to begin testing - exactly how well (or not well) was she now? We were desperate to learn whether or not that awful chemotherapy had killed off the cancer cells. One of our favourite midday walks whilst we had been busy with bed and breakfasts was just a mile or so along the edge of Loch Ewe to the NATO pier. By now we had not been able to do that short walk for well over a year but were set on giving it a go. It was heartbreaking to see her efforts, aided by two walking sticks. This was a woman who had walked all her life and for the sheer pleasure of it, who had always *noticed* things of nature, who had never been put off by adverse weather - indeed I sometimes thought had relished it. Delia Mary Smalley nee Perry nee Islip was for me the free spirit of the wilderness.

In July came a summons to attend Aberdeen General hospital. Dee was to have a nuclear test of some kind presumably to determine if and how the chemotherapy had worked. The appointment was for ten in the morning. Aberdeen is a minimum four hours hard driving away. We made it on time and those long four hours back home again after ... won't bore you further with all that! Day by day we awaited some kind of message. Nothing. I called Raigmore. An appointment for us was made. No explanations of course and of course no apologies at being left swinging in the wind. We waited way past the schedule for the consultant finally to let us in to his room and presumably deliver news of our fate. It at once became clear that he knew nothing - had not even spent a prior minute looking at his computer screen (with its computer graphics of Dee's Aberdeen scan) or at Delia's bulky paper files. So now he spent at least five silent minutes trying to get the picture on screen in focus. Both Dee and I could read the bloody red splodges around her pelvic girdle long before he opened his mouth. Perhaps that was his way of breaking the news gently, I don't know.

Finally he looked up, seeming as grave as did his well practiced nurse. He made some irrelevant noises and then announced that there was nothing more to be done. Even then she had to ask him, *how long do I have?* The answer, for the first time not obfuscated; *you have three months, Mrs Islip.*

On being shown the way out the consultant shook my hand and told me quietly; *she can have as many pain killers as she wants.*

Thank you doctor, I said; I hope without irony..

80. Delia's gone

In her mid/late teens Delia hd become a friend of the similarly aged Rod Stewart. This was even before Rod joined up with his pals to form *The Small Faces* - the rest, as they say, being history. At that time he had scripted on his guitar the American Blues title *Delia's Gone*. Quite what had been on his mind with that I have no idea and if Dee knew she didn't tell me. But as I have reported in the previous episode, on September 9th 2013 we were informed that her cancer was terminal. She had but three months to live. Delia was indeed going.

There are four district nurses attached to our surgery. All of them became very good friends as well as essential support, and Mary Ann, the Macmillan CancerCare nurse was an especially welcome visitor. It is difficult to explain her role because she didn't do 'nursing' as such, other than as a specialist go-between with the local doctors. But the effect of her visits on my wife's morale (and therefore mine) was palpable indeed. She and Dee's close friend Brenda Peace, or one or other of the district nurses shared much of her personal care, showering etc with me. One by one or couple by couple all the children came up to say their goodbyes. So did Delia's sister Gloria and her husband Peter. So did the two Hickey brothers, our good friends and landlords (who spontaneously and without any kind of asking had refused our house rental for six months!). Of course our local friends also wished to come in and sit by her bedside, especially Michelle and Yvonne, owners of the village shop who had been bringing her baskets of goodies throughout her illness - most of which she couldn't eat but which I surely could. And our principal Burns Club friends, Ian, Jean, Tony and Ann. These were, of course, very emotional visits. Towards the end Delia wrote personal letters to each of our sons and daughters and her closest friends, sending the daughters also some pieces of her jewellery. She was a brilliant writer. (Long since I had urged her to have a shot at writing stories for a living but she was always too self-effacing for anything like that.)

All of her life Dee had professed a non-belief in the hereafter. Nevertheless amongst her many friends was one rather gloriously irreverent reverend by the name of Pam Shinkins. One day she asked me to contact Pam and ask her please to come over. During those final three months Pam was a frequent visitor. I usually left the two of them together so cannot be sure if my wife ever modified her spiritual beliefs / non-beliefs. I would not have dreamt of asking that question of either lady at the time and I will not now. But what I do know is that Dee was always happier when Pam had been than she had been, beforehand.

All the while the magnificent conservatory (aka 'sunhouse') addition to Kirkhill House was going on apace. Not ideal of course because of the noise and the inevitable dirt and dust, but we had agreed to this building work before moving in and we knew it would enormously enhance the living quality of our home when it was finished.. We were not to know how long it would take, nor that one of us would never live to feel its benefit.

In early November Dee asked to go into the Highland Hospice. The Hospice is situated in the centre of Inverness. I was informed she made this request not to get away from my tender care but to afford her husband a rest. It is true that, without realising it, the constant exposure to Dee's agony and to a lesser extent the physical wear and tear of looking after everything was eating away at me. Subsequently, although the daily drives for Hospice visitations were wearing in themselves, the week she spent there proved enormously beneficial for both of us. It is quite impossible to adequately praise its staff. Sufficient to say that a private ten minute talk with the head doctor there left me on a totally elevated plane, all mystery removed, a certain conviction about the inherent goodness of humankind firmly in place. His answer to that most important question; *how long does she have, doctor?* He told me, with ultimate kindness and without unecessary sentiment; *Days, not weeks.* She whispered that she now wanted to come home to die and insisted I drive her - *no more ambulances, Bryan, please.*

We made the passenger seat in our car as comfortable as possible for her. I shall never forget that drive back over the hills, most of the time in a perfect silence and holding hands, just like lovers do. At a tiny drive-in called Tarvie she wanted her usual Walls Magnum ice cream but could only eat a small portion of it and of course would not be able to leave her seat in the car until we reached home. By the time we got as far as the Inchbae hotel she was desperate for a drink of water. Shortly thereafter I stopped the car to allow her to empty her stomach. I told her if she didn't stop apologising I would finish her off myself. At least we could still have a laugh. When we reached the highest point of the journey she again asked me to stop. She (and I) spent five minutes looking around at the array of mighty Highland mountains, sun-kissed this day, then another ten minutes talking in the most relaxed way about our past and my future. When we got home I was so glad of help from our friend Chris Wood, who happened to be passing by, in getting Dee out of the car and upstairs into bed. She was never to leave that bed.

Delia Mary Islip died at 13.01 hours on Tuesday 29th November 2013. I had been by her bedside as she lay unconscious for three days and almost all of three long nights. I distinctly heard the slow shuddery expulsion of that last breath, then I stood up, straightened her bedclothes, bent over to kiss her cooling forehead (not her lips; my Dee didn't like lip kissing too much). I said some things to her - some things for her alone, then picked up the telephone. One of the nurses answered. It took me a few seconds to get myself together enough to say; *Dee's gone.*

81. In the aftermath

As I have said, and now say again, Delia Mary Islip died at 13.01 hours on Tuesday 29th November 2013. The Reverend Pam Shinkins very soon arrived at the bedside. She was of great comfort to me. My girl's hand was so very, very cold as, at Pam's suggestion I removed her wedding ring. This was for me probably the lowest of the low points. Before that I had gone downstairs and asked the workmen who were busy finishing the sunhouse extension please to pack up and go home. I called George the undertaker and over the succeeding days put into action all the funeral arrangements for the 5th December church (kirk) service next door, then, ably helped by Dee's best friend Lynne Benstead, the arrangements for the 11th December memorial gathering in the Anglesey Hotel, down south in Gosport.

When my wife Joan died I had had Delia to lean on. Now I was on my own - and yet I was not on my own for the good folk of Aultbea gathered round to lend me their hands and their strength. The weather was particularly vile overnight and on the morning of the funeral service. I would have forgiven anybody for staying at home, yet come they did, parking their cars all along the roadway and filling up the church. Dee's sons Rudi and Max had driven up and I had collected my daughter Julie from Inverness rail station the evening prior. My son Stuart had come from his home in Spain with his wife Lorraine and daughters Jadine and Sinead. I delivered the eulogy in church, the readings were delivered by Adrian Hollister, Stuart Islup and Ian Macmillan. The music was Dee's choice and all in attendance were invited by Adrian and Katie afterwards to the wake in their Perfume Studio / Amora Cafe. Almost a thousand pounds were collected on that day for donation to the Highland Hospice and Macmillan CancerCare and then another several hundreds of pounds at the Gosport gathering.

Seeing Dee

I see her still, and will
so long as I have seeing eyes alive
to the hills we walked,
with those beloved dogs.
So many, many lovely days;
so many, many trackless ways.
The hills are winter muted now,
their lovely colours sombre
as if in respect or tribute
to she who, leaving me alone,
embarked on that adventure
that all that lives well knows,
each harder, emptier year that goes.

I see her still, and will
so long as I have seeing eyes alive
to the stony, bouldery shores
or riverside woods
where we would each day
in all weathers find a seat
to eat our picnic lunch
often in silence, content
to watch the play of light,
oft-times the drift of rain or snow
on hill or moving water, smile at
the play of otters, divers, others,
listening to the crying of the gulls.

I see her still, and will
so long as I have seeing eyes alive
to the crystal seas of Wester-Ross
cold, clear, summertime blue,
'remote', where she would
take off her clothes and, breathless,
slip nymph-like in to swim,
framed by deep, dark-waving weeds,
laughing at me, at the cold;
or for the simple joy of it,
lithe mermaid in a perfect zone,

*the zone, forever gone
that had become our own.*

The December of two thousand and thirteen was a blur. I recall attending as many of the parties as I could, especially Ian and Jean's, trying very hard not to be the spectre at the feast. At Adrian and Katie's invitation I had my Christmas Day lunch with a group of friends at the Aultbea Hotel. Everywhere I went Delia was there also in spirit. One of the last things she said to me was; *change nothing for a year after I die and then change whatever makes sense with your new life.* I'll get back to that before the end of this autobio. Suffice to say right now, two years later, that I still have no wish to change any damn thing.

Months before Delia died I had become aware that I too was in the grip of a cancer. I had kept the knowledge to myself but in August of 2014 I finally went to see a doctor. After the usual protracted series of probes and scans back at Raigmore, yes, it was confirmed; I had a prostrate cancer which had advanced from the gland itself into some of my bones - and yes, it was terminal. However, the customary hormone tablets and injections could delay the inevitable indefinitely. Pressed on the definition of 'indefinitely' the oncologist said *months, years or even a normal lifespan.* Not terribly helpful. He added that the treatment would deprive me of my 'libido' and cause me to experience hot flushes plus enlargement of the breasts. To the latter I responded there was always a silver lining and to the former that at least the ladies of Aultbea would hernceforth be able to sleep safely in their beds. He did mention the word 'chemotherapy' but I cut short that one in a big hurry. (Death where is thy sting when compared with chemo).

I said I had changed nothing since the loss of my wife but that isn't quite true, for I have not lifted a paint brush nor confronted my easel since before she went. Nevertheless I still sell the residual cards, prints and booklets etc that have emerged from my sixty or so Highlands and seascape paintings and I still write both prose and verse; just as I have had the urge to write since the age of seventeen. In fact I have thought of this blog primarily as an exercise in writing since my friend Jackie West suggested it in 2008. It has morphed into this autobiography since last Autumn when my son Stuart said; *Dad, why don't you write about your early life. None of us know anything about it.* If you're reading these episodes, Stu, and I think you are, I hope this helps. And another thing! Since coming to the Highlands I have written and published two novels, two collections of short stories and two non-fiction booklets of my paintings, poems and narratives. In 2010 I began writing a third novel and was three quarters through it when for various reasons including Delia's illness I stopped. Some months after my world collapsed I looked again at it and began a re-write. So, alongside this autobio I have been working solidly on the work that had the original title *'The Book'* and has, since then, had several differing titles until now, at some 100,000 words in length and with about another 10,0000 to go it is called *Like An Angel Sings*. If a writer feels no excitement I would guess its probably rubbish. I am very excited by *Like An Angel Sings*. It is the novel I should have written thirty and more years ago.

There is another novel that I did start to write thirty years ago then abandoned for various reasons. It was / is called *'Rose Feather'*. If I am, as they say, spared beyond the publication of *Like An Angel Sings* and this bio ...it will be back to dear Rose and her father, star snooker player American Henry Feather. We shall see...

82. These last pages

One year after being finally on my own, 2015 began for me as a classic Highlands Hogmanay. At nine in the evening of December 31 I found myself seated in a very subdued village hall with just a few mostly elderly couples and a rather good, local, two piece band doing mostly Scottish country music. An hour later the place was packed with people of all ages, the majority of whom had come straight from the Aultbea Hotel so were already well in the mood. The music had ratchetted up into all kinds of dance, rock and Scottish traditional including the ever more violent *strip the willows*, *jolly white sergeants*, etc. Cancer or no, and by the way I had not made any secret of my condition, I was dragged on to the dance floor and for a while was able to imagine myself of a different age and stage. The beer and whisky helped. By two in the morning I had had my fill of the glorious home-made food on offer and felt it unsafe to partake of any more alcohol so I went home feeling great even as the party went swinging ever onwards. Young ladies were being thrown around like rag dolls, screaming with laughter even though sometimes falling and sliding on the drink sodden floor as if on ice!

It seemed that the hormone treatment had worked - or was working - very well indeed, and clearly my condition was a source not just of interest but of genuine local concern. The questions from friends in the post office or village store by now were morphing from a truly interested, *how are you?*, into the *how are you?* of mere politeness. After all there are only so many times one can answer, 'Oh, fine, and how are you?' To keep the pennies rolling in this year I have been able, thus far, to maintain the stocks of my cards, prints, books etc and as winter ended and springtime begins I did my customary rounds of the shops with fair sales results. But as for painting; time after time I have stood quite still in front of that empty easel and stacks of canvasses and row upon row of oil paints, mentally planning the painting that I now know I shall never create. Why not? I had and have no idea. I was and am at time of writing (December 2015) physically fit enough and the painting I wanted to create of Delia was there, clear enough in my head, but it was and is as if Bryan Islip, the painter was a different person, now lost. Writing these memoirs has become my principal interest along with the novel I began four years ago and have now re-written - and intend continuing on to its conclusion / publication.

Those who may have tried unsuccessfully to call me will know that I do still get out and about a lot. Mobile reception is so variable around here that the carrying of these devices is of doubtful value. But I am invariably to be found on Sunday mornings with Mike and Heather at Connie and Mike's Bridge Cafe in nearby Poolewe. My products are still on display and sold there and by by my friend Alison at her Tuesday Poolewe Market, where I will almost always go for a chat with friends and a bacon roll or a bowl of home-made soup. On Wednesdays I am to be found at the Morefields Motel in Ullapool at lunch with my friends Ian and Tony and the other eight or ten Rotarians. Did I mention that last back end I was invited to join Ullapool Rotary? Perhaps not. I should have, for it has been a source of great pleasure for me and I hope of some benefit to others less fortunate as are helped by the Rotary Club of Ullapool, myself now included.

Rarely a week goes by without an invitation to lunch, or dinner or drinks - either that or my invitation to others in return. In the evenings I will generally be sitting in the new sunhouse watching the glorious sunsets over Loch Ewe and distant mountains and/or watching the TV - mostly programs I have recorded; almost invariably my favourite sports or (non-soap) drama. I will most often be in bed by eleven, reading a book - possibly the Arden edition of a Shakespeare play - or watching on my Kindle one or other of the Fawlty Towers episodes. For me these things are an ever constant joy.

In June Mike and Gerry Hickey (my friends and landlords) and three of their more well-heeled friends did their customary car tour of Scotland. I always look forward to these very occasional visits. They are a window on a different world. I asked Mike what motor cars I might expect this time. I should explain that they put all five motors on a car transporter and have them driven up to Scotland, having themselves flown Gatwick - Edinburgh. Mike's answer: *my Lambourgini, an Aston, a Porche and two Ferraris!* That Saturday the cavalcade arrived in a gutteral roar of high performance engines. After a brief look at the sunhouse extension we all repaired for lunch to the Aultbea Hotel. Mike invited me to get a lift; *jump into my Lambourgini, Bryan.* Unfortunately either the car was too low to the ground or my back had become far too inflexible to get in! I had to make do with a Ferrari for a lift - that was OK because, low to the ground as it also was, it had lift up gull wing doors. Its driver asked me the question, *Bryan, do you have any problem with speed?* Replied I; *good lord no, I'm one of the fastest drivers around here.* The next thing I all but blacked out under the G Force of a foot down Ferrari! After lunch they all roared off around Scotland's north coast then down to Edinburgh; back to work in Kent or London on Monday.

Mike had e-mailed me early in the year, inviting me to have a google on the twelfth century 'Ralthaldron Castle' near Dublin in Ireland. He had seen it come up for sale whilst on holiday in Australia and, after due diligence from afar, had bought it on line! He had said he would show me around it if I was OK to fly. You might expect that amidst a life as crowded as his, such a passing comment might be forgotten. Not a bit of it. Like most highly successful businessmen he has a marvellous mind for detail and would never forget or renege on even a half promise. Soon I got the call; *I'm having my fifty'th birthday party in the castle, 22nd August. Want to come?* No sooner had I accepted, which was pretty well straight away, than came the rider: *It's fancy dress obligatory; Game of Thrones or Medieval!*

Well, this proved to be one of the very best birthday parties I can remember. I was met at Dublin Airport by Serena, Mike's personal assistant, and generally well looked after by her all weekend. I went as King Arthur - one of two King Arthurs as it transpired, the other being Mike and Gerry's Uncle Morty. I have no recollection of the names of the lovely ladies (except of course my escort, Serena) with whom I danced and chatted that night. They were mostly Guenevieres. It was a two a.m. effort with one hundred and fifty or so guests, most of whom had clearly not bothered the fancy dress shops, preferring proper theatrical costumiers!. Marvellous food and drink, beautiful old castle, three different bands culminating in a hard rock brass ensemble loud enough to shake the place to its ancient foundations! I have to say I surprised myself with my energy levels. At one in the morning Mike walked up as I was in full swing and muttered the memorable words; *Bryan, I thought you were dying!*

The next day, on the Sunday, I was looked after by Mike and Gerry's uncle Morty. We visited another very large old castle where a brass band was in full swing. On the way out to Morty's farm and home he asked me, how would you like to visit a typical Irish pub? Would I? Well, whyever the hell not? I think I was becoming addicted to the Guinness! Lo and behold, sitting inside were Mike and Gerry and their father Mike and another uncle and. They toldc me this meeting was a co-incidence ….

The day after I got home I guess it all caught up with me, for I felt pretty rotten. A reminder that my friend the cancer was still somewhere inside, eating away at me. But listen, I wouldn't have changed anything about my Irish adventure. For a man so unlucky I really am the luckiest, if you see what I mean!

83. Thinking of it so far

Ernie Wise used to ask his partner Eric Morecambe, *Well, what d'you think of it so far?* to which Eric would invariably reply, *Rubbish!* I guess all of us at times would respond in similar vein when asked how they felt about their lives, and I am no exception. On the other hand we all know and marvel that our lives on planet Earth have at times been filled with so much of that sweet harmony. That great beauty that I imagine in my current novel-in-progress, is a glimmering, pinpoint reflection of the everlasting Music of the Spheres.

In these pages I have been able to revisit some of the immense joys as well as to face up to its hurts and its disappointments. I here include even the personal short-comings - the disappointing way in which I have all too often played the good cards handed to me at birth. But until writing this I have never spent much time looking within myself. Indeed I have, I suppose, been more of a stargazer than an ingazer.

So with what gifts and what handicaps, can I now conclude, was I endowed? And how well or badly would I conclude I have used them? I think I was given my fair share of looks, physical fitness and imagination - and perhaps no more than above average of intelligence. Measured in terms of fame and fortune I have undoubtedly under-used such assets. Perhaps the key word here is 'character'; perhaps it is the force and strength of character that decides how well or how less well we are / have been able to use ourselves. One can after all be congenitally disabled - mentally or physically - and at the same time a person most would recognise as being 'good' or even 'great' for any one of a thousand reasons. Or on the other hand some genius Greek-god-like figure who by general consent is a 'bad' person - in the vernacular, 'a right bastard'! Only time will tell how well or badly I have used my own endowments. That is, of course, should time care to tell anything at all about that Mister Bryan Henry Islip. None of us can, nor should ever pretend to be our own judge and jury.

But I do know what has made me especially happy to be me and to be alive. Amongst many, many things that might qualify, most if not all of them are or were of no importance whatsoever to anybody else ... for instance, and forgetting about chronology, being allowed to walk a young lady named Joan Wood to her home after the Saturday night dance in York's De Grey Ballroom ... coming home from work mid-week then taking Robert and Stuart and our boat down to the cold winter night-time Solent to fish for cod ... finding the perfect nest and collecting the perfect little egg of a golden-crested wren ... being in Picadilly Circus with my father at the end of World War Two, one of an enormous crowd listening to and singing along with Ida Lupino on her hotel balcony *I'm gonna get lit up when the lights go on in London* ... coming out of that Newmarket cinema into the night after seeing the marvellous movie, On The Waterfront; (Brando: *'I could've been a contender'*) ... smelling the dizzying, exciting smells inside my grandfather's fishing tackle box on Hastings Pier ... walking to work in Cambridge filled with enthusiasm and conviction; a twenty one years old married man with nothing else but utter confidence in the future ... holidays camping by the beach on Shell Island in West Wales, there lying in my sleeping bag listening to the spatter pattering of rain on tight canvas and the eternal shushing of wave of shingle... the constantly replenishing heat of sex with wondrous love, (but never, ever without it) ... the pure perfection of sight and smell (not necessarily of sound!) of our babies, one by one ... overcoming with that first significant order from Jack's Hill Cafe the early fear of business failure ... reading the final pages of Hemingway's *For Whom The Bell Tolls* ... being presented with my first national short fiction award for *Willie's Place* in that Tottenham Court Road book store ... the all too rare perfection of one particular golf shot (amongst so many, many far less perfect!) ... the take-off from Riyadh airport in the Heathrow-bound red eye and that first malt whisky after a dry business fortnight under the harsh Saudi sun, order book nicely filled ... reading the very favourable review in the Ross-shire Journal of my first published novel, *More Deaths Than One* ... that first time, after dinner, when I stood up to address a group of people knowing they were really listening, really wanting me somehow to make things better or at least plainer ... watching Stuart in that great big dog show ring with his lovely young vizsla dog Seth in all their pomp ... reading Tennison or Hemingway to Karen and Julie over the breakfast table ... my first ever sale in an Ullapool street market of a greetings card bearing my painting on its front and my verse on its rear ... standing on the beach at Hillhead that heart-stoppingly beautiful morning after I had been advised that my new bosses had no further use for my services and that therefore for the first time in my adult life I was free to do anything, go anywhere within my means and my reason ... admiring myself in the mirror wearing the light tan harris tweed jacket earned from first earnings at Boots the Chemist in Cambridge, the jacket that my father said made me look like a 'spiv' ... walking into the Stratford-on-Avon restaurant as the guest of my daughter and son-in-law on the occasion of my eightieth birthday to find waiting there my grandson and granddaughters with their various partners (Am I really, really responsible for all this? thought I) ... being the first schoolboy to gain the topmost branches of a certain great tree in the grounds of Abingdon School ... the quiver of my beach caster rod tip announcing the arrival of a hungry sea bass ...etcetera and so on and etcetera.

I was planning next to set out a contrary series of miserable low-lights and/or disappointments in my life but have decided against it, having already made myself sufficiently unhappy through their narration within these many pages.

I have tried to tell the truth as faithfully and as well if not as completely as I possibly could, or as I have the courage so to do. I cannot tell the truth completely for to do so would be to hurt myself and others to an unnecessary degree. Besides, the size and weight of such a tome would be impractical! Neither have I set out here to state my general views on life and the affairs of mankind (although that may come in the next and final postscript episode). In any case Bryan Islip's views would truly be only one man's opinions and are therefore as worthless as is today's newspaper editorial - which is indeed only the opinion of some anonymous other. My grandfather was an evangelist but I am not. Perhaps that makes him a better person than I. But telling it as it is, that's one thing; telling it in ways and words that can, if one is lucky, sometimes transcend the content - that is what I have tried to do whether in this or in my other writings, fiction or non-fiction. Ernest Hemingway wrote about how prose, to be any good must be truer *than the truth* ... and (in his *Death in the Afternoon*) ... *Prose is architecture, not interior decoration, ... A good writer should know as near everything as possible. Naturally he will not. There are some things which cannot be learned quickly and time, which is all we have, must be paid heavily for their acquiring. They are the very simplest things and because it takes a man's life to know them the little new that each man gets from life is very costly and the only heritage he has to leave.*

The End

(but not quite my own end)

Bryan Islip

84. Post script

The fifteen years old boy in *Like An Angel Sings*, my novel in progress, was born with a spina bifida condition and an exceptional brain and an exceptional mother who is educating him at home. This boy has used the internet extensively to research and has learned, out of the company of other children to think differently than others. He might well have read these words of *Hamlet* ... *What a piece of work is a man! How noble in reason, how infinite in faculty! In form and moving how express and admirable!* In composing the pages of this autobiography I have often thought, yes, what a marvellous piece of bio-mechanical engineering I am - and you are - and are we all! What a marvellous mystery lies behind all of us that propels our individual and group actions through each and every millisecond of our lives here on planet earth!

I suppose the lucky ones are they who would dispute that previous paragraph because for them human bio-mechanics are of but secondary interest. We are what we are, such folk would argue, and no underlying mystery exists because all is either explained by my God or not explained by It / Him. In either event, they would say, I shall do well not to bother about it.

I suppose through my years I've gone like most of us through the usual arc of thinking on such things; beginning with *dear father which art in heaven hallowed be thy name* ... etc, which morphs into natural scepticism *- there's only what's here and when you're dead there's nothing else*. After that, *this is not as good as I had hoped so what's it all about? Is this really it? This cannot be it!* But at the age of eighty one my personal conclusions are that there is indeed something ultimately mysterious that goes by the title of a soul and, furthermore, there is no reason why this ephemera should have to die with the body corporate. That being so - hey - there realy is a hereafter, therefore this life must be a hereunder! The transition from the hereunder to the hereafter - aka one's death - that will surely be the most powerful of any conceivable adventures; a thing to anticipate with a healthy degree of relish.

Here I go again; the not so beautiful dreamer!

At any rate it has become clear to me that although the species of animal of which I am one is a marvel amongst creatures great and small it is at the same time deeply flawed. I and my fellow man have consistently sought to damage as well as to create. Nothing has been safe from our depredations. We have sometimes hurt our fellow man and woman and how deeply our fellow man and woman has sought to hurt us in return. Not only that, but we have, either consciously or carelessly extended our destructive force to other life forms. We even seek to destroy the host planet itself. Yes, even today when we do know what we are doing! I cannot think of a single way in which the air, the sea and the main substance of this planet is anything other than damaged right now compared with how it was on the day I was born. I take no pleasure in saying this but in truth if we were, all of us, to disappear overnight all the millions of other forms of life on earth would no doubt heave one almighty sigh of relief.

In writing this accidental autobiography; (I say 'accidental' for in answering my youngest son's question about my early life I had no idea that an autobiography would be the outcome), I have tried to stick to straight reportage, albeit couched in the most careful language at my command. I have for the most part avoided the temptation to comment on things in general or the world at large. I have left alone such things, as I have left alone until now that which I see as our saving grace.

Our saving grace, it seems to me, is this ... You and I are a part of the one and only species that has it in its power to create things beautiful, to recognise such creation for what it is and to find within it a proper and personal raison d'etre. Most importantly we have it in our power to amend our own behaviour so as to accentuate the constructive and the beautiful and eliminate the destructive and the ugly. Will we ever seek positively so to do? Perhaps if we do then indeed we shall have created Milton's Paradise. If we do not then perhaps we shall be no more. So sorry.

Science (aka curiosity) is what ratchets up the degree of difficulty on the road to redemption. I posit that, even if we could find through our science the answers to each and every question thrown up by our combined intelligence and imagination, we would know not one billionth of what there is to know. So perhaps we should wise up, learn to live well with the blessings already given, bloody well stop trying to become our own selfish possessor of a personal security and comfort (aka 'wealth') greater than that belonging to our neighbour. Perhaps we should listen to the music, i.e. the creations, only some of them musical, of those who have preceded us. Each generation produces beauty in many, many forms even though that may seem - to me - to be so in steadily diminishing scale. Today there is no Socrates, (he who told his accusers that yes, he was the wisest in all Athenians because he was the only one wise enough to know that he knew nothing), there is no Jesus of Nazareth, no Mohammed, no Confucius, no Shakespeare. There is no Da Vinci, no Picasso, no Beethoven, no Mozart. Or perhaps I am wrong about this; perhaps they are indeed here, below the radar of our much vaunted media. How I hope so!

Anyway I look out of the window and I see the jagged skyline of ancient Torridian mountains (today against a powder blue sky for a welcome change!). It uplifts me as does Brahms symphony number four that's playing on the radio or the sight of that ragged V of barnacle geese that overflew this place a few moments ago, or as does the snatch of Shakespeare in paragraph one of this postscript. I may shock you by saying what I think makes it difficult, perhaps even impossible for the vast majority of us to access this saving grace in these modern times ... but, for me, these things go to make it less possible, perhaps even impossible …

- science because science feeds our perpetual curiosity and claims that nothing exists until 'proven'. Science cannot prove the existence or non-existence of the human soul any more than a thermometer can prove the colour red or King Henry the eighth could discourse on electronics.
- the media because it is most often better for the soul and the personal wellbeing simply not to know those things that are beyond individual power to change, ennoble or even influence. It seems to me that the only validation for the existence of the media is the profitable preservation of the established order and the useless feeding of valueless humn curiosity.
- money because it does not actually exist and can do nothing to nourish, then satisfy the soul much less justify its own or our own existence. The acquisition of money and the comforts that money can bring should not be our primary raison d'etre. It does nothing to prevent the bad stuff. One day an alternative will emerge, I trust.

I cannot think many or indeed any of us will ever really be able to get behind these screens truly to smell the flowers. I hope I'm wrong about this. After eighty plus years of close observation it seems to me that we have constructed too many obstacles of too severe a difficulty through the ways in which we, as a tribe within a species, have historically chosen to live our lives.

But as I turn over to this last page of my own life at least I can imagine how it really could be, given enough of individual vision and enough determination to actually realise it. And I can have my young Jamie Case in *Like An Angel Sings* succeed where all of us in real life must fail.

I am, after all, a writer and a painter and a parent and many kinds of a lover. Oh yes, these things have been and are good enough for me.